Graphic Standards
for Landscape
Architecture

Graphic Standards
for Landscape
Architecture

Richard L. Austin, ASLA
Thomas R. Dunbar, ASLA
J. Kip Hulvershorn, Ph.D.
Kim W. Todd, ASLA

 VAN NOSTRAND REINHOLD COMPANY
——————————————————————————— New York

Printed in the United States of America

Designed by Rose Delia Vasquez

Van Nostrand Reinhold Company Inc.
115 Fifth Avenue
New York, New York 10003

Van Nostrand Reinhold Company Limited
Molly Millars Lane
Wokingham, Berkshire RG11 2PY, England

Van Nostrand Reinhold
480 La Trobe Street
Melbourne, Victoria 3000, Australia

Macmillan of Canada
Division of Canada Publishing Corporation
164 Commander Boulevard
Agincourt, Ontario M1S 3C7, Canada

16 15 14 13 12 11 10 9 8 7 6 5 4 3 2 1

Library of Congress Cataloging-in-Publication Data

Graphic standards for landscape architecture.

   Includes index.
   1. Landscape architecture—Standards. 2. Landscape
architecture—Standards—United States. I. Austin,
Richard L.
SB472.G73 1986   712'.0218   86–7760
ISBN 0-442-20834-0

Contents

Preface

J. Kip Hulvershorn, Ph.D.

This reference was developed in response to the need for a single guide for site-specific design data. It is intended to be used by those working in the fields of landscape architecture, architecture, urban planning, as well as engineering.

Each of the contributing authors has been involved not only in private practice but also in the education of students in the various targeted disciplines. The combined experience of these experts in site design, together with extensive designer-needs research, has guided the gathering of this valuable resource.

Although it is important to approach each design site issue on an individual basis, local development restrictions often vary from locale to locale. The standards within this text therefore promote the development of site-specific facilities from a more common, national basis. On this premise, the designer can use these *standards* to refine specific improvements to a site project.

The contributors to this guide are committed to the principle that the most functional site facilities are designed by the combined expertise of the various professional disciplines. Therefore, the standards within this document are presented for the following reasons:

- Standards allow site design activities to function at their peak effectiveness.
- Standards are tested and evaluated by usage.
- Standards provide site uniformity for certain design activities, such as transportation systems, recreation activities, and site modifications.
- Standards allow efficient use of client resources.
- Standards provide for user familiarity and security.
- Standards provide accessibility for all user groups.
- Standards result in facilities that are easier to maintain and operate.
- Standards are based upon time-tested design.

This text does not guarantee good physical site design, but it does provide additional resources and design components to aid in the development of more effective exterior environments.

Acknowledgments

We wish to express our appreciation to the following organizations and agencies for the use of their material in the preparation of this manuscript:

University of Nebraska—Lincoln, Department of Grounds, for information on walks and walkway components, site furniture, drinking fountains, and landscape irrigation systems; University of Nebraska—Lincoln for information on recreation systems and retaining walls; the United States Department of Transportation for information on transportation systems; the National Park Service for information on recreation systems; Theraplan, Incorporated, for information on barrier-free design and plant material for the visually handicapped; Applewood Seed Company, Colorado, for information on native wildflowers; and the United States Department of Agriculture for information on environmental systems.

Contributing Editors _____

Richard L. Austin, ASLA
Associate Professor/University of Nebraska—Lincoln

Thomas R. Dunbar, ASLA
The DeBord Dunbar Partnership
Des Moines, Iowa

J. Kip Hulvershorn, Ph.D.
Associate Professor/University of Nebraska—Lincoln

Kim W. Todd, ASLA
Assistant Professor/University of Nebraska—Lincoln

1

Site Design Systems

Transportation Systems _____

In the forefront of the major design issues is the effective use of transportation resources. The following systems information is presented to assist the professional in addressing these issues, and the standards given—from the overall factors of mass transit facilities to the specific components of streets and parking areas—can be used as guides to more creative site improvement solutions.

A. MASS TRANSIT
1. BUS PASSENGER SHELTER POLICY
a) Shelter Location

(1) Bus Routes: Passenger shelters should be located only along existing or soon-to-be-implemented (i.e., within three months) regular service routes.

(2) Bus Stops: Passenger shelters should be located only at designated bus stops. For purposes of this policy, bus stops are considered to be at or near intersecting streets along each regular service route. Exceptions to this definition may include locations otherwise designated as bus stops through the installation of bus stop signs and/or appropriate markings.

(3) Curbs: Passenger shelters should be located a minimum of 4 feet from the curb and, where possible, set back 6 feet from the curb (as measured from the curb face to the nearest point of the shelter). Shelters should be positioned in such a way that they do not obstruct access to or use of any wheelchair ramp generally located in the surrounding curb/sidewalk area.

(4) Traffic Conditions: Passenger shelters should not interfere with the safe and orderly movement of vehicular traffic. Determination of location should be made in accordance with local traffic conditions and sound engineering judgment.

(5) Sidewalks: Passenger shelters should be situated on the site to permit the safe and orderly movement of pedestrians in front of (or behind, as appropriate), beside, into, and out of the shelter. A minimum of 4 feet of unobstructed sidewalk should be maintained in front of or behind the shelter in residential areas. Additional sidewalk space may be required in commercial areas.

(6) Utilities and Landscaping: In the placement of passenger shelters, consideration should be given to existing and proposed public and private utility systems and landscaping, including, but not limited to:
   (a) Fire hydrants and standpipes (shelters should be located a minimum of 15 feet from all fire hydrants and standpipes)
   (b) Overhead power and/or telephone lines and poles
   (c) Underground power and/or telephone lines
   (d) Water and sewer lines
   (e) Other underground conduits
   (f) Utility easements
   (g) Lawn sprinkler systems
   (h) Existing and proposed street trees

(7) Wind Patterns: Passenger shelters should be positioned so that they provide waiting bus passengers with the maximum feasible protection from prevailing winds.

(8) Existing Shelter: Passenger shelters should make maximum feasible use of existing shelter at each site. This may include the integration of passenger shelters with existing structures.

(9) Visibility into and out of Shelter: Passenger shelters should be positioned so that existing structures, trees, shrubs, utility poles, signs, and other natural or man-made obstructions do not substantially interfere with visibility into and out of the shelter.

(10) Public Right-of-Way: Passenger shelters should generally be locted on public rights-of-way.

(11) Clustering of Street Features: Passenger shelters should be clustered together with other street features, such as benches, pay telephones, waste receptacles, and letter drops.

b) Shelter Design and Dimensions

(1) Shelter Length: Passenger shelters should be a minimum of 10 feet and a maximum of 16 feet in length, as measured from the exterior of the shelter walls.

(2) Shelter Width: Passenger shelters should be a minimum of 5 feet and a maximum of 8 feet in width, as measured from the exterior of the shelter walls.

(3) Overall Shelter Dimensions: Exceptions to the above shelter length and width standards are permissible, provided that the overall shelter dimensions generally maintain a minimum of 50 square feet, to a maximum of 128 square feet. Such exceptions should be based on existing and projected average daily and maximum boardings and unique conditions or features of the site and/or proposed shelter.

(4) Shelter Height

    (a) Interior Height: Passenger shelters should maintain an interior ceiling height of at least 7 feet, but should not generally exceed 8 feet 6 inches in height.

    (b) Exterior Height: Passenger shelters should maintain an exterior roof height of at least 7 feet but should generally not exceed 8 feet in height. The design of the roof (including degree of slope) should permit adequate drainage and prevent the unreasonable accumulation of snow on the shelter roof.

(5) Windscreens: Passenger shelters should provide for windscreens along the front of the shelter, especially if the shelter will be generally facing north or west. Windscreens should be maintained at the same length and height as other shelter walls, with allowances for door openings.

(6) Door Openings: Passenger shelters should have unobstructed door openings with a minimum 32-inch clearance. For shelters with a windscreen, a minimum of two openings should be provided, one at each end of the shelter. Shelters located between the curb and sidewalk should provide easy access into and out of the shelter from both the street and the sidewalk sides of the shelter.

(7) Shelter Design: The design of the passenger shelters and amenities should be compatible with the character of the surrounding environment in terms of style, materials, scale, and mass.

c) *Shelter Materials*

(1) Structural Framing: Passenger shelters should be constructed or fabricated with structural framing elements of sturdy and durable material. Acceptable structural framing materials for passenger shelters include:

    (a) Extruded aluminum alloy (2½- by 2½-inch hollow aluminum tubes of 0.125-inch thickness)

    (b) Painted or stained milled lumber (minimum 4 by 4 inches, nominal)

    (c) Brick

(2) Walls/Glazing: Enclosed passenger shelters should use wall/glazing materials of acrylic or polycarbonate plastics (commonly referred to by the trade names of Plexiglas, Lexan, or Margard) or tempered glass. Bronzed or tinted glazing materials should be abrasion-resistant. Each wall, except the back wall if the shelter is backing against a building or other structure, should generally be transparent from 18 inches above the floor to the ceiling or should have an overall minimum transparency of 70 percent, excluding structural members. This includes any windscreen on the shelter. Passenger shelters should have a minimum of three sides. Open-sided passenger shelters are not acceptable.

(3) Roof: The shelter roof should be constructed or fabricated of leakproof materials able to withstand approximately 40 pounds per square foot without permanent or non–self-correcting deformities. The roof must be fastened to the shelter's structural framing without holes or other fastenings into the roof material. The roof should provide adequate drainage of water from its surface so that water does not drip over door openings. The roof should not extend more than 1 foot beyond the wall of the shelter.

(4) Finish: The shelter finish should be compatible with the character of the surrounding area. Painted or stained wood, brick, and bronzed or natural-color aluminum are generally acceptable as finish materials.

(5) Floor: Passenger shelter floors should be constructed or fabricated of a hard surface material, preferably concrete or laid brick (asphalt is generally unacceptable as a flooring material). The floor should not exceed a slope of ½ inch rise per 1 foot in any direction, and should not have a slope of less than ¼ inch per 1 foot run perpendicular to the street in order to provide drainage toward the street. The passenger shelter should be firmly anchored to the floor.

(6) Walkway: A walkway should be constructed or fabricated between the entrance(s) of passenger shelters and the curb where buses are boarded. The walkway should be constructed or fabricated of a hard surfacing material, preferably concrete or brick (asphalt is generally unacceptable as a walkway material). The width of the walkway preferably should not be less than standard sidewalk width (4 to 5 feet).

(7) Level: Passenger shelters should be leveled where possible to be perpendicular to the horizon.

d) *Passenger Amenities*

(1) Seating: Passenger shelters should provide seating, generally in the form of benches permanently attached to either the shelter wall(s) or to the shelter flooring, or both. The bench should be constructed or fabricated of a single-, double-, or triple-plank seat made of wood, aluminum, or galvanized metal. A similar plant backrest of the same material should be provided. The bench seat should be 16 to 18 inches in height where possible, as measured from the shelter floor.

(2) Schedule and Route Map Holders: Passenger shelters should provide a mechanism for displaying route and schedule information. The holder(s) should not obstruct the view of the approaching buses for waiting passengers.

(3) Bus Stop Signs: Bus stop signs or other appropriate markings or signs should be installed on or near each passenger shelter.

(4) General Graphics: General graphics, other than required signage and information, should not be placed on or near passenger shelters. No commercial advertising should be allowed.

(5) Lighting: Passenger shelters should have adequate ambient lighting available whenever possible so that a separate lighting source inside the shelter will not be necessary.

(6) Heating: Passenger shelters are not required to provide passenger heating for the interior of the shelter.

(7) Trash Receptacles: Passenger shelters should provide trash receptacles on the interior and/or exterior of the shelter, where possible.

e) Bus Passenger Shelter Warrants

(1) Shelter evaluation factors and weightings for proposed passenger shelter sites are given in table 1–1.

Table 1–1. Bus Shelter Evaluation Factors

Planning Categories		Value
Priority Allocation		15 pts.
Safety		15 pts.
Review Areas		60 pts.
Property Owner	(15)	
Neighborhood	(15)	
Bus Operator's	(15)	
Urban Design	(15)	
Physical Aspects		30 pts.
Site Characteristics	(15)	
Nearby Shelters	(15)	
Usage		20 pts.
Passenger	(15)	
Route Density	(5)	
Planning Compatibility		10 pts.
	Total	150 pts.

(2) The Shelter Site Evaluation Form is shown in figure 1–1.

(3) Shelter Placement Review

(a) Evaluation Criteria: Shelter placement shall be determined after reviewing and evaluating the following information:

i) Origin of Request: The individual, group, or organization requesting the shelter placement.

ii) Feasibility: Number of shelters available, location of proposed site, allocation category, safety, local and neighborhood acceptance, other existing shelters, site characteristics, urban design review.

iii) Potential Use: The service near the site (route density), average weekday riders, rider characteristics.

iv) Compatibility with Future Route Planning: Insurance that the route on which the shelter is to be located is not programmed for abandonment or change.

v) Coordination with Accessible Improvements: Coordination of shelter placement with other passenger boarding improvements to enhance the effectiveness of accessible transit service.

(b) Shelter Allotment: Shelter priorities shall be developed to serve a variety of transit markets based on the allocations formula shown below:

i) 15 percent elderly and handicapped (retirement facility, nursing home, hotel, etc.).

ii) 15 percent medical facilities, hospitals, other community medical facilities.

iii) 15 percent public and semipublic institutions (i.e., court house, city hall, federal buildings, coliseum, or sports arenas).

iv) 15 percent major trip generators (shopping centers, multiple-family dwellings, industrial parks, large residential developments).

v) 15 percent major transfer points.

vi) 15 percent fixed route accessibility improvements.

vii) 10 percent unallocated reserve.

(c) Processing of Shelter Requests

i) Passenger counts at the affected bus stop shall be taken by operators. The cutoff point of shelter consideration shall normally be ten or more daily passengers boarding at the requested location. Requests for locations that generate fewer than ten daily passengers will be given a low priority and will generally receive no further consideration, unless special circumstances dictate further study.

ii) Each shelter request that satisfies the daily-use criteria (10 or more passengers) shall then be evaluated using the Shelter Site Evaluation Form (Figure 1–1). Any shelter request that does not receive at least a minimum total score of 125 on the feasibility study will be disqualified for shelter placement unless special consideration is requested of and received from the Advisory Board.

iii) The evaluation shall include a field visit, and the potential for private shelter investment shall be investigated to eliminate duplication of effort.

iv) Any parentheses on the Shelter Site Evaluation Form indicate automatic disqualification of a shelter request for a period of six months.

v) Based on this evaluation process, each shelter request shall be assigned a priority rating, based on a final score from the SSE form. Within each shelter allocation, ranked sites will be assigned priority on the basis of productivity as measured by overall route performance statistics.

vi) This shelter priority list will be continually updated as new requests are processed, and highest-ranking sites within each allocation will be assigned priority for shelter installation as construction funds become available.

vii) When shelter funds become available, the current list of shelter priorities will be reviewed before letting a construction contract.

See figure 1–2.

f) *Procedure for Requesting and Reviewing Shelters*

(1) Constructed/Installed Shelters

(a) Individual(s) or organization(s) desiring to construct or install a bus passenger shelter at an existing or soon-to-be-constructed bus stop should submit a written request to the Chair of the Advisory Board of and/or the Director of the Transportation Department, clearly indicating the specific location of the bus stop and any other pertinent information related to the request.

(b) Upon receiving the request, the Transportation Department will conduct an in-field investigation of the proposed shelter site. A Shelter Site Evaluation Form should be completed by the Transportation Department in assessing the shelter request.

(c) As appropriate, the Director of Transportation should request oral or written reports from Departments, Advisory Committees, and/or individual(s) or organization(s) (including affected property owners) concerning any problems foreseen in the placement of a bus passenger shelter at the site.

(d) Based upon this review, the Director of Transportation shall report to the Advisory Board within 60 days from receipt of the request and make recommendations concerning the construction or installation of a shelter at the site.

(e) The Board should then take such action upon the request as deemed appropriate.

(2) Non–Agency-Constructed/Installed Shelters

(a) Individual(s) or organization(s) desiring to construct or install a bus passenger shelter at an existing or soon-to-be-constructed bus stop should submit a written request to the Chair of the Advisory Board of and to the Director of the Transportation Department with the following information:

i) The specific location of the bus stop.

ii) Detailed drawings/diagrams of the proposed shelter. The Director of Transportation may request the individual(s) or organization(s) to submit such additional information concerning the shelter as deemed necessary.

iii) Upon receiving the request, the Transportation Department shall conduct an in-field investigation of the proposed shelter site. A Shelter Site Evaluation Form should be completed by Transportation Department staff in assessing the shelter request.

iv) As appropriate, the Director of Transportation should request oral or written reports from Departments, Advisory Committees, and/or individual(s) or organization(s) (including affected property owners) concerning any problems foreseen in the placement of a bus passenger shelter at the site and/or with the shelter design. Any design other than commercial prefabricated shelters must be approved by the Codes Administration Division of the government agency for structural integrity.

v) Based upon this review, the Director of Transportation shall report to the Advisory Board within 60 days from the receipt of the request and make recommendations concerning the construction or installation of a shelter at the site and the shelter design.

vi) The Board should then take such action upon the request as deemed appropriate.

(3) Future Shelter Sites: In undeveloped areas of the City without current or imminent fixed-route service, individual(s) or organization(s) desiring to (1) construct or install a bus passenger shelter, and/or (2) designate/dedicate a portion(s) of property for the purpose of possible future placement of a bus passenger shelter(s) should request the Planning Director of the government agency to inform the Director of Transportation of this desire as part of the Procedure for Processing Subdivisions. Upon receiving such notification from the Planning Director, the Director of Transportation should direct Transportation Department staff to review the request and to prepare and submit a written response to the Planning Director within 15 days concerning the desirability and feasibility of the proposal.

g) *Shelter Construction or Installation and Maintenance*

(1) Constructed or Installed Shelters: The City should assume total financial responsibility for bus passenger shelters constructed or installed by the City. This includes the cost of materials and labor used in constructing or installing the shelter.

(2) Non–Agency-Constructed/Installed Shelters: Individual(s) or organization(s) desiring a shelter in advance of the scheduled construction or installation

date should assume total financial responsibility for constructing or installing the bus passenger shelter. This includes the cost of materials and labor used in constructing/installing the shelter. Individual(s) or organization(s) desiring a special design shelter in place of a previously scheduled standard bus passenger shelter would be required to pay the incremental cost of the special design shelter.

(3) Maintenance of Shelter: The City should assume total responsibility for the continued maintenance (e.g., repairs, trash removal) of all designated bus passenger shelters, including concrete work and passenger amenities directly related to the shelter.

(4) Shelter Removal: The Transportation Department retains sole discretion in determining when a bus passenger shelter should be removed (e.g., maintenance problems, vandalism, reroutings).

2. BUS-LOADING AREAS/BAY LOCATIONS
See figures 1–3 to 1–10.

3. BUS-PASSENGER BENCH POLICY
a) Bench Location
(1) Bus Stops: Passenger benches should be located only at designated bus stops (designated as such by the installation of an authorized bus stop sign).
(2) Curbs: Passenger benches should be located a minimum of 4 feet from the face of the curb. Where possible, benches should be set back 6 feet from the curb face and a maximum of 30 feet from the curb face.
(3) Obstructions: The location of passenger benches should not interfere with the safe and orderly movement of vehicular traffic or with access to and use of, but not limited to, such facilities as wheelchair ramps, sidewalks, fire hydrants, and water, sewer, or utility lines.
(4) Public Rights-of-Way: Passenger benches generally should be located on public rights-of-way.
b) Bench Material
(1) Structural Materials: Passenger benches should be constructed of sturdy and durable materials, such as wood, steel, or concrete.
(2) Bench Floor and Walkways: Passenger benches should be installed into or on concrete floors, and access should be provided from the sidewalk to the bench and from the bench to the curb where buses are boarded by means of a concrete walkway. The width of the walkway preferably should not be less than standard sidewalk width (4 to 5 feet).
c) Bus-Passenger Bench Criteria
(1) The major criterion for placement of benches at a bus stop is that ten or more persons board there during an average day.
(2) Each bench request that satisfies the daily-use criterion (ten or more passengers) should then be evaluated using a Bench Site Evaluation Form (see

Figure 1–11). Any bench request that does not receive at least a minimum total score of 60 on the feasibility study will be disqualified from bench placement unless special circumstances warrant other consideration. All other requests should be placed on a priority list according to their numerical ratings.

(3) Any parentheses on the Bench Site Evaluation Form indicate automatic disqualification of a bench request for a period of at least six months.
d) Bench Placement
(1) Bench Sites: The list of current bench priorities should be reviewed in order to make final determination of bench placements.
(2) Bench Maintenance and Removal: The Government Agency or Contractor assumes total responsibility for the continued maintenance of all designated passenger benches and retains sole discretion in determining when a bench should be removed.
(3) Bench Site Evaluation Form: See figure 1–11.

B. STREETS, ROADS, AND PARKING
1. STREET DESIGN STANDARDS
Supplemental design requirements for public street systems are established as follows:
a) Location of Major, Collector, and Local Streets
(1) The locations of collector streets are governed by the following criteria:
  (a) The purpose of a collector street is to collect traffic from a system of local streets and to provide a convenient connection to a major street. The primary points of access to major streets should be collector streets.
  (b) Intersections of collector streets with major streets should be located at approximately ½-mile intervals. The actual spacing should depend on the layout of the system of local streets and the vertical grades of the major streets from which the collector streets take access.
(2) Intersections of local streets with major streets must be located at approximately ¼-mile points on the major street.
(3) Local and collector streets intersecting a major street shall be located so that adequate sight distance is provided along the major street. The required sight distance is determined by the speed limit and grade of the major street and the acceleration rate of an average vehicle. All designs shall provide minimum safe stopping sight distance as well as permit a vehicle to enter the major street and accelerate to the speed limit without interfering with the traffic flow on the major street. The design sight-distance values that should be used for residential or nonresidential areas are provided in table 1–2. The sight-distance values for nonres-

idential districts are considerably higher due to the higher truck volumes.

Table 1-2. Sight-Distance Values*

| Speed Limit on Major Street (mph) | MINIMUM SIGHT DISTANCE REQUIRED (FT.) | |
	Residential (Auto)	Nonresidential (Truck)
25	175	300
30	265	400
35	360	625
40	435	850
45	565	1,225
50	730	1,660
55	865	2,050

*Enabling vehicles to *enter* a street from a *stop*.

(a) Intersections of local or collector streets with major streets should be in line with streets intersecting on the opposite side of the major street or offset by at least 600 feet.

(b) Streets intersecting on opposite sides of a local or collector street should be either directly across from each other or offset by at least 120 feet between centerlines.

(c) The design of local streets should be such that traffic is directed toward a collector street.

(d) Local streets should also adequately provide for vehicular circulation and movement within the subdivision while discouraging through-traffic movement.

(4) Angle of Intersection: Streets should intersect as near as possible to right angles. In no case should the angle of intersection vary more than 10 degrees from a right angle.

(5) T Intersections: For intersections of local streets, T-type intersections are preferred over four-way intersections because of the greatly reduced number of conflict points.

(6) Horizontal Radius: All changes in horizontal alignment should be connected by horizontal curves of such degree as to provide safe operation for the established speed limit for the classification of the street. The minimum horizontal centerline radius of a street shall not be less than 125 feet.

(7) Minimum Tangent Length for Horizontal Alignment: Whenever a local or collector street approaches any other street with an angle of Delta greater than 10 degrees, a tangent length, measured from the nearest right-of-way line of the intersected street to the point of curvature in the intersecting street, shall be provided for sight distance and safe traffic operation. The tangent length required is determined by the centerline radius of the approach street. The minimum tangent lengths are listed in table 1-3.

Table 1-3. Minimum Tangent Lengths for Horizontal Alignment

Centerline Radius (ft.)	Tangent Length (ft.)	Centerline Radius (ft.)	Tangent Length (ft.)
125	90	375	45
120	90	400	40
175	85	425	35
200	80	450	30
225	75	475	25
250	70	500	20
275	65	525	15
300	60	550	10
325	55	575	5
350	50	600	0

(a) T-type intersections may be permitted along a horizontal curve if the intersecting street is on the *outside* of the curve and the intersected street is a nonmajor street and has the 175 feet of necessary sight distance.

(b) T-type intersections may be permitted on the *inside* of a horizontal curve if the intersected street is a nonmajor street and has a centerline radius of 525 feet or greater.

(c) A minimum tangent length of 100 feet should be provided between horizontal curves to allow for the smooth flow of traffic. This tangent distance is not required where the sum of the radii is 600 feet or greater.

(8) Vertical Grades
(a) Terrain Classification
    i) Ordinary, natural ground slope of 0 to 8 percent.
    ii) Rolling, natural ground slope of more than 8 percent.

The maximum grades for new construction of public ways are listed in table 1-4.

Table 1-4. Maximum Grades for New Construction of Public Ways

| | TERRAIN CLASSIFICATION | |
	Ordinary (%)	Rolling (%)
Major Streets	4	6
Collector Streets	5	7
Local Streets	6	8
Cul-de-sacs	6	8
Alleys	6	8

(b) The minimum street grade should be 0.5 percent. This is required to allow adequate street drainage.

(c) The grade of any street approaching a major street should not exceed a slope of 2 percent within 100 feet of the right-of-way of the major street.

(d) The grade of local streets approaching a collector street should not exceed a slope of 2 percent within 50 feet of the right-of-way of the collector street.

(e) At the intersection of two local through streets, the grade of each street should not exceed a maximum slope of 2 percent within 50 feet of the right-of-way of the intersected street. The grades of a through street at an intersection with a cul-de-sac or a T-type intersection may exceed 2 percent.

(f) The grading of the property adjacent to a major street or the intersection of any street with the major street should be designed to meet the ultimate street grades of the major street. This street grade in the city limits will be provided by the City Engineer's Office upon request.

(9) Vertical Curves

(a) All changes in street grade should be connected by parabolic vertical curves of such lengths as to provide the minimum safe stopping sight distance.

(b) Vertical curves connecting relatively flat grades should be kept to a minimum length to facilitate proper drainage.

(10) Minimum Curb Radius at Intersections

(a) At the intersection of two local or collector streets, the minimum curb radius should be 20 feet, except in industrial, commercial, or business zoning districts, where the minimum curb radius should be 30 feet.

(b) At the intersection of a local or collector street and a major street, the minimum curb radius should be 30 feet. In addition, some intersections with a major street may require turn lanes, tapers, medians, and other special treatment.

(c) At the intersection of two major streets, a minimum curb radius of 40 feet, or equivalent three-centered curve, etc., should be provided.

(11) Cross Section and Material

(a) Local streets in residential zoning districts should be constructed with 6-inch-thick Portland cement concrete or 5-inch-thick Portland cement concrete base with a 2½-inch-thick asphalt concrete surface course. Pavement thickness for local streets in commercial, business, or industrial zoning districts and collector streets is related to the expected traffic loads.

(b) The roadway widths that should be provided are listed in table 1–5 (the widths are from face of curb to face of curb).

(12) Street Projections For Future Adjoining Subdivisions

(a) The location of temporary dead end streets for future projected streets should allow for the

Table 1–5. Residential Street Classifications

Street Classification	Zoning	Width
Local	Residential	26 ft.
	Commerical, Business, Industrial, or Office	38 ft. (With Parking) 32 ft. (With No Parking)
Collector	All—Without Median	38 ft.
	With Median (4–8 ft. Median Width Possible in 80-ft. Right-of-Way)	2–20 ft. Roadways
Major (i)	All—2 Lane	32 ft.
	2 Lane (Extra Width for Bicycles)	38 ft.
	4 Lanes (Typical)	67 ft.
Cul-de-Sacs	Residential	43 ft. Radius
	Commerical, Business, Industrial, or Office	49 ft. Radius (With No Parking) 55-ft. Radius (With Parking)

1. The actual street width for major facilities is generally determined through the City's Street Project Selection Procedure.

2. Allows for optional center island of 20-ft. radius when maintenance is provided by associations or individuals other than City.

   a. All changes in street width should be connected by tapers of minimum length $(L) = WS$, where W is the shift in the curb alignment and S is the speed limit on the street.

   b. Pavement crown is required for streets as follows:

    26-ft.-wide paving: 5 in.
    32-ft.-wide paving: 6 in.
    38-ft.-wide paving: 7 in.
    44-ft.-wide paving: 8 in.
    67-ft.-wide paving: 9 in.

Roadway crowns on local and collector streets are parabolic.

proper projection of the storm sewer and sanitary system as well as street systems into adjacent natural drainage areas.

(b) Temporary dead end streets shall be paved to the property line of the subdivision. The developer should provide the legal descriptions and shall be financially responsible for obtaining the easements necessary for any earthwork grading required beyond the limits of the plat. This should include providing satisfactory temporary drainage at the property line of the subdivision.

2. PRIVATE ROADWAY SYSTEM

a) Connections to Public Street

(1) The private roadway system should provide convenient and reasonable access from the public street system to each dwelling unit, lot, commercial or community building, and adjacent property.

b) Maximum Block Length

(1) No block should be longer than 1,320 feet between cross streets or roadways. Cul-de-sacs or dead ends should not be longer than 1,000 feet as measured

from the termination of the cul-de-sac to the intersection with a cross street or roadway.

c) *Dead End Roadways*

(1) All dead end roadways more than 300 feet in length from the nearest intersection or other turnaround should be terminated with a vehicular turnaround with a minimum outside radius of 30 feet.

d) *Sight Distance at Intersections*

(1) Intersections of private roadways with public streets should be located so that adequate sight distance along the public street from the intersection with a private roadway is provided. The required sight distance is determined by the speed limit and grades of the public street and the acceleration rate of an average vehicle. The design shall provide minimum safe stopping sight distance and permit a vehicle to enter the public street and accelerate to the speed limit without interfering with the traffic flow on the public street. The design/sight-distance values that should be used for residential or nonresidential areas are provided in table 1–2. The sight-distance values for nonresidential areas are considerably higher due to higher truck volumes.

(2) No obstruction to the view should be permitted higher than 2 feet 6 inches above the centerline grade of the adjacent roadways:

(a) At through intersections on any property within that triangular area bounded by the curbs of the intersecting roadways and a diagonal line between two points located 60 feet back along the curbs of the two intersecting roadways.

(b) At T-type intersections on any property within the triangular area 17 feet back on the terminating roadway from the near side of the through roadway and 175 feet back on the through roadway from the point of intersection of the centerline of the terminating roadway.

e) *Angle of Intersection*

(1) The minimum angle at which a roadway intersects another roadway or street should be 80 degrees.

f) *Offset Intersections*

(1) The centerline of a roadway entering on opposite sides of a roadway or street should be either directly across from the centerline of the opposite roadway or street or offset by at least 120 feet.

g) *Minimum Tangent Lengths for Horizontal Alignment*

(1) Whenever a private roadway approaches any street with an angle of Delta greater than 10 degrees, a tangent length measured from the nearest right-of-way line of the intersected street to the point of curvature in the approach roadway should be provided for sight distance and safe traffic operation. The tangent length required should be determined by the centerline radius of the approach roadway. The minimum required tangent lengths are listed in table 1–3.

h) *Horizontal Radius*

(1) The centerline radius for any horizontal curve in a private roadway should be at least 125 feet.

(2) Roadways shall not intersect other roadways or streets on the outside of a horizontal curve without providing the 175 feet of necessary sight distance or on the inside of a horizontal curve with a centerline radius of less than 525 feet.

(3) There should be a minimum of 100 feet of tangent length between all horizontal curves; where the sum of the radii exceeds 600 feet, however, no tangent is required.

i) *Vertical Grades*

(1) The maximum vertical grades are listed in table 1–6.

Table 1–6. Maximum Vertical Grades

Terrain Classification	Maximum Grade
Ordinary Natural Ground Slope, 0%–8%	6%
Rolling Natural Ground Slope, over 8%	8%

(2) The *maximum* grade for a roadway that provides primary service in the area should be plus or minus 2 percent within 50 feet of the right-of-way on an intersected public street. The *minimum* grade should be 0.5 percent to provide adequate drainage.

j) *Vertical Curve*

(1) All changes in roadway grades should be connected by parabolic vertical curves of lengths that provide the minimum safe stopping sight distance. The minimum sight distance should be determined using the following formula:

$$L = KA$$

Where: L = Required length of the vertical curve (this distance is measured on a horizontal plane)

A = The algebraic difference of the grades of the two tangents

K = Constant: crest curves, $K = 28$; sag curves, $K = 35$

3. ROADWAY SPECIFICATIONS

a) *Dimensions*

(1) Roadways should be at least 26 feet in width, have a 5-inch crown, and have a curb. The roadway width may be reduced to 20 feet for residential roadways serving fewer than 30 parking spaces.

b) Surfaces

(1) Roadways may be surfaced by any of the following methods:

    (a) Portland cement concrete, 6 inches thick

    (b) Portland cement concrete base, 5 inches thick, with an asphaltic concrete surface course 2½ inches thick

    (c) Asphaltic concrete, 6 inches thick

    (d) Paver brick

    (e) Grasscrete

    (f) Other stable surface

4. GENERAL SPECIFICATIONS FOR ROADWAYS

a) Angle or Perpendicular Parking

(1) Angle or perpendicular parking should not be permitted along private roadways since accident rates tend to be much higher than with parallel parking. Therefore:

    (a) Driveways and parking areas for commercial or business districts should be designed to allow vehicles to enter and leave the private roadway in a forward motion.

    (b) Driveways to property used for residential purposes may have a maximum of 6 garage units or parking stalls (without a minium separation of 20 feet) where vehicles back out onto the private roadway. All other parking should be designed such that vehicles can reasonably leave and enter the roadway in a forward motion.

b) Traffic Signs and Pavement Markings

(1) All traffic signs and pavement markings along the private roadway should conform to the latest edition of the Federal Highway Administration's *Manual on Uniform Traffic Control Devices.*

5. EASEMENTS

a) Requirements

(1) An easement may be required by the governing agency; it shall be dedicated to allow public use of the private roadways.

b) Design Speed

(1) Roads should be designed for a minimum of 30 miles per hour.

c) Vertical Grades

(1) The maximum grade should be 60 percent and the minimum grade 5 to 10 percent.

(2) The maximum grade may be increased only when a request to deviate, reasons for the deviation, and solutions to erosion of roadside ditches are submitted with the preliminary plat.

d) Vertical Curves

(1) All changes in roadway grades should be connected by parabolic vertical curves of such length as to provide the minimum safe stopping distance.

(2) The minimum sight distance should be determined using the following formula:

$$L = KA$$

Where: L = Required length of vertical curve (measured in horizontal plane)

    A = Algebraic difference in grades in percent of the two tangents

    K = Constant (see table 1–7)

Table 1–7. Minimum *K* Values

Design Speed (mph)	30	40	50	60
Crest Vertical Curves	28	55	85	160
Sag Vertical Curves	35	55	75	105

e) Horizontal Alignment

(1) The maximum degree of curvature is limited by the design speed selected. The maximum rate of superelevation should be .08 feet per foot. The degree of curvature should not exceed those listed in table 1–8.

Table 1–8. Horizontal Alignment

Design Speed (mph)	30	40	50	60
Maximum Degree of Curvature	23.0	12.5	7.0	4.5

$$\frac{5729.58}{\text{Degree of Curvature}} = \text{Centerline Radius}$$

f) Angle of Intersection

(1) The minimum angle of intersection between roads should be 80 degrees.

g) Roadway Cross Section

(1) All roads should conform to the Local Roads RL-1 classification standard set by the State Board of Public Roads.

h) Road Surfacing

(1) Roads should be surfaced per the applicable standards as follows: When roads are located within a platted area in which the lots average 2 acres or less but more than ½ acre, or there are fewer than two dwelling units per acre but more than one dwelling unit per 2 acres, such roads should be hard surfaced with 3 inches of asphalt/concrete base course as designated and 2 inches of asphalt/concrete surface course as specified.

i) Surfacing Exceptions

(1) Roads located in areas that are not included in (1) above should be surfaced with 3 inches of crushed rock embedded as specified.

See figures 1–12 to 1–15.

6. INTERSECTION DESIGN
   See figures 1–16 to 1–22.

7. TYPICAL ROAD LAYOUT
   See figures 1–23 to 1–25.

8. TURNING RADIUS
   See figure 1–26.

9. PARKING: STANDARD LAYOUT
   See table 1–9 and figure 1–27.

Table 1–9. Standard Layout for Parking

Parking Angle	Stall Width	Stall Depth*	Aisle Width	Skew Width
90°	8' 0"	18' 0"	28'–32'	—
	8' 6"	18' 0"	25'–29'	—
	9' 0"	18' 0"	23'–27'	—
60°	8' 0"	19' 7"	19' 0"	9' 3"
	8' 6"	19' 10"	18' 0"	9' 10"
	9' 0"	20' 0"	17' 0"	10' 5"
45°	8' 0"	18' 5"	12' 0"	11' 4"
	8' 6"	18' 8"	11' 0"	12' 0"
	9' 0"	19' 1"	11' 0"	12' 9"
30°	8' 0"	15' 11"	11' 0"	16' 0"
	8' 6"	16' 5"	10' 0"	17' 0"
	9' 0"	16' 10"	9' 0"	18' 0"

Parallel	W	D	A
	7' 0"	22' 0"	10' 0"
	8' 0"	22' 0"	10' 0"

*Perpendicular to aisle, except parallel parking

10. PARKING: ACCESSIBILITY FOR THE
    HANDICAPPED
    See figures 1–28 to 1–30.

11. PARKING: TYPICAL AUTO SIZES
    See figure 1–31.

12. PARKING: WHEEL STOP (TYPICAL)
    See figures 1–32 to 1–36.

C. BICYCLE SYSTEMS
1. DESIGN EVALUATION/NEEDS ANALYSIS
a) *Evaluation of Community Cycling Activity*
(1) Consult with law enforcement agencies for auto-bike conflicts and problems.
(2) Interview school officials and school safety committees that determine cycling patterns in the community.
(3) Consult with local planning commissions and personnel.
(4) Solicit opinions from civic organizations and service clubs.

(5) Request input from cycling clubs in the community.
(6) Consult authorities in other communities and states.
(7) Review state and local outdoor recreation plans.
b) *Survey Factors*
(1) Individual and group interests in cycling.
(2) Number and ages of cyclists in neighborhoods.
(3) Existing cycling patterns.
(4) Traffic problems with cyclists using streets.
(5) Existing laws and ordinances affecting cyclists.
(6) Community-wide distribution.
(7) Traffic counts.
(8) Plans for future developments that may include cycling facilities.
c) *Available Facilities and How Used for Bicycling*
(1) Inventory of park and recreation areas:
    (a) Roads
    (b) Walks
    (c) Hiking trails
    (d) Paved multiple-use areas
    (e) Parking lots
(2) Community facilities not under park and recreation departments that have potential for cycling:
    (a) Side streets
    (b) Secondary and little-used roads
    (c) School grounds
    (d) School and college tracks
    (e) Fairgrounds
    (f) Parking lots
    (g) Utility rights-of-way
(3) Facilities that can be converted, expanded, or improved for bicycling:
    (a) Dry canals
    (b) Dry riverbeds
    (c) Abandoned railroad beds
    (d) Existing little-used pedestrian or riding paths and trails
d) *Evaluation Factors*
(1) In terms of general facilities
(2) In terms of facilities for bicycling

2. EXISTING FACILITIES
a) *Preliminary Evaluations*
(1) Evaluate planned bicycle programs in light of community survey to determine needs for expansion.
(2) Experiment with marking roads and streets as bike routes.
(3) Experiment using walks, hiking trails, etc., signed and marked as bike routes.
(4) Try multiple uses of facilities.
(5) Evaluate use to determine additional need.

3. EVALUATING NEW BIKE ROUTE FACILITIES
a) *Suitability Check*
(1) Topography.
(2) Scenic qualities.
(3) Points of interest.
(4) Passing other activity points.

(5) Proximity to service facilities.

(6) Using perimeter areas.

(7) Following canal, creek, or riverbanks.

(8) Paralleling roads.

(9) Compatability with overall plan or ultimate goal.

b) *Plan Layout*

(1) Sketch approximate route.

(2) Possible additional engineering necessary (topography, etc.) for detailed layout.

(3) Design variety into trail to ensure repeat use.

(4) Determine length of trail (avoid a short facility).

(5) Determine width of trail.

(6) Consider maintenance.

(7) Consider lighting.

(8) Consider street crossings and alternatives.

(9) Plan markings and signs.

4. GENERAL CONSIDERATIONS FOR DESIGN AND CONSTRUCTION OF FOOTPATHS AND BIKE ROUTES

a) *Bike Routes for Varying Conditions*

(1) An independent trail for exclusive bicycle/pedestrian use that may be entirely independent of other facilities (or use highway right-of-way).

(2) A bike route that uses city streets, secondary roads, and other existing facilities and is so designated by signs, striped lanes, and/or physical barriers such as guard rails, special fencing, curbed sections, etc.

(3) A bike route using same as above, but signed only (no provisions made for separation).

(4) A bike route to be constructed as part of a new structure, signed and separated from the travel way by a physical barrier.

(5) Extra width on sidewalks, usually 2 to 3 feet, with markings or signing to allow bicycle traffic.

b) *Features of Interest*

(1) A footpath and bike route, while providing a means for reaching one point from another, should provide stops and access to and near parks, viewpoints, or items of cultural interest. It should allow bikers to ride through a diverse and dynamic landscape. The following are some of the items to be considered in route selection:

    (a) Physical Features

        i) Terrain

        ii) Vegetative cover, open areas, deep woods

        iii) Lakes, streams, ponds, rivers, waterfalls

        iv) Geologic formations

        v) Highways

        vi) Canals, utilities

        vii) Railroads

        viii) Bridges

    (b) Cultural Features

        i) Historic sites

        ii) Rest areas

        iii) Shopping centers

        iv) Parks

        v) Civic centers

        vi) School campuses

(2) If a route cannot pass close to or through some items of interest, spurs or connecting loops may be considered as additions to the main trail to create diversity and stimulate interest.

c) *Length of Facility*

(1) Generally speaking, the proposed route should be in excess of 5 miles in length to assure continued interest and use by the pedestrian and bicyclist. If the proposal serves largely commuting traffic, and if large sources or generators of use (e.g., college campus, large factory) are present at the termini, short-distance and direct routes may become a primary consideration. Ideally, a bike route should serve a commuting and overall transportation use, with segments or all of that trail being used for recreation purposes.

(2) Other proposals may specifically serve the racing and competition bicyclists.

d) *Width Considerations*

(1) The recommended width for bike routes is 8 feet, but heavily used urban bike routes can exceed this width. For a two-way bike facility, the minimum width is 5 feet. Where conditions warrant one-way trails, sections with widths of 3 to 4 feet would be considered adequate, but minimal.

(2) If the bike route is to be established in conjunction with sidewalks, it is desirable to add extra width to accommodate bicycles. A minimum of 2 to 4 feet is recommended, generally extending the total width of the sidewalk to 7 to 9 feet.

e) *Bridges*

(1) Bridges will need to be wider than the bike routes they connect, particularly if two-way traffic is to be accommodated. A survey shows that an average width of bicycle bridges is 7½ feet; therefore, a basic minimum of 8 feet is undesirable.

(2) Consideration should be given to pull-off areas either on or abutting the bridge to take advantage of scenery or other interesting features of the crossing.

f) *Horizontal and Vertical Alignment*

(1) Development of the horizontal alignment, in many respects, is similar to that used for highways, roads, or streets. Where the bike route is contiguous with such existing facilities, it assumes the same alignment, with deviations to create interest (the extent of deviation would depend on topography, culture, and available right-of-way). When the facility is not contiguous to an existing roadway, transition (spiral) curves are not needed. The bike route in this instance can follow the prevalent topography in the area, keeping cuts and fills to a minimum to ensure proper drainage of the trail. It may be desirable to split the trail, creating a one-way condition to avoid

trees or other obstacles (this also adds interest to the trail). Curve radius should be selected to provide a smooth transition in the change of direction. In some instances, where the angle between adjacent tangents is slight (10 degrees or less), curves are not necessary. Short, sharp curves and sharp angles should be avoided if possible, particularly in areas where high speeds can be attained (e.g., at the bottom of a long descending grade). The cyclist should be given opportunities to permit him- or herself to slow down and not brake while in the curve.

(2) A bicycle is a versatile machine and is capable of negotiating a 6-foot radius; the range of minimum turning radii reported in a recent survey varied from 6 to 50 feet, with an average minimum radius of 17⅔ feet. On this basis, the minimum turning radius should be 20 feet.

(3) Grades should vary on a bike route, particularly one serving recreation cyclists. The main condition to avoid is long, steep uphill grades. A 15 percent uphill grade for short distances may be considered a working maximum; a 10 percent grade is a desirable maximum. The grade and its length must be judged together. Long climbs, even though gradual, should be avoided.

g) Land Acquisition Fundamentals

(1) There are five methods of acquiring land or arranging for its use in the development of trails:
   (a) Purchase of title in fee simple
   (b) Lease arrangements
   (c) Purchase of easements
   (d) Gifts or dedications
   (e) Zoning

(2) Fee simple acquisition is generally the most expensive method, but it guarantees the fullest use of property. Acquiring lands or rights for bike route use may be complicated by many factors due to the linear aspects of a trail, and several methods of acquisition may be necessary for establishing one facility. Purchase of fee title should be used where major use areas, such as rest stops, mini parks, campgrounds, or parking areas, are anticipated. Less than fee-title arrangements can then be made for intervening areas where only bike route use itself is warranted.

(3) Width of right-of-way will vary considerably and, as a minimum, needs to be only as wide as the trail itself. In most cases, this minimum should be surpassed to afford some protection from encroachment. Where scenic qualities, anticipated use, and/or physical features warrant, right-of-way may be extended considerably. Generally, 15 feet could be considered a working minimum.

5. CONSTRUCTION

a) Clearing

(1) Any vegetation, except grasses, should be cleared to a minimum of 3 feet from the edge of the bike route surfacing. Overhead clearance should be maintained for a 10-foot minimum.

(2) All dead branches and trunks should be removed from above the trail. All vegetation, including roots, on the subgrade should be removed down to bare earth.

b) Drainage

(1) Drainage should be properly handled to prevent washouts and to avoid ground saturation beneath the trail. The trail should be sloped to provide run-off, and ditches should be provided where necessary. Underdrains may be necessary in very wet places in order to prevent frost action with resultant heaving.

(2) In special instances, catch basins and drains may be needed.

c) Bases

(1) Bases and sub-bases need to be adequately prepared to protect the surface. Removal of topsoil, stumps, and roots and compaction of subgrade will normally be adequate.

(2) In wet or otherwise poor conditions, crushed stone or slag may be necessary for stability. General specifications for sidewalks, light-duty roads, or driveways will generally be applicable.

d) Sight Distances

(1) The sight distance to any hazard or potential hazard must be a minimum of 50 feet at 10 mph. This allows the rider 4 seconds to react to any obstacle or hazard. If this sight distance cannot be provided, warning signs must be posted.

e) Grade

(1) Bike paths shall not exceed a 5 percent grade (except for very short distances). If difficult grade problems cannot be overcome, measures should include the provision of rest stops or lower grade switchbacks.

f) Radius of Curvature

(1) In this standard, a design speed of 20 mph is recommended for bike paths. The following simple linear equation, which relates curve radius to design speed at the relatively low speeds bicycles normally travel, will be used to arrive at radius of curvature:

$$R = 1.25 V + 1.4$$

Where: V = Speed MPH
R = Curve radius in feet

(2) The equation in (1) allows for a minimum R of 58 feet at a V of 20 mph. Since bike paths in parks are used for both pedestrians and bicycles, a maximum of .06 foot per foot superelevation should be used.

g) Width of Path

(1) The minimum width is 6 feet. This allows a cyclist going in one direction to meet and pass a cyclist going in the opposite direction.

h) Bridges

(1) Bridge widths need to be the minimum width of the path.

i) Bike Path Graphics

(1) Route Signing: Adequate signs should be posted at all decision points along a bikeway. This includes both signs informing the cyclist of directional changes and confirmatory signs to ensure that route change has been correctly perceived.

(2) Bike, Pedestrian, and Roadway Crossing Signs: Warning signs indicating to motorists that bicycles should be anticipated and to cyclists that motor vehicles or pedestrians may be encountered should be installed on the approaches to points of potential conflict and at high-activity areas. Included are:

(a) Points where a bikeway crosses a roadway or sidewalk

(b) Bikeway starts and terminations or transition areas involving potential conflict movements

(c) Intense activity areas such as the vicinity of parks, schools, recreational facilities, and community centers

Motorist-directed warning signs on urban streets should be placed at least a half block in advance of the conflict point, and in all circumstances such signs, whether directed to motorists or cyclists, should be placed sufficiently in advance of the conflict point to permit appropriate perception and reaction. Additional cyclist-directed warning signs may be installed as required to warn cyclists of specific hazardous conditions.

See figures 1–37 to 1–46.

D. PEDESTRIAN WALKWAYS

1. RAMPS AND RAMPING COMPONENTS
See figures 1–47 to 1–52.

2. WALKS AND WALKWAY COMPONENTS: SLOPE
See figure 1–53.

3. WALKS AND WALKWAY COMPONENTS: SECTIONS
See figures 1–54 to 1–66.

4. WALKS AND WALKWAY COMPONENTS: CURB CUTS
See figures 1–67 to 1–69.

5. INTEGRAL CONCRETE CURB AND GUTTER
See figure 1–70.

6. STEPS AND ELEVATION CHANGES
See figures 1–71 to 1–76.

7. PEDESTRIAN ACCESS IMPEDIMENTS

All building sites used by the public should be fully accessible to all people. This includes entry to the site for those walking, using a wheelchair, driving, or using public transportation.

a) Site Entrances

(1) High-quality design requires that the location of all site entrances be clearly evident to individuals arriving on foot, by automobile, or via public transportation. The main site entrance should generally provide a direct connection to the accessible building entrance.

b) Walkways

(1) Walkways should provide clearly defined, unobstructed, direct routes through the site, interconnecting site entrances, parking areas, waiting areas, and accessible building entrances. Walking surfaces need to be reasonably firm and level, and curb ramps should be provided as necessary. Walkway widths are generally sized to correspond to projected pedestrian traffic volume.

(2) Any pedestrian path with a gradient of less than 5 percent is a walkway. Wherever possible, walkway gradients should be held to 3 percent or less to prevent excessive fatigue for individuals using wheelchairs. If 4 to 5 percent slopes are necessary, level resting areas 60 inches or longer should be provided at 100-foot intervals. The widths of walkways should be sized to meet projected pedestrian traffic demands. Two-way walkways at least 66 inches wide are recommended; a walkway should not be narrower than 48 inches. Heavily traveled walkways need to be at least 72 inches wide.

c) Parking

(1) For many sites, the primary access for the disabled is vehicular. Parking areas should be related directly to the buildings they serve and connected to accessible building entrances via the wide walkway system. It is recommended that specially designed parking stalls for the physically disabled be located within 100 feet of the accessible building entrance.

(2) Head-in or diagonal parking spaces for the physically disabled should be at least 144 inches (12 feet) wide. Parallel parking may also be used, provided that at least 48 inches of clear space is available beside the car, at the same level as the parking space. Some of these spaces should be on the driver's side and some should be on the passenger's side. Parking spaces that are reserved for the disabled should be clearly identified with the International Symbol of Access. The importance of parking accessibility to the disabled cannot be overemphasized. Given current conditions in public transit, the primary means of travel for most disabled people is a vehicle with operating controls that are modified to meet user needs. The basic requirement for accessible parking is additional space (the standard car and a wheelchair). Extra space between cars is also necessary for the passage of individuals using crutches, canes, and other mobility aids.

(3) At least 2 percent of all parking spaces in any project (with a minimum of two spaces) should be designed and designated as parking for the physically disabled. These spaces should be located as close as possible to an accessible building entrance or should be located centrally in parking lots between

two buildings. Maximum recommended travel distance between accessible parking spaces and building entrance is 200 feet.

d) Building Entrances

(1) Accessible building entrances need to be clearly identifiable. In new construction, the accessible entrance—if all cannot be accessible—should be the main entrance into the lobby or vestibule. This provides convenient access for all building users to public facilities within the structure, such as restrooms, telephones, or drinking fountains, without grade changes.

e) Signage

(1) Adequate directional and informational signage must be provided for pedestrian and vehicular site access. Signs designating accessible building entrances, parking, and specific destinations within the site are especially important. Site signage should be illuminated after dark. Accessible building entrances should be marked with the International Symbol of Access.

(2) For reasons of durability as well as for maximum accessibility, surfaces of walkways should not be "soft" materials such as earth, grass, crushed rock or gravel, or tan bark. Such materials present difficulties to individuals with mobility impairments. The intent of this section, however, is not to prohibit such materials where their textures and colors are appropriate additions to the environment. The suggestion is that soft materials be used judiciously with respect to traffic volume and expected users.

(3) For general use, walkway surfaces of concrete or asphalt are best. Brick, tile, cobbles, and flagstones are good if laid on a concrete bed with full joints (hairline joints when possible). When properly installed, these surfaces remain firm and relatively stable through freeze-thaw cycles. In urban spaces, where several paving surfaces are contemplated, it is suggested that textured materials such as cobbles be reserved for areas out of the mainstream of pedestrian traffic. Concrete walkways require nonslip surfaces for safety. The recommended treatment is a broom finish, with the striations perpendicular to the direction of travel. The number of expansion joints should be minimized, and such joints should not exceed ½ inch in width.

8. PEDESTRIAN ACCESS AREAS

a) Outdoor Ramps

(1) A ramp is any walkway surface sloped more than 5 percent. Ramps should be designed as alternate routes for those who have difficulty using stairs. Ramps should not, however, take the place of outdoor stairs, because some people have difficulty using ramps. The maximum acceptable gradient for accessible ramps is 8.33 percent. Thus, all ramps usable by individuals in wheelchairs fall in a 5 to 8.33 percent gradient range. Ramp length should not exceed 30 feet of run without a landing. In long ramps, the landing serves as a resting place for wheelchair users. Ramps should be at least as wide as the walkways they serve, and in no case should a ramp be narrower than 36 inches.

(2) Handrails should be provided on both sides of ramps to aid individuals using walking aids or wheelchairs. Top rails should be 34 to 36 inches above the ramp surface. On ramps that will be used extensively by children, an intermediate rail at 24 inches is suggested. Ramp handrails should extend horizontally at least 18 inches beyond the upper and lower edges of the sloping ramp surface.

b) Entry Platforms/Vestibules

(1) A level platform at the building entrance allows those with restricted mobility a landing for operating a door. In order for these platforms to be usable, a minimum size of 5 feet square (60 inches across) should be provided, with the platform extending 18 inches beyond the strike jamb of the door.

(2) Shallow vestibules prohibit or restrict maneuvering for those with mobility limitations. A sufficiently deep vestibule permits the operation of one door at a time.

c) Doorways

(1) Doors in the accessible route of travel should be sufficiently wide to allow passage of wheelchairs and individuals on crutches. The doors should be easily operated with a pressure not to exceed 8 pounds when applied by the user. They should have an accessible International Symbol of Access. There should be levered door handles, a 12-inch-high kick plate at the bottom, and a threshold maximum height at the bottom of the door frame of no greater than $\frac{1}{2}$ inch. Should there be a floor mat or carpet, it must be flush with the finished door.

d) Stairs/Handrails

(1) The size and shape of handrails should be such that they can be easily grasped. They should be located no closer to the wall than $1\frac{1}{2}$ inches and, at the same time, should not exceed a diameter of $1\frac{1}{2}$ inches. Various configurations can be used.

(2) Some individuals with mobility limitations are able to use stairways. However, since many semiambulatory people have problems with foot drag when ascending stairs, a closed riser system, with the nose of the tread rounded, reduces the hazard of tripping and is the preferred type. Stairs should be no greater than 7 inches in height and no greater than 11 inches in depth. From the top and bottom of the stairs, there should be a handrail that extends at least 18 inches horizontally at a level no higher than 34 inches in height.

e) Toilet Compartments

(1) Toilet compartments for the disabled should have sufficient depth and width to allow for the needed

maneuvering and should be arranged to provide lateral transfer space for those in wheelchairs. Grab bars should be wall-mounted to avoid obstructing such maneuvering areas. Grab bars should be placed approximately 33 inches off the ground and should be horizontal to the ground. The height of the toilet seat should be approximately 20 to 22 inches from the ground. The ideal width for the doorway to the toilet compartment should be a minimum of 32 inches; the interior operating space inside the doorway should be 54 inches across. The compartment should have a minimum depth of 58 inches. The door to the bathroom should pull out.

(2) Many companies and users are finding that where space considerations do not permit additional room for the accessible toilet compartment, a curtain in lieu of a door is acceptable. An open area to the left *or* to the right of the toilet is considered accessible and will permit transfer from a wheelchair to the toilet and back again.

f) Toilet Rooms

(1) Toilet rooms with one or more compartments should allow sufficient maneuvering space for the disabled. When privacy screens are provided, allowance should be made for turning space, which will vary with the direction of the door swing. Single walk-in toilet rooms, for use by either sex, may be an alternative to conversion of compartments in multiple-use facilities.

(2) In any toilet rooms for use by the disabled, at least one each of such fixtures as mirrors, dispensers, or shelves should be at a usable height for those in wheelchairs. The tops of sinks should be no higher than 34 inches from the ground. Sufficient protection should be provided to prevent legs from burning on pipes underneath the sink. Towel bars, shelves, and dispensers should be located no higher than 40 inches, and the bottoms of mirrors should be located at the same height.

9. TYPICAL PEDESTRIAN BARRIERS

The following discussion is meant to be an aid to visualizing specific kinds of common barriers. These are arranged according to an individual's typical progression up to and through a building. *They must be seen as part of the whole and are broken down here for convenience only.* The listing of barriers is not intended as a checklist, but rather is designed to offer a composite profile of barriers that typically face the disabled person.

a) Parking and Approaches to Building Entrances

(1) Parking

  (a) Space too narrow to permit transfer to wheelchair or crutches

  (b) Space not level

  (c) A curb or step from space to paved walk

  (d) Parking meter out of reach

(2) Approach

  (a) Street between parking space and building entrance

  (b) No curb cut or traffic light at crossing

  (c) Curb cut blocked by a car

  (d) No snow removal

  (e) Step between sidewalk and entrance

  (f) Ramp, if provided, too steep for wheelchair or crutches

(3) Entrance

  (a) Doors too narrow to admit wheelchair

  (b) Revolving doors that operate while flush side doors are locked

  (c) Distance between outer and inner door too short

  (d) Excessive pressure needed to operate doors

b) Travel within Building

(1) Stairs

  (a) Steps open or with projecting nosing under which toes may be caught

  (b) Risers exceeding 7 inches

  (c) Handrail too high or low to use, hard to grasp due to its size or shape, or not extending beyond the steps

(2) Elevators

  (a) Entrance too narrow to admit wheelchair

  (b) Floor level out of alignment with building floor

  (c) Controls for upper floors out of reach

  (d) Buttons flush, precluding unaided use by blind

  (e) Audible arrival signal that does not tell blind whether cab is on way up or down

(3) Architectural Elements to Add or Modify

  (a) Concrete access ramps

  (b) Ramped sidewalks

  (c) Concrete access bridges

  (d) Wooden ramps

  (e) Access to swimming pools

  (f) Water fountains

  (g) Public telephones

  (h) Concrete retaining walls

  (i) Curb cuts

  (j) Grading

  (k) Toilet stalls

  (l) Shower cubicles

  (m) Lavatories

  (n) Bathrooms

  (o) Door clearances

  (p) Elevators

  (q) Automatic doors

  (r) Instrumentation and controls

  (s) Tactile and audible warnings

10. PEDESTRIAN CROSSWALKS

See figures 1–77 and 1–78.

SHELTER SITE EVALUATION FORM

_____   _____
Origin of Request   Date

_____   _____
Location   Bus Route

Preferred Shelter Allocation Categories   Check One
                                              ( )

Elderly and handicapped   _____
Retirement facility, nursing home   _____
Medical facility   _____
Public institution   _____
Major trip generator: shopping center _____
Apartments, industrial park, large   _____
residential development   _____
Major transfer points   _____
Fixed route accessibility improvements _____

Passenger Counts

                                                      Total
   Date   On Count   Off Count   Passengers
_____   _____   _____   _____
_____   _____   _____   _____
_____   _____   _____   _____
_____   _____   _____   _____
_____   _____   _____   _____

Compatibility with Plans
(10) _____ No programmed change in route or service
(5) _____ Programmed decrease in service
( ) _____ Programmed change in route within 1 year
TOTAL SCORE: _____
             (Possible 150)

Final Dispensation: _____
_____
_____
_____
_____
_____

                          _____
                          Prepared by

                          _____

1-1. Shelter Site Evaluation Form

A. MASS TRANSIT

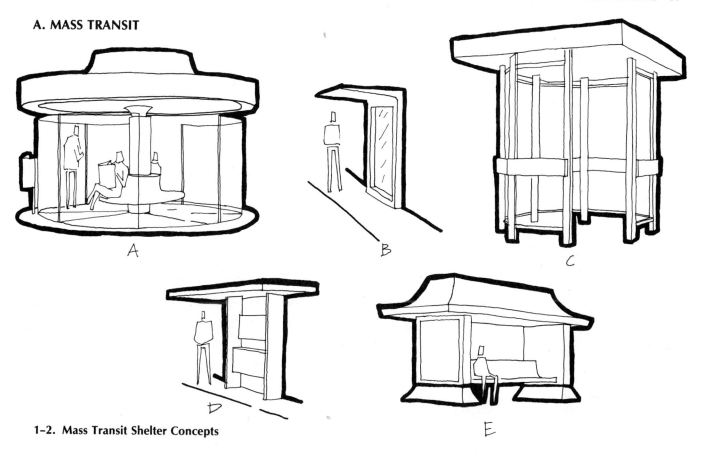

1-2. Mass Transit Shelter Concepts

Capacity Required (Bays) When Service Time at Stop Is Seconds

Peak Hour Bus Flow	10	20	30	40	60
15	1	1	1	1	1
30	1	1	1	1	2
45	1	1	2	2	2
60	1	1	2	2	3
75	1	2	2	3	3
90	1	2	2	3	4
105	1	2	3	3	4
120	1	2	3	3	5
150	2	3	3	4	5
180	2	3	4	5	6

1-3. Bus Stop and Bay Capacity Requirements

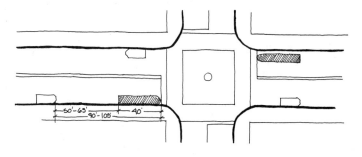

1-5. Near-Side Bus Stop

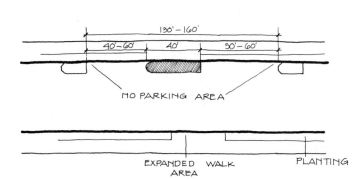

1-4. Midblock Bus Stop

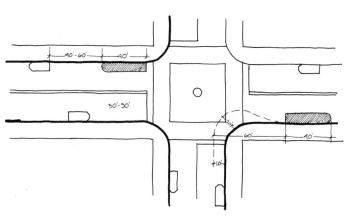

1-6. Far-Side Bus Stop

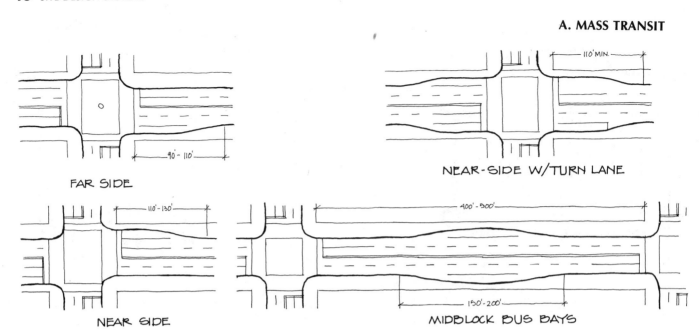

FAR SIDE

NEAR-SIDE W/TURN LANE

NEAR SIDE

MIDBLOCK BUS BAYS

1-7. Arterial Bus Bay Locations

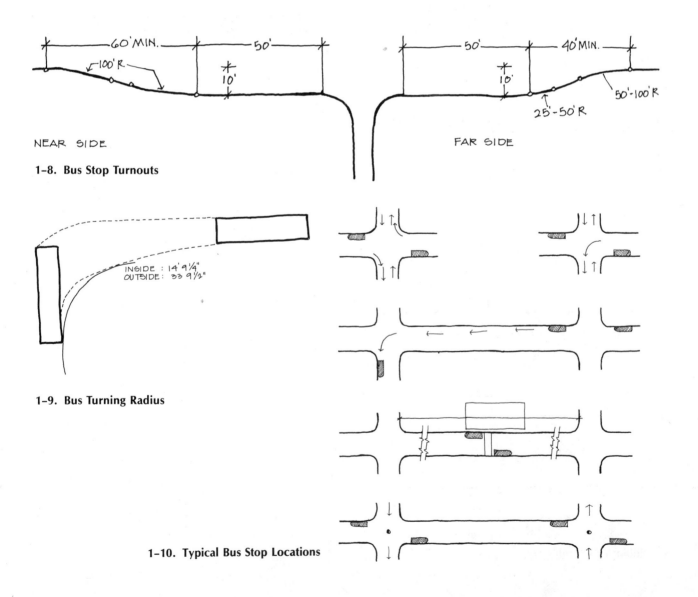

NEAR SIDE

FAR SIDE

1-8. Bus Stop Turnouts

INSIDE : 14' 9¼"
OUTSIDE: 33 9½"

1-9. Bus Turning Radius

1-10. Typical Bus Stop Locations

A. MASS TRANSIT

BENCH SITE EVALUATION FORM

Origin of Request _____   Date _____

Location _____   Bus Route _____

Passenger Counts

Date	On Count	Off Count	Total Passengers
_____	_____	_____	_____
_____	_____	_____	_____
_____	_____	_____	_____
_____	_____	_____	_____

Feasibility

(a) Safety (Traffic Engineer's Review)

    (10) __ No hazards

    (5) __ Some hazards: _____

                       (Explain)

    ( ) __ Very hazardous _____

                       (Explain)

(b) Adjacent Property Owner's Acceptance

    (10) __ Yes

    (5) __ Conditional

    (0) __ No

(c) LTS Assessment

    (10) __ Greatly needed

    (5) __ Slightly needed

    ( ) __ Not needed

(d) Site Characteristics

    (10) __ Desirable, minimum preparation required

    (5) __ Desirable, major preparation required

    ( ) __ Undesirable, not feasible: _____

                       (Explain)

(e) Bench or Shelters Already Installed

    (10) __ More than 5 blocks away

    (5) __ Within 5 blocks

    (0) __ Within 1 block

(f) Passenger Usage

    (10) __ High (15+)

    (5) __ Medium (10+)

    ( ) __ Low (below 10), not needed

(g) Compatibility with Plans

    (10) __ No programmed change in route or service

    (5) __ Programmed decrease in service

    ( ) __ Programmed change in route within 1 year

(h) Route Density

    (5) __ Site served by two or more routes

TOTAL SCORE: _____ (Possible 75)

FINAL DISPENSATION: _____

_____

_____

_____

_____

Prepared by _____

(Date) _____

1-11. Bench Site Evaluation Form

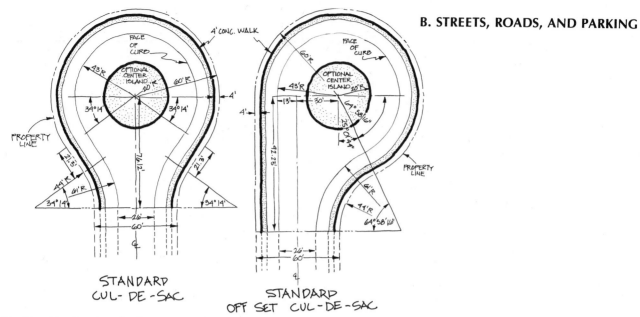

STANDARD
CUL-DE-SAC

STANDARD
OFF SET CUL-DE-SAC

1–12. Street Design Standards, 60-Ft. Radius

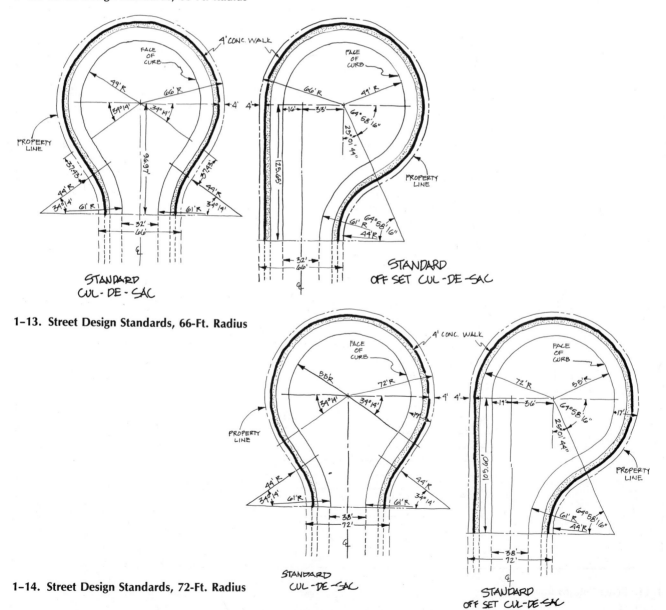

STANDARD
CUL-DE-SAC

STANDARD
OFF SET CUL-DE-SAC

1–13. Street Design Standards, 66-Ft. Radius

1–14. Street Design Standards, 72-Ft. Radius

STANDARD
CUL-DE-SAC

STANDARD
OFF SET CUL-DE-SAC

B. STREETS, ROADS, AND PARKING

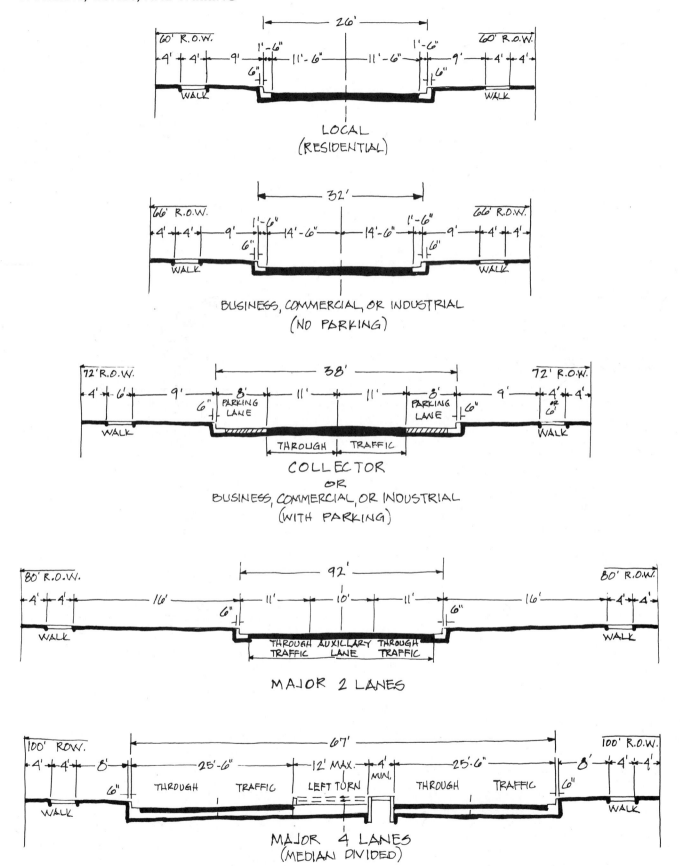

1–15. Typical Residential/Commercial Street Sections

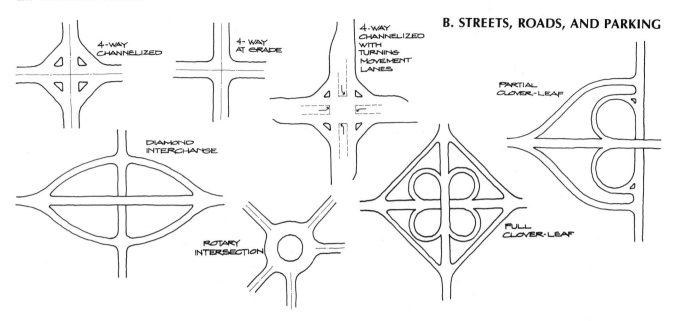

1-16. Typical Intersections

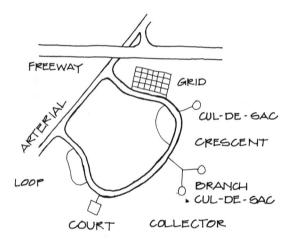

1-17. Arterial Types

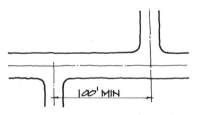

ALLOW 100' BETWEEN ALL INTERSECTIONS

1-18. Converging Intersections

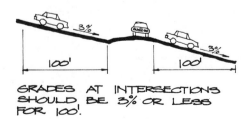

GRADES AT INTERSECTIONS SHOULD BE 3% OR LESS FOR 100'.

1-19. Intersection Grades

AVOID INTERSECTIONS BELOW THE BROW OF A HILL

1-20. Below-Grade Intersections

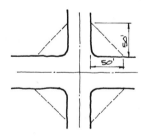

A 50' TRIANGLE ON ALL SIDES OF AN INTERSECTION SHOULD BE CLEAR OF VISUAL OBSTRUCTIONS

1-21. Intersection Sight-Distance

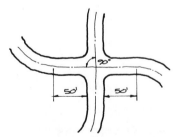

INTERSECTIONS SHOULD ENTER AT 90° WITHIN 50' EACH DIRECTION. ANGLED INTERSECTIONS ARE SELDOM JUSTIFIED.

1-22. Angled Intersections

B. STREETS, ROADS, AND PARKING

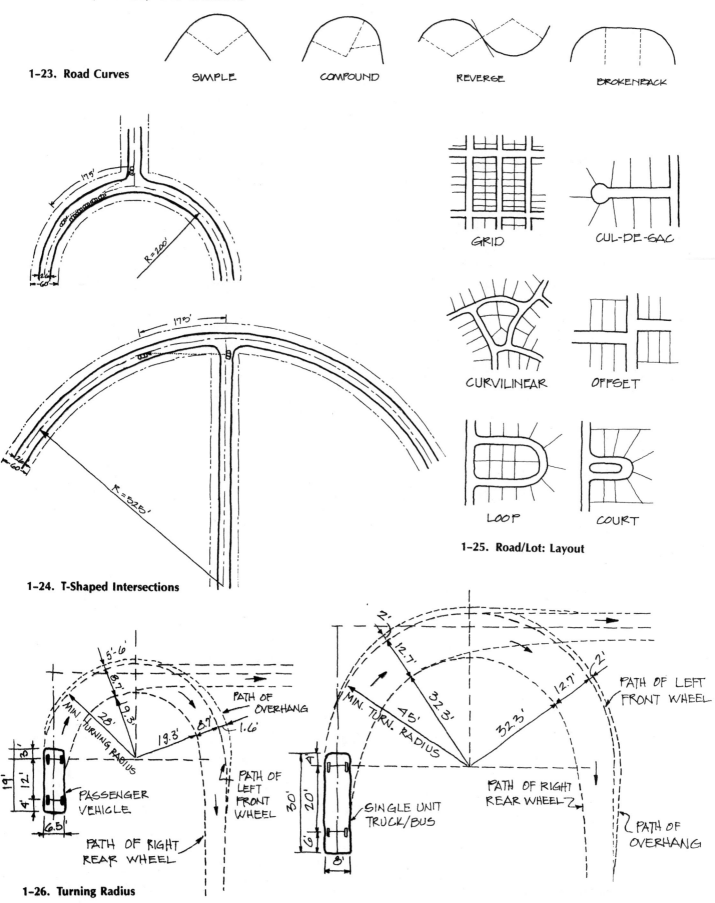

1–23. Road Curves

SIMPLE   COMPOUND   REVERSE   BROKENBACK

1–24. T-Shaped Intersections

GRID   CUL-DE-SAC

CURVILINEAR   OFFSET

LOOP   COURT

1–25. Road/Lot: Layout

1–26. Turning Radius

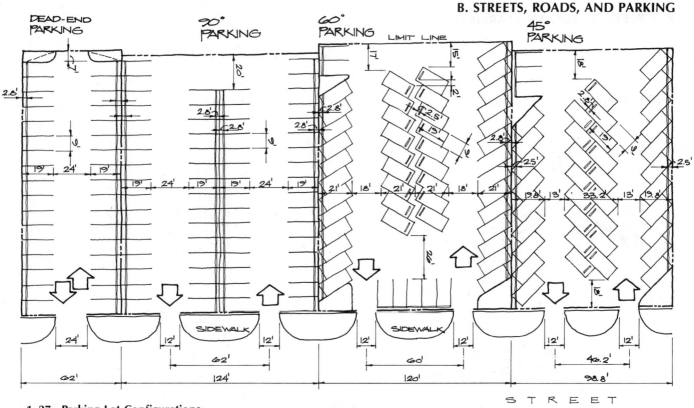

1-27. Parking Lot Configurations

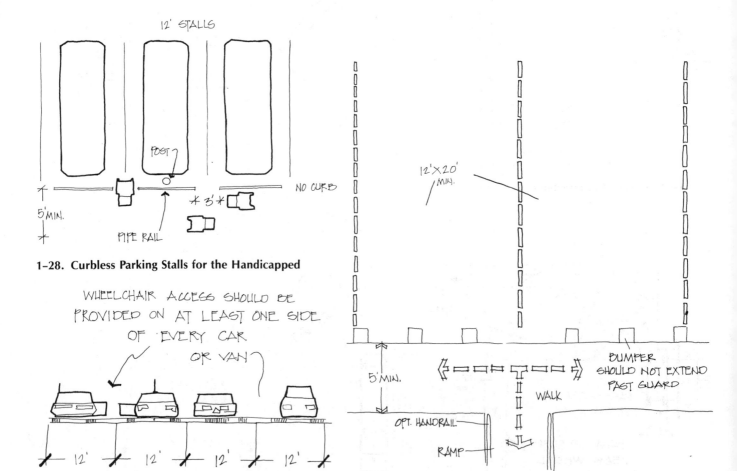

1-28. Curbless Parking Stalls for the Handicapped

WHEELCHAIR ACCESS SHOULD BE
PROVIDED ON AT LEAST ONE SIDE
OF EVERY CAR
OR VAN

1-29. Parking Stall for the Handicapped: Section

1-30. Parking Stall for the Handicapped: Plan

B. STREETS, ROADS, AND PARKING

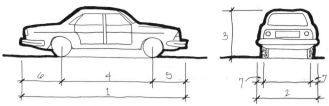

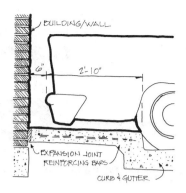

Small Cars		Size		Standard Auto		Size	
1.	Length	15' 5"		1.	Length	17' 9"	
2.	Width	5' 10"		2.	Width	6' 8"	
3.	Height	4' 10"		3.	Height	5' 2"	
4.	Wheelbase	9' 2"		4.	Wheelbase	10' 7"	
5.	Overhang (f)	2' 6"		5.	Overhang (f)	2' 10"	
6.	Overhang (r)	3' 9"		6.	Overhang (r)	4' 4"	
7.	Overhang (s)	0' 7"		7.	Overhang (s)	0' 9"	
8.	Track	4' 9"		8.	Track	5' 2"	

Compact Cars		Size		Large Auto		Size	
1.	Length	16' 11"		1.	Length	18' 0"	
2.	Width	6' 3"		2.	Width	6' 8"	
3.	Height	5' 1"		3.	Height	5' 4"	
4.	Wheelbase	10' 1"		4.	Wheelbase	10' 8"	
5.	Overhang (f)	2' 7"		5.	Overhang (f)	2' 10"	
6.	Overhang (r)	4' 3"		6.	Overhang (r)	4' 6"	
7.	Overhang (s)	0' 9"		7.	Overhang (s)	0' 8"	
8.	Track	4' 11"		8.	Track	5' 3"	

Dimensions will vary witih model/year

1–31. Typical Auto Sizes

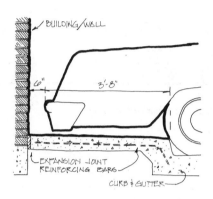

1–34. Parking Lot, Head-In Parking Stop

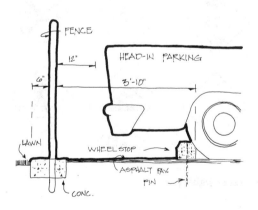

1–32. Parking Lot, Wheel Stop

1–35. Parking Lot, Back-In Parking

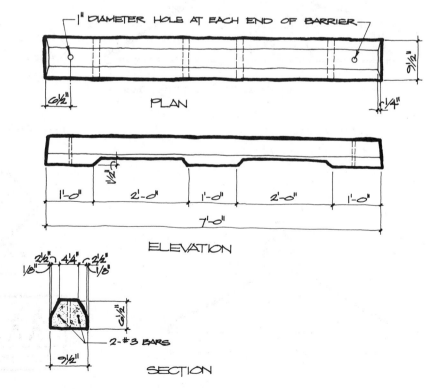

1–36. Parking Lot, Wheel Stop: Detail

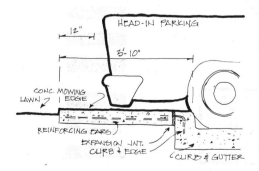

1–33. Parking Lot, Curb and Gutter Wheel Stop

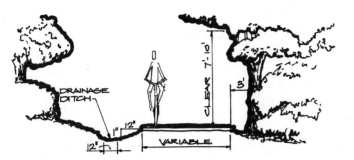

1-37. Clearing and Drainage: Typical Section

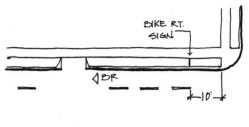

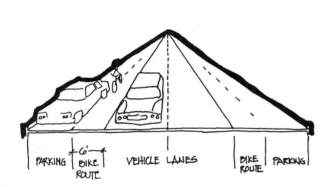

1-38. Bicycle Lane in Residential Street

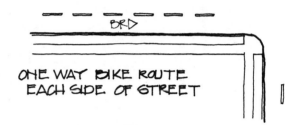

1-41. One-Way Bike Route Each Side of Street

1-39. Interior Bicycle Lane

1-42. Typical Bikeway Signing

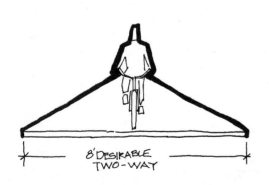

1-40. Typical Bicycle Lane

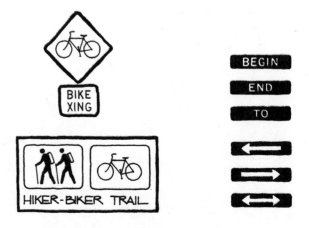

1-43. Sign Graphics, Typical

C. BICYCLE SYSTEMS

RIDER WIDTH

2'-2"

TIRE WIDTH
7/8"

1-44. Rider Width, Typical

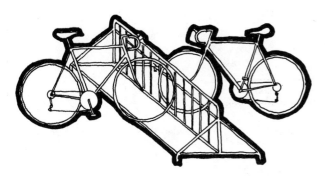

1-45. Bike Rack, Typical

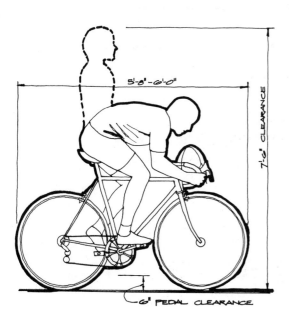

5'-8"-6'-0"

7'-6" CLEARANCE

6" PEDAL CLEARANCE

1-46. Rider Profile, Typical

D. PEDESTRIAN WALKWAYS

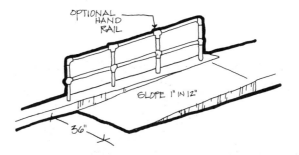

OPTIONAL HAND RAIL

SLOPE 1" IN 12"

36"

1-47. Ramped Curb with Handrail

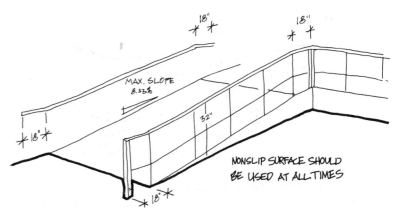

18"

18"

MAX. SLOPE
8.33%

32"

18"

18"

NONSLIP SURFACE SHOULD
BE USED AT ALL TIMES

1-48. Typical Entry Ramp

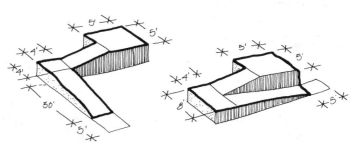

5'

5'

4'

4'

30'

5'

5'

5'

4'

8'

5'

1-49. Typical Ramp Systems

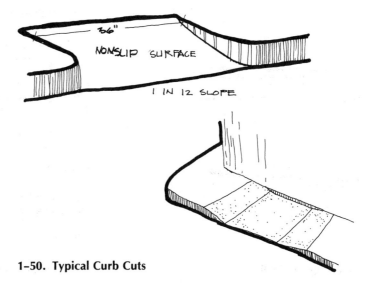

36"

NONSLIP SURFACE

1 IN 12 SLOPE

1-50. Typical Curb Cuts

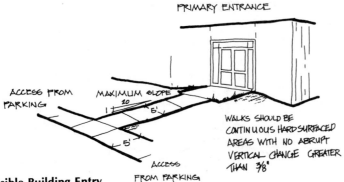

PRIMARY ENTRANCE

ACCESS FROM PARKING

MAXIMUM SLOPE 1 20 6'

5'

ACCESS FROM PARKING

WALKS SHOULD BE CONTINUOUS HARD SURFACED AREAS WITH NO ABRUPT VERTICAL CHANGE GREATER THAN 3/8"

1-51. Accessible Building Entry

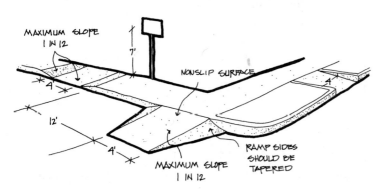

MAXIMUM SLOPE 1 IN 12

7'

NONSLIP SURFACE

4'

12'

4'

MAXIMUM SLOPE 1 IN 12

RAMP SIDES SHOULD BE TAPERED

1-52. Typical Curbed Ramp Approach

5%

LONGITUDINAL SLOPE ON WALKS

10%

MAXIMUM LONGITUDINAL SLOPE ON WALKS

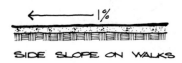

1%

SIDE SLOPE ON WALKS

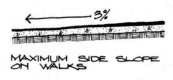

3%

MAXIMUM SIDE SLOPE ON WALKS

1-53. Slope on Walks

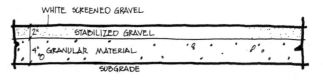

CONTRACTION JOINT

1½" EXPANSION JOINT
½" DOWEL

WIRE MESH

6" POURED CONCRETE W/COMPACTED SUBGRADE

1-54. Poured Concrete Walk, 6"

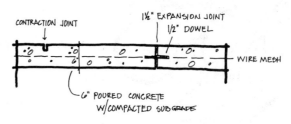

WHITE SCREENED GRAVEL

2" STABILIZED GRAVEL

4" GRANULAR MATERIAL

SUBGRADE

1-55. Stabilized Gravel Walk

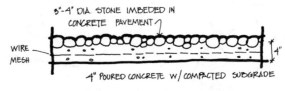

3"-4" DIA. STONE IMBEDED IN CONCRETE PAVEMENT

WIRE MESH

4"

4" POURED CONCRETE W/ COMPACTED SUBGRADE

1-56. Stone Walk

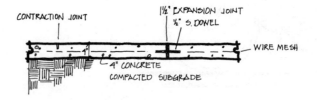

CONTRACTION JOINT

1½" EXPANSION JOINT
½" S. DOWEL

WIRE MESH

4" CONCRETE COMPACTED SUBGRADE

1-57. Poured Concrete Walk, 4"

D. PEDESTRIAN WALKWAYS

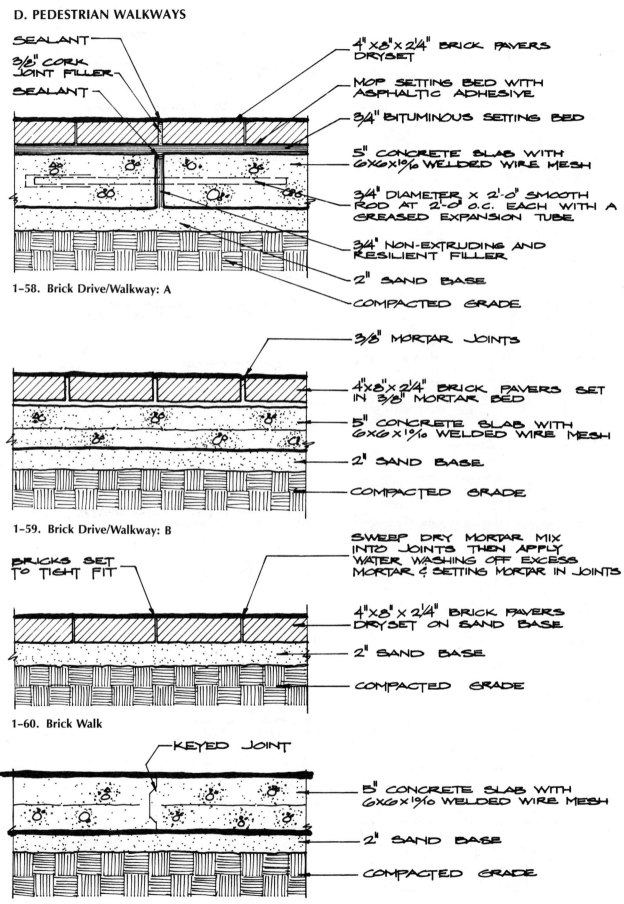

SEALANT

3/8" CORK JOINT FILLER

SEALANT

4" x 8" x 2¼" BRICK PAVERS DRYSET

MOP SETTING BED WITH ASPHALTIC ADHESIVE

3/4" BITUMINOUS SETTING BED

5" CONCRETE SLAB WITH 6 x 6 x 10/10 WELDED WIRE MESH

3/4" DIAMETER x 2'-0" SMOOTH ROD AT 2'-0" O.C. EACH WITH A GREASED EXPANSION TUBE

3/4" NON-EXTRUDING AND RESILIENT FILLER

2" SAND BASE

COMPACTED GRADE

1-58. Brick Drive/Walkway: A

3/8" MORTAR JOINTS

4" x 8" x 2¼" BRICK PAVERS SET IN 3/8" MORTAR BED

5" CONCRETE SLAB WITH 6 x 6 x 10/10 WELDED WIRE MESH

2" SAND BASE

COMPACTED GRADE

1-59. Brick Drive/Walkway: B

BRICKS SET TO TIGHT FIT

SWEEP DRY MORTAR MIX INTO JOINTS THEN APPLY WATER WASHING OFF EXCESS MORTAR & SETTING MORTAR IN JOINTS

4" x 8" x 2¼" BRICK PAVERS DRYSET ON SAND BASE

2" SAND BASE

COMPACTED GRADE

1-60. Brick Walk

KEYED JOINT

5" CONCRETE SLAB WITH 6 x 6 x 10/10 WELDED WIRE MESH

2" SAND BASE

COMPACTED GRADE

1-61. Construction Joint, Concrete Sidewalk

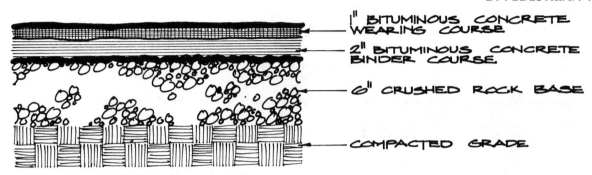

1" BITUMINOUS CONCRETE WEARING COURSE

2" BITUMINOUS CONCRETE BINDER COURSE

6" CRUSHED ROCK BASE

COMPACTED GRADE

1-62. Bituminous Concrete Walk

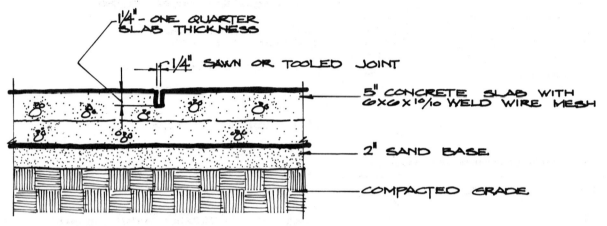

1/4" - ONE QUARTER SLAB THICKNESS

1/4" SAWN OR TOOLED JOINT

5" CONCRETE SLAB WITH 6×6 × 10/10 WELD WIRE MESH

2" SAND BASE

COMPACTED GRADE

1-63. Control Joint, Concrete Sidewalk

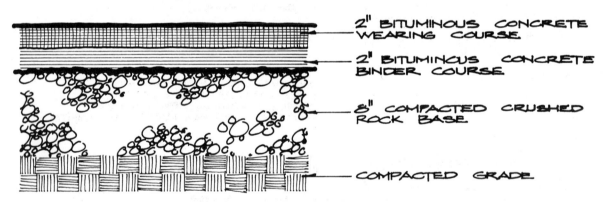

2" BITUMINOUS CONCRETE WEARING COURSE

2" BITUMINOUS CONCRETE BINDER COURSE

8" COMPACTED CRUSHED ROCK BASE

COMPACTED GRADE

1-64. Bituminous Concrete Walk/Drive

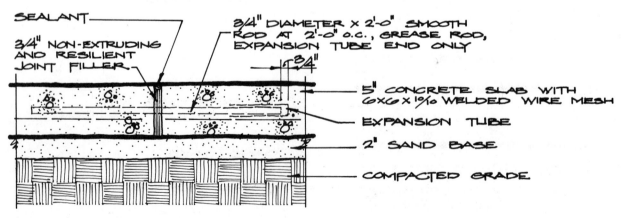

SEALANT

3/4" NON-EXTRUDING AND RESILIENT JOINT FILLER

3/4" DIAMETER × 2'-0" SMOOTH ROD AT 2'-0" O.C., GREASE ROD, EXPANSION TUBE END ONLY

3/4"

5" CONCRETE SLAB WITH 6×6 × 10/10 WELDED WIRE MESH

EXPANSION TUBE

2" SAND BASE

COMPACTED GRADE

1-65. Expansion Joint, Concrete Sidewalk

D. PEDESTRIAN WALKWAYS

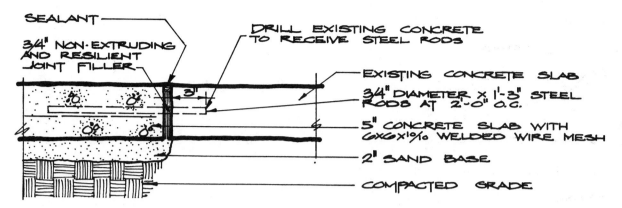

SEALANT

3/4" NON-EXTRUDING AND RESILIENT JOINT FILLER

DRILL EXISTING CONCRETE TO RECEIVE STEEL RODS

3"

EXISTING CONCRETE SLAB

3/4" DIAMETER X 1'-3" STEEL RODS AT 2'-0" O.C.

5" CONCRETE SLAB WITH 6X6X10/10 WELDED WIRE MESH

2" SAND BASE

COMPACTED GRADE

1-66. New Pavement at Existing Walk

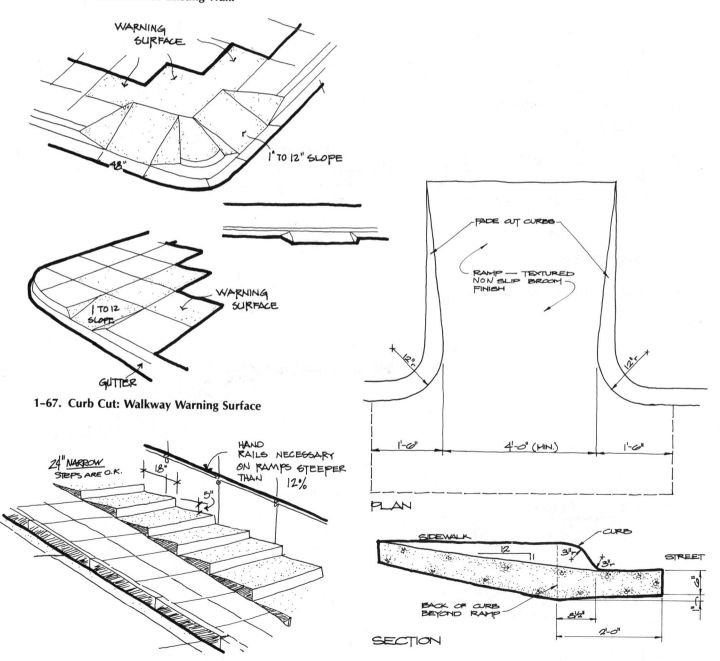

WARNING SURFACE

1" TO 12" SLOPE

48"

WARNING SURFACE

1 TO 12 SLOPE

GUTTER

1-67. Curb Cut: Walkway Warning Surface

24" NARROW STEPS ARE O.K.

18"

HAND RAILS NECESSARY ON RAMPS STEEPER THAN 12%

5"

1-68. Ramp/Walk Combination

FADE OUT CURBS

RAMP — TEXTURED NON SLIP BROOM FINISH

12"r

12"r

1'-6"   4'-0" (MIN.)   1'-6"

PLAN

SIDEWALK

12
11

CURB

3"r

3"r

STREET

6"

BACK OF CURB BEYOND RAMP

8½"

2'-0"

SECTION

1-69. Street/Sidewalk Ramp: Section

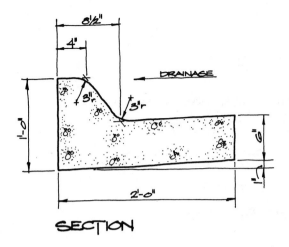

SECTION

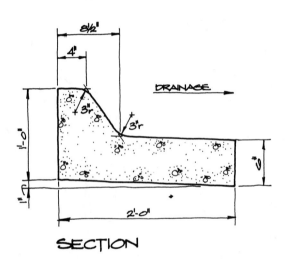

SECTION

1-70. Integral Concrete Curb and Gutter

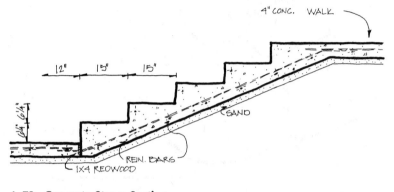

1-72. Concrete Steps: Section

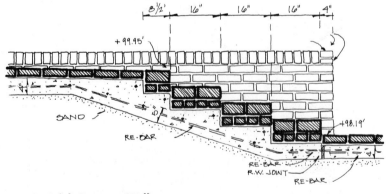

1-73. Brick Steps on Wall

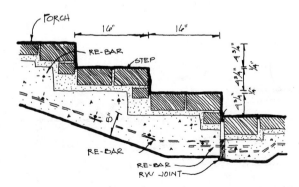

1-71. Brick Steps: Section

D. PEDESTRIAN WALKWAYS

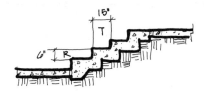

STEP PROPORTION

STEPS SHOULD OCCUR
IN PAIRS

LANDING

MORE THAN 9 STEPS
SHOULD BE SEPARATED
BY A LANDING

STEPS

1-74. Step Components

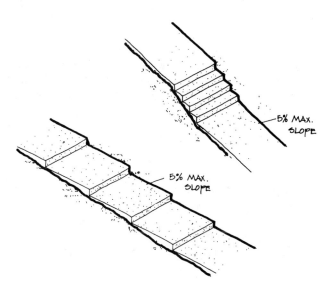

5% MAX.
SLOPE

5% MAX.
SLOPE

1-76. Steps in Walks

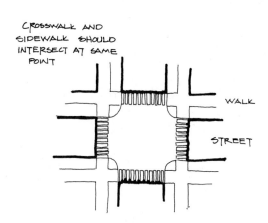

CROSSWALK AND
SIDEWALK SHOULD
INTERSECT AT SAME
POINT

WALK

STREET

1-77. Typical Crosswalk Design

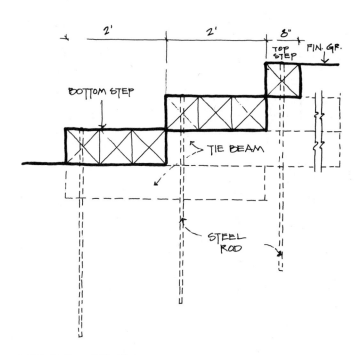

TOP
STEP

FIN. GR.

BOTTOM STEP

TIE BEAM

STEEL
ROD

1-75. Railroad Tie Steps

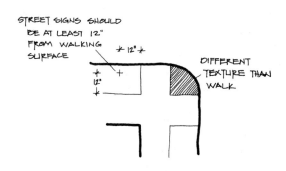

STREET SIGNS SHOULD
BE AT LEAST 12"
FROM WALKING
SURFACE

DIFFERENT
TEXTURE THAN
WALK

1-78. Typical Crosswalk Corner

Environmental Systems ____

The environmental considerations for site design are numerous and varied. The following reference components have been compiled to assist the site designer in relating the issues of national standards to the specific project values of location, climate, and vegetation ecosystem.

A. STATE REFERENCE MAPS
See figures 1–79 to 1–127.

B. GENERAL REFERENCE SYSTEMS
1. PLANT-MATERIAL GROWTH REGIONS
   See figure 1–128.

2. HARDINESS ZONES
   See figure 1–129.

3. FROST PENETRATION
   See figure 1–130.

4. SUN ANGLE/ORIENTATION
   See figure 1–131.

5. TERMITE DAMAGE LIMITATIONS
   See figure 1–132.

6. AVERAGE DESIGN TEMPERATURE (OUTSIDE)
   See figure 1–133.

7. RAINFALL INTENSITY MAP
   See figure 1–134.

8. HEATING/COOLING HOURS PER YEAR
   See figure 1–135.

9. WARM/HUMID REGIONS OF THE UNITED STATES
   See figure 1–136.

10. MAJOR TERMITE INFESTATION AREAS
    See figure 1–137.

11. COMMON GRASS ZONES OF THE UNITED STATES
    See figure 1–138.

12. U.S. TIME ZONES
    See figure 1–139.

13. EARTH MOTION/SOLAR CONSTANT
    See figure 1–140.

14. DRY/HOT REGIONS OF THE UNITED STATES
    See figure 1–141.

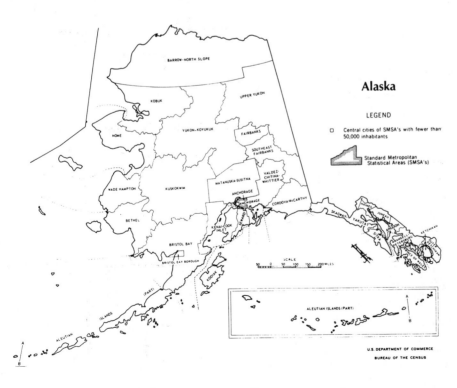

1-79.

A. STATE REFERENCE MAPS

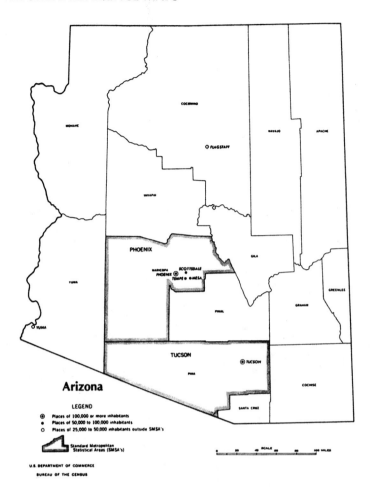

1–80.

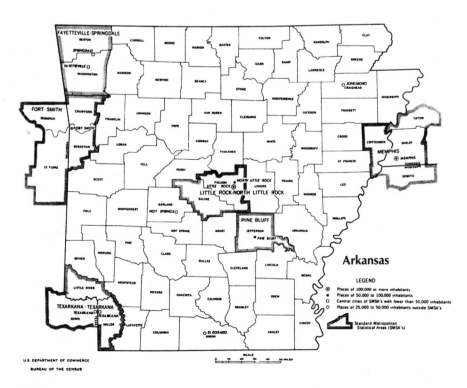

1–81.

California

LEGEND
- ⊚ Places of 100,000 or more inhabitants
- ● Places of 50,000 to 100,000 inhabitants
- □ Central cities of SMSA's with fewer than 50,000 inhabitants
- ○ Places of 25,000 to 50,000 inhabitants outside SMSA's

Standard Metropolitan
Statistical Areas (SMSA's)

U.S. DEPARTMENT OF COMMERCE   BUREAU OF THE CENSUS

1–82.

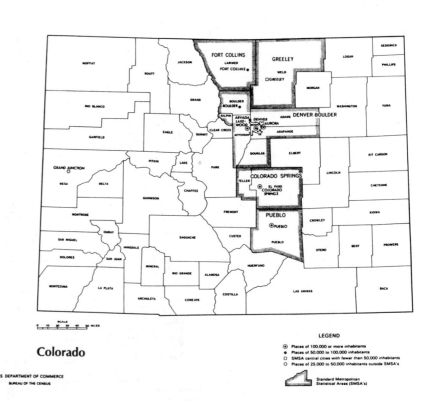

Colorado

U.S. DEPARTMENT OF COMMERCE
BUREAU OF THE CENSUS

LEGEND
- ⊚ Places of 100,000 or more inhabitants
- ● Places of 50,000 to 100,000 inhabitants
- □ SMSA central cities with fewer than 50,000 inhabitants
- ○ Places of 25,000 to 50,000 inhabitants outside SMSA's

Standard Metropolitan
Statistical Areas (SMSA's)

1–83.

A. STATE REFERENCE MAPS

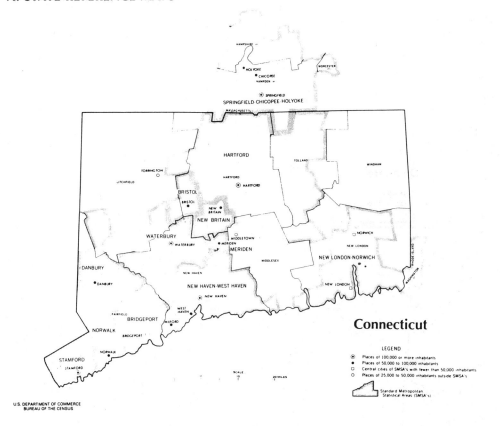

Connecticut

LEGEND
- Places of 100,000 or more inhabitants
- Places of 50,000 to 100,000 inhabitants
- Central cities of SMSA's with fewer than 50,000 inhabitants
- Places of 25,000 to 50,000 inhabitants outside SMSA's

Standard Metropolitan
Statistical Areas (SMSA's)

SCALE
0   10   20 MILES

U.S. DEPARTMENT OF COMMERCE
BUREAU OF THE CENSUS

1–84.

District of Columbia

LEGEND
- Places of 100,000 or more inhabitants

Standard Metropolitan
Statistical Areas (SMSA's)

SCALE
0   10 MILES

U.S. DEPARTMENT OF COMMERCE
BUREAU OF THE CENSUS

1–85.

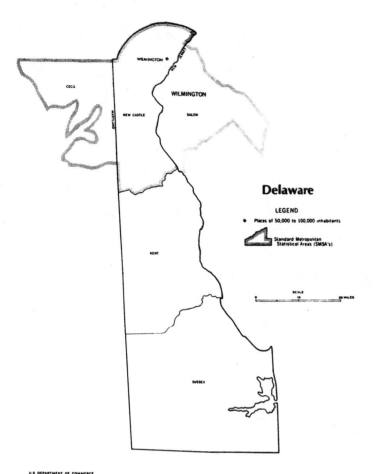

Delaware

LEGEND

● Places of 50,000 to 100,000 inhabitants

Standard Metropolitan
Statistical Areas (SMSA's)

SCALE
10   20 MILES

U.S. DEPARTMENT OF COMMERCE
BUREAU OF THE CENSUS

1–86.

Florida

LEGEND

⊚ Places of 100,000 or more inhabitants
● Places of 50,000 to 100,000 inhabitants
□ SMSA central cities with fewer than 50,000 inhabitants
○ Places of 25,000 to 50,000 inhabitants outside SMSA's

Standard Metropolitan
Statistical Areas (SMSA's)

U.S. DEPARTMENT OF COMMERCE
BUREAU OF THE CENSUS

1–87.

A. STATE REFERENCE MAPS

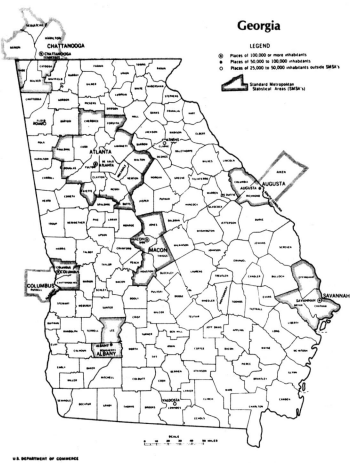

Georgia

LEGEND

⊙ Places of 100,000 or more inhabitants
● Places of 50,000 to 100,000 inhabitants
○ Places of 25,000 to 50,000 inhabitants outside SMSA's

Standard Metropolitan
Statistical Areas (SMSA's)

SCALE
0 10 20 30 40 50 MILES

U.S. DEPARTMENT OF COMMERCE
BUREAU OF THE CENSUS

1-88.

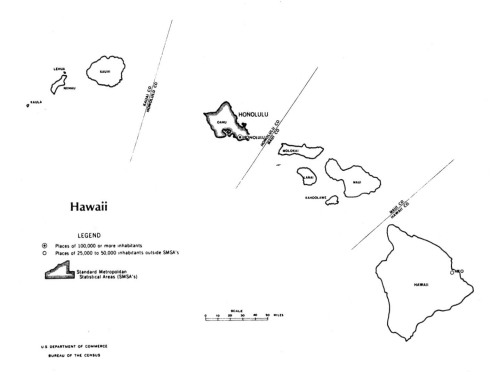

Hawaii

LEGEND

⊙ Places of 100,000 or more inhabitants
○ Places of 25,000 to 50,000 inhabitants outside SMSA's

Standard Metropolitan
Statistical Areas (SMSA's)

SCALE
0 10 20 30 40 50 MILES

U.S. DEPARTMENT OF COMMERCE
BUREAU OF THE CENSUS

1-89.

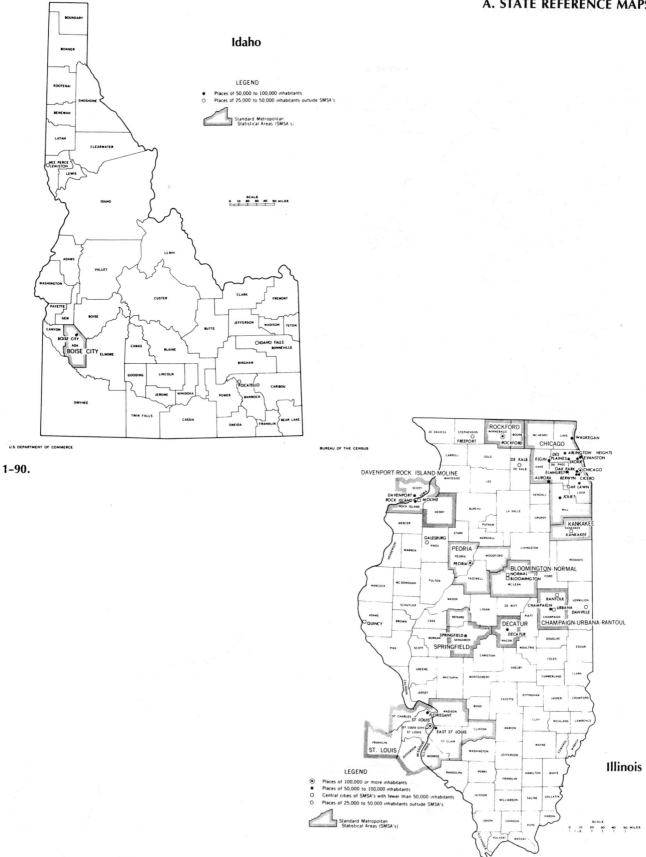

Idaho

LEGEND

● Places of 50,000 to 100,000 inhabitants
○ Places of 25,000 to 50,000 inhabitants outside SMSA's

Standard Metropolitan
Statistical Areas (SMSA's)

SCALE
0 10 20 30 40 50 MILES

U.S. DEPARTMENT OF COMMERCE

BUREAU OF THE CENSUS

1-90.

Illinois

LEGEND

⊙ Places of 100,000 or more inhabitants
● Places of 50,000 to 100,000 inhabitants
□ Central cities of SMSA's with fewer than 50,000 inhabitants
○ Places of 25,000 to 50,000 inhabitants outside SMSA's

Standard Metropolitan
Statistical Areas (SMSA's)

SCALE
0 10 20 30 40 50 MILES

U.S. DEPARTMENT OF COMMERCE

BUREAU OF THE CENSUS

1-91.

A. STATE REFERENCE MAPS

Indiana

LEGEND

◉ Places of 100,000 or more inhabitants
● Places of 50,000 to 100,000 inhabitants
□ SMSA central cities with fewer than 50,000 inhabitants
○ Places of 25,000 to 50,000 inhabitants outside SMSA's

Standard Metropolitan
Statistical Areas (SMSA's)

U S DEPARTMENT OF COMMERCE
BUREAU OF THE CENSUS

1–92.

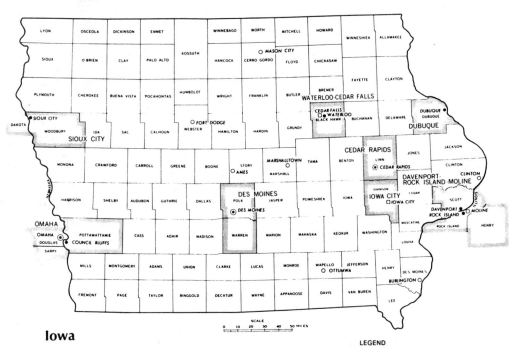

Iowa

LEGEND

◉ Places of 100,000 or more inhabitants
● Places of 50,000 to 100,000 inhabitants
□ SMSA central cities with fewer than 50,000 inhabitants
○ Places of 25,000 to 50,000 inhabitants outside SMSA's

Standard Metropolitan
Statistical Areas (SMSA's)

1–93.   U S DEPARTMENT OF COMMERCE
BUREAU OF THE CENSUS

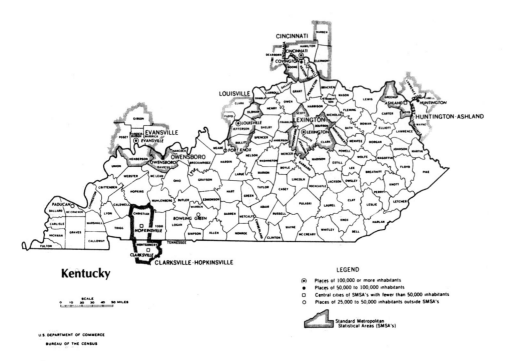

Kentucky

SCALE
0 10 20 30 40 50 MILES

LEGEND
⊙ Places of 100,000 or more inhabitants
● Places of 50,000 to 100,000 inhabitants
☐ Central cities of SMSA's with fewer than 50,000 inhabitants
○ Places of 25,000 to 50,000 inhabitants outside SMSA's

Standard Metropolitan
Statistical Areas (SMSA's)

U.S. DEPARTMENT OF COMMERCE
BUREAU OF THE CENSUS

1–94.

Louisiana

LEGEND
⊙ Places of 100,000 or more inhabitants
● Places of 50,000 to 100,000 inhabitants
☐ Central cities of SMSA's with fewer than 50,000 inhabitants
○ Places of 25,000 to 50,000 inhabitants outside SMSA's

Standard Metropolitan
Statistical Areas (SMSA's)

U.S. DEPARTMENT OF COMMERCE
BUREAU OF THE CENSUS

1–95.

A. STATE REFERENCE MAPS

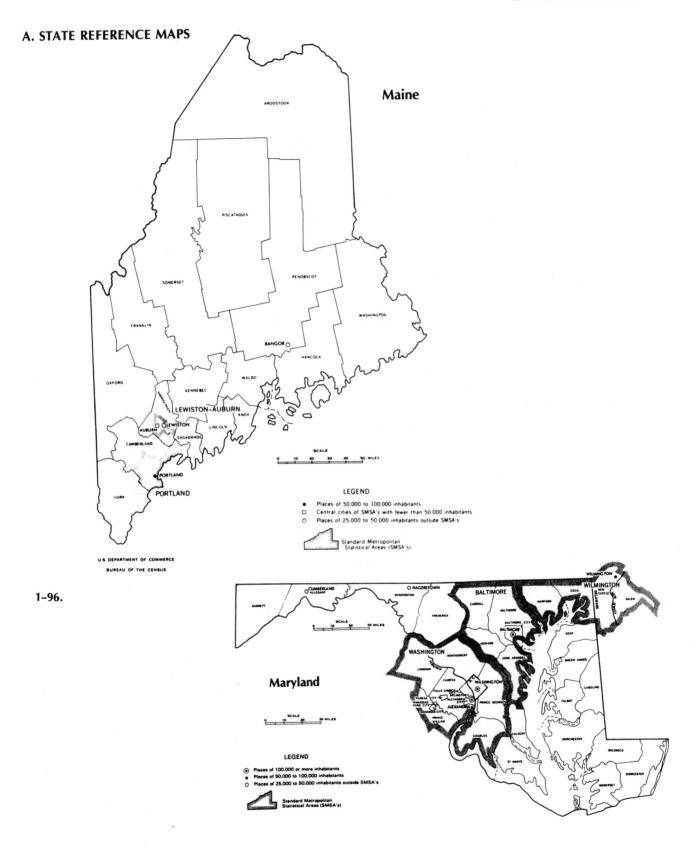

Maine

LEGEND

● Places of 50,000 to 100,000 inhabitants
□ Central cities of SMSA's with fewer than 50,000 inhabitants
○ Places of 25,000 to 50,000 inhabitants outside SMSA's

Standard Metropolitan
Statistical Areas (SMSA's)

U.S. DEPARTMENT OF COMMERCE
BUREAU OF THE CENSUS

1-96.

Maryland

LEGEND

◉ Places of 100,000 or more inhabitants
● Places of 50,000 to 100,000 inhabitants
○ Places of 25,000 to 50,000 inhabitants outside SMSA's

Standard Metropolitan
Statistical Areas (SMSA's)

U.S. DEPARTMENT OF COMMERCE
BUREAU OF THE CENSUS

1-97.

A. STATE REFERENCE MAPS

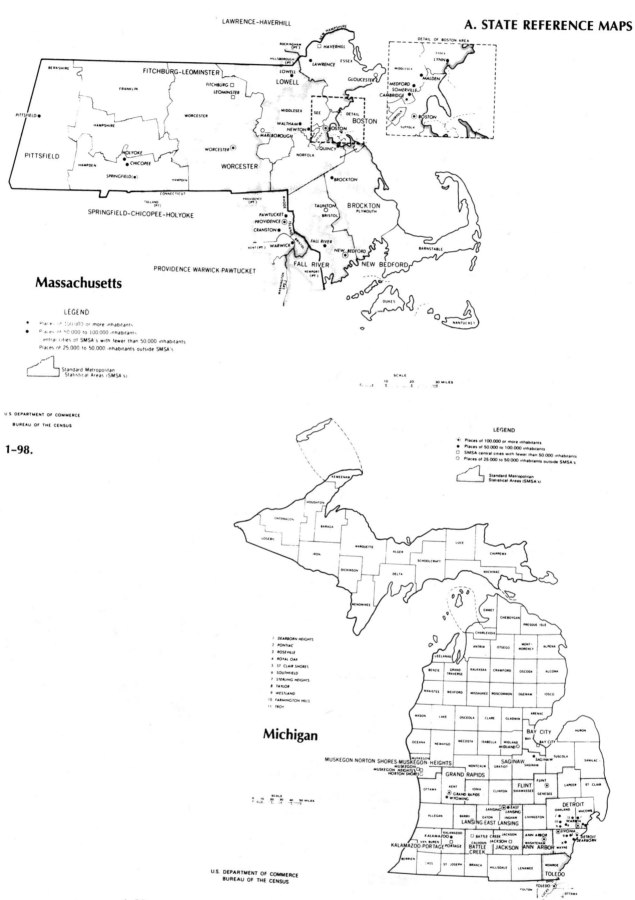

Massachusetts

LEGEND

- Places of 100,000 or more inhabitants
- Places of 50,000 to 100,000 inhabitants
  Central cities of SMSA's with fewer than 50,000 inhabitants
  Places of 25,000 to 50,000 inhabitants outside SMSA's

  Standard Metropolitan
  Statistical Areas (SMSA's)

SCALE
0 10 20 30 MILES

U.S. DEPARTMENT OF COMMERCE
BUREAU OF THE CENSUS

1-98.

LEGEND

- Places of 100,000 or more inhabitants
- Places of 50,000 to 100,000 inhabitants
- □ SMSA central cities with fewer than 50,000 inhabitants
- ○ Places of 25,000 to 50,000 inhabitants outside SMSA's

  Standard Metropolitan
  Statistical Areas (SMSA's)

1 DEARBORN HEIGHTS
2 PONTIAC
3 ROSEVILLE
4 ROYAL OAK
5 ST CLAIR SHORES
6 SOUTHFIELD
7 STERLING HEIGHTS
8 TAYLOR
9 WESTLAND
10 FARMINGTON HILLS
11 TROY

Michigan

SCALE
0 10 20 30 40 50 MILES

U.S. DEPARTMENT OF COMMERCE
BUREAU OF THE CENSUS

1-99.

A. STATE REFERENCE MAPS

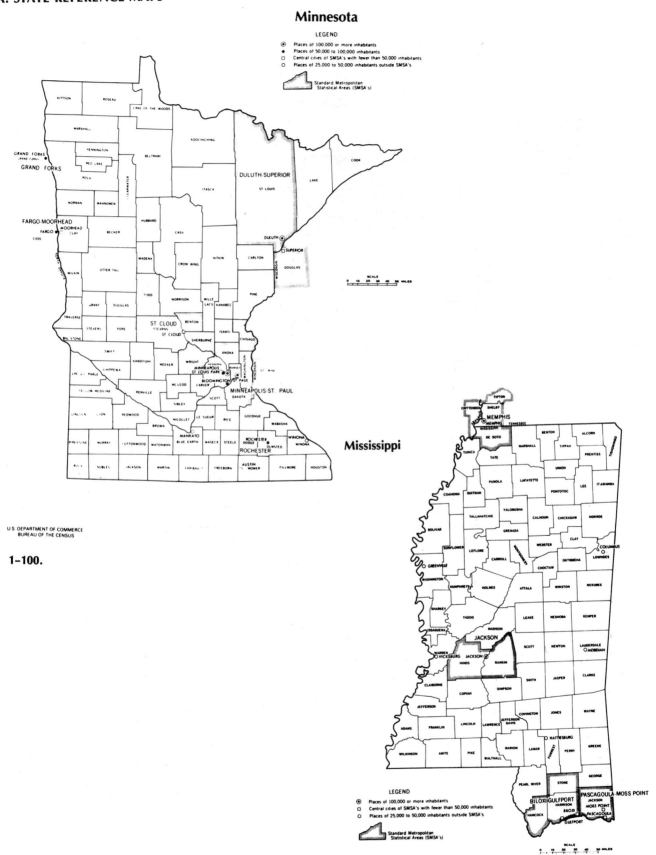

Minnesota

LEGEND

⊙ Places of 100,000 or more inhabitants
● Places of 50,000 to 100,000 inhabitants
□ Central cities of SMSA's with fewer than 50,000 inhabitants
○ Places of 25,000 to 50,000 inhabitants outside SMSA's

Standard Metropolitan
Statistical Areas (SMSA's)

U.S. DEPARTMENT OF COMMERCE
BUREAU OF THE CENSUS

1–100.

Mississippi

LEGEND

⊙ Places of 100,000 or more inhabitants
□ Central cities of SMSA's with fewer than 50,000 inhabitants
○ Places of 25,000 to 50,000 inhabitants outside SMSA's

Standard Metropolitan
Statistical Areas (SMSA's)

U.S. DEPARTMENT OF COMMERCE
BUREAU OF THE CENSUS

1–101.

U.S. DEPARTMENT OF COMMERCE
BUREAU OF THE CENSUS

1-102.

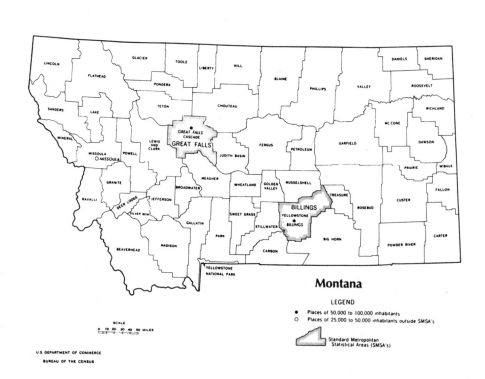

U.S. DEPARTMENT OF COMMERCE
BUREAU OF THE CENSUS

1-103.

A. STATE REFERENCE MAPS

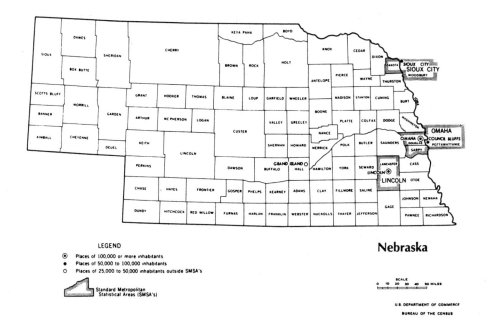

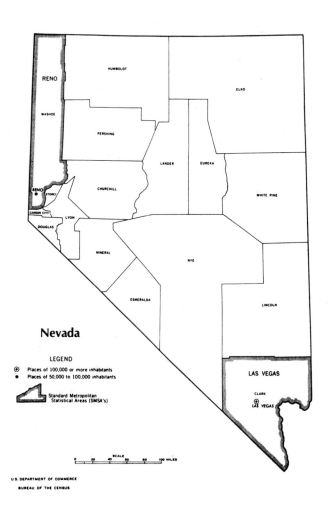

LEGEND
⊙ Places of 100,000 or more inhabitants
● Places of 50,000 to 100,000 inhabitants
○ Places of 25,000 to 50,000 inhabitants outside SMSA's

Standard Metropolitan
Statistical Areas (SMSA's)

Nebraska

SCALE
0 10 20 30 40 50 MILES

U.S. DEPARTMENT OF COMMERCE
BUREAU OF THE CENSUS

1–104.

Nevada

LEGEND
⊙ Places of 100,000 or more inhabitants
● Places of 50,000 to 100,000 inhabitants

Standard Metropolitan
Statistical Areas (SMSA's)

SCALE
0 20 40 60 80 100 MILES

U.S. DEPARTMENT OF COMMERCE
BUREAU OF THE CENSUS

1–105.

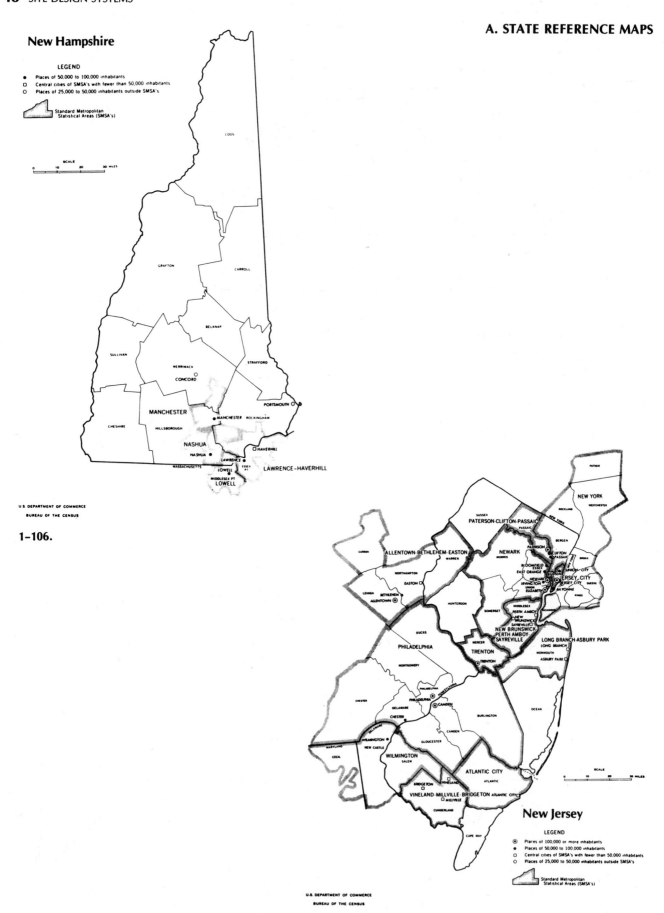

New Hampshire

LEGEND

- Places of 50,000 to 100,000 inhabitants
- Central cities of SMSA's with fewer than 50,000 inhabitants
- Places of 25,000 to 50,000 inhabitants outside SMSA's

Standard Metropolitan
Statistical Areas (SMSA's)

SCALE
0   10   20   30 MILES

U S DEPARTMENT OF COMMERCE
BUREAU OF THE CENSUS

1–106.

New Jersey

LEGEND

- Places of 100,000 or more inhabitants
- Places of 50,000 to 100,000 inhabitants
- Central cities of SMSA's with fewer than 50,000 inhabitants
- Places of 25,000 to 50,000 inhabitants outside SMSA's

Standard Metropolitan
Statistical Areas (SMSA's)

U.S. DEPARTMENT OF COMMERCE
BUREAU OF THE CENSUS

1–107.

A. STATE REFERENCE MAPS

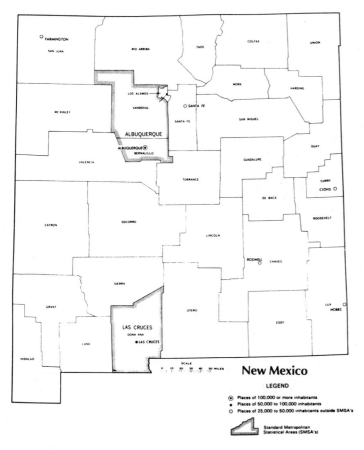

New Mexico

LEGEND

⊙ Places of 100,000 or more inhabitants
• Places of 50,000 to 100,000 inhabitants
○ Places of 25,000 to 50,000 inhabitants outside SMSA's

Standard Metropolitan
Statistical Areas (SMSA's)

U.S. DEPARTMENT OF COMMERCE
BUREAU OF THE CENSUS

1–108.

New York

LEGEND

⊙ Places of 100,000 or more inhabitants
• Places of 50,000 to 100,000 inhabitants
□ Central cities of SMSA's with fewer than 50,000 inhabitants
○ Places of 25,000 to 50,000 inhabitants outside SMSA's

Standard Metropolitan
Statistical Areas (SMSA's)

U.S. DEPARTMENT OF COMMERCE
BUREAU OF THE CENSUS

1–109.

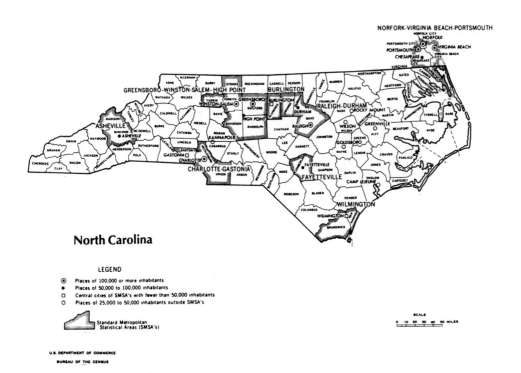

North Carolina

LEGEND

⊙ Places of 100,000 or more inhabitants
● Places of 50,000 to 100,000 inhabitants
▫ Central cities of SMSA's with fewer than 50,000 inhabitants
○ Places of 25,000 to 50,000 inhabitants outside SMSA's

Standard Metropolitan
Statistical Areas (SMSA's)

SCALE
0   10   20   30   40   50 MILES

U.S. DEPARTMENT OF COMMERCE
BUREAU OF THE CENSUS

1–110.

North Dakota

LEGEND

● Places of 50,000 to 100,000 inhabitants
▫ SMSA central cities with fewer than 50,000 inhabitants
○ Places of 25,000 to 50,000 inhabitants outside SMSA's

Standard Metropolitan
Statistical Areas (SMSA's)

SCALE
0   10   20   30   40   50 MILES

U S DEPARTMENT OF COMMERCE
BUREAU OF THE CENSUS

1–111.

A. STATE REFERENCE MAPS

Ohio

LEGEND

⊙ Places of 100,000 or more inhabitants
● Places of 50,000 to 100,000 inhabitants
□ SMSA central cities with fewer than 50,000 inhabitants
○ Places of 25,000 to 50,000 inhabitants outside SMSA's

Standard Metropolitan
Statistical Areas (SMSA's)

U.S. DEPARTMENT OF COMMERCE
BUREAU OF THE CENSUS

1–112.

Oklahoma

LEGEND

⊙ Places of 100,000 or more inhabitants
● Places of 50,000 to 100,000 inhabitants
□ SMSA central cities with fewer than 50,000 inhabitants
○ Places of 25,000 to 50,000 inhabitants outside SMSA's

Standard Metropolitan
Statistical Areas (SMSA's)

U.S. DEPARTMENT OF COMMERCE
BUREAU OF THE CENSUS

1–113.

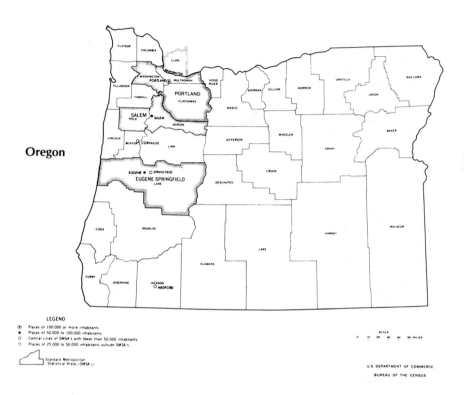

Oregon

LEGEND

⊙ Places of 100,000 or more inhabitants
● Places of 50,000 to 100,000 inhabitants
□ Central cities of SMSA's with fewer than 50,000 inhabitants
○ Places of 25,000 to 50,000 inhabitants outside SMSA's

Standard Metropolitan
Statistical Areas (SMSA's)

SCALE
0   10   20   30   40   50 MILES

U.S DEPARTMENT OF COMMERCE
BUREAU OF THE CENSUS

1–114.

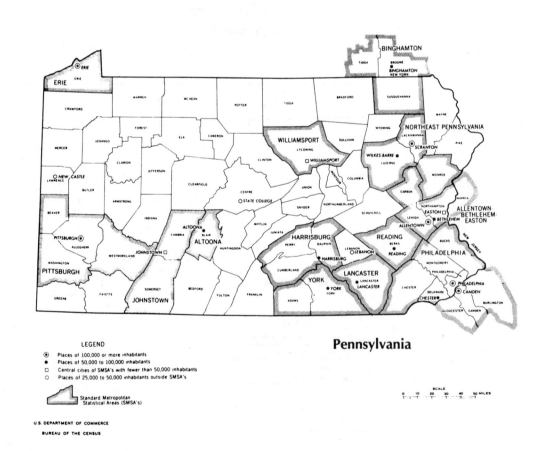

Pennsylvania

LEGEND

⊙ Places of 100,000 or more inhabitants
● Places of 50,000 to 100,000 inhabitants
□ Central cities of SMSA's with fewer than 50,000 inhabitants
○ Places of 25,000 to 50,000 inhabitants outside SMSA's

Standard Metropolitan
Statistical Areas (SMSA's)

U.S. DEPARTMENT OF COMMERCE
BUREAU OF THE CENSUS

SCALE
0   10   20   30   40   50 MILES

1–115.

A. STATE REFERENCE MAPS

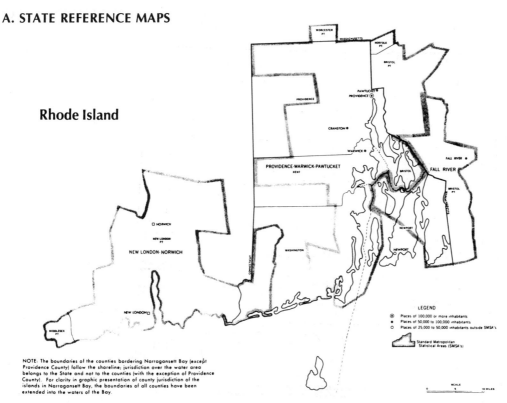

Rhode Island

LEGEND

⊙ Places of 100,000 or more inhabitants
● Places of 50,000 to 100,000 inhabitants
○ Places of 25,000 to 50,000 inhabitants outside SMSA's

Standard Metropolitan
Statistical Areas (SMSA's)

SCALE
0   5   10 MILES

NOTE: The boundaries of the counties bordering Narragansett Bay (except
Providence County) follow the shoreline; jurisdiction over the water area
belongs to the State and not to the counties (with the exception of Providence
County). For clarity in graphic presentation of county jurisdiction of the
islands in Narragansett Bay, the boundaries of all counties have been
extended into the waters of the Bay.

U.S. DEPARTMENT OF COMMERCE
BUREAU OF THE CENSUS

1–116.

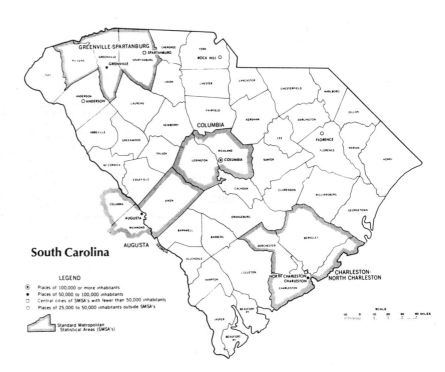

South Carolina

LEGEND

⊙ Places of 100,000 or more inhabitants
● Places of 50,000 to 100,000 inhabitants
□ Central cities of SMSA's with fewer than 50,000 inhabitants
○ Places of 25,000 to 50,000 inhabitants outside SMSA's

Standard Metropolitan
Statistical Areas (SMSA's)

SCALE
10   0   10   20   30   40 MILES

U.S. DEPARTMENT OF COMMERCE
BUREAU OF THE CENSUS

1–117.

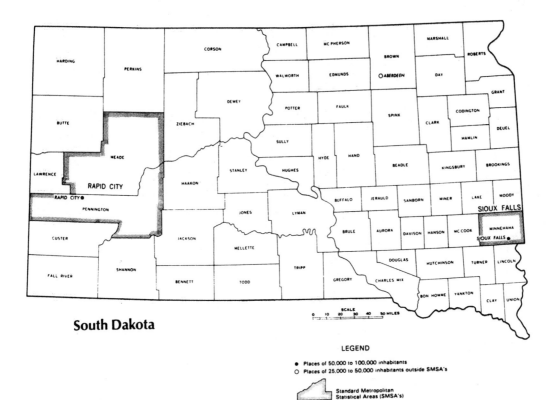

South Dakota

LEGEND

● Places of 50,000 to 100,000 inhabitants
○ Places of 25,000 to 50,000 inhabitants outside SMSA's

Standard Metropolitan
Statistical Areas (SMSA's)

U.S. DEPARTMENT OF COMMERCE
BUREAU OF THE CENSUS

1-118.

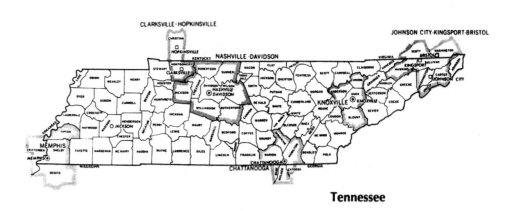

Tennessee

LEGEND

⊙ Places of 100,000 or more inhabitants
○ Places of 25,000 to 50,000 inhabitants outside SMSA's
□ Central cities of SMSA's with fewer than 50,000 inhabitants

Standard Metropolitan
Statistical Areas (SMSA's)

U.S. DEPARTMENT OF COMMERCE
BUREAU OF THE CENSUS

1-119.

A. STATE REFERENCE MAPS

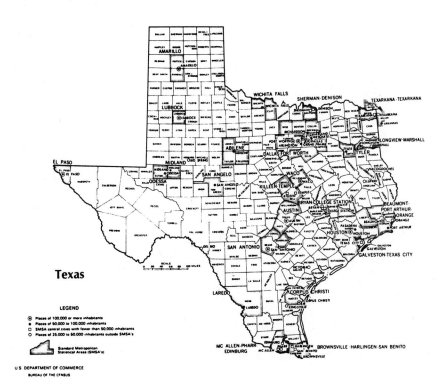

Texas

LEGEND
- Places of 100,000 or more inhabitants
- Places of 50,000 to 100,000 inhabitants
- SMSA central cities with fewer than 50,000 inhabitants
- Places of 25,000 to 50,000 inhabitants outside SMSA's

Standard Metropolitan
Statistical Areas (SMSA's)

U.S. DEPARTMENT OF COMMERCE
BUREAU OF THE CENSUS

1-120.

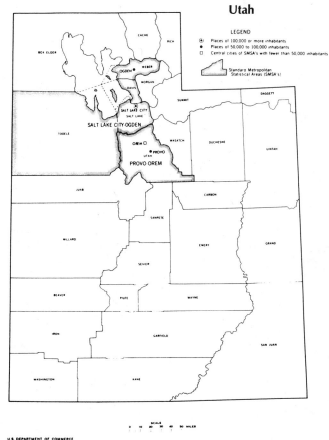

Utah

LEGEND
- Places of 100,000 or more inhabitants
- Places of 50,000 to 100,000 inhabitants
- Central cities of SMSA's with fewer than 50,000 inhabitants

Standard Metropolitan
Statistical Areas (SMSA's)

U.S. DEPARTMENT OF COMMERCE
BUREAU OF THE CENSUS

1-121.

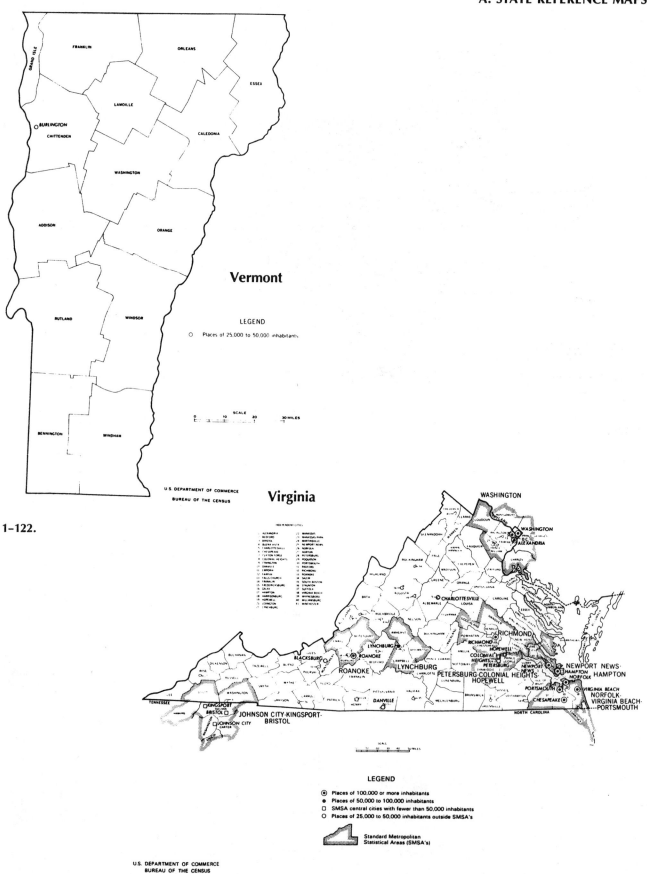

Vermont

LEGEND

○   Places of 25,000 to 50,000 inhabitants

SCALE
0   10   20   30 MILES

U.S. DEPARTMENT OF COMMERCE
BUREAU OF THE CENSUS

1–122.

Virginia

LEGEND

⊙   Places of 100,000 or more inhabitants
●   Places of 50,000 to 100,000 inhabitants
□   SMSA central cities with fewer than 50,000 inhabitants
○   Places of 25,000 to 50,000 inhabitants outside SMSA's

Standard Metropolitan
Statistical Areas (SMSA's)

U.S. DEPARTMENT OF COMMERCE
BUREAU OF THE CENSUS

1–123.

A. STATE REFERENCE MAPS

Washington

LEGEND

⊙ Places of 100,000 or more inhabitants
● Places of 50,000 to 100,000 inhabitants
□ SMSA central cities with fewer than 50,000 inhabitants
○ Places of 25,000 to 50,000 inhabitants outside SMSA's

Standard Metropolitan
Statistical Areas (SMSA's)

U.S. DEPARTMENT OF COMMERCE
BUREAU OF THE CENSUS

1-124.

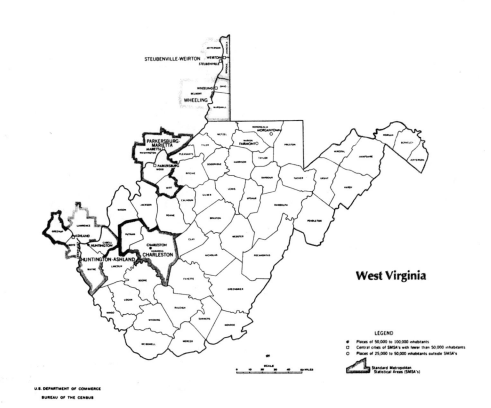

West Virginia

LEGEND

● Places of 50,000 to 100,000 inhabitants
□ Central cities of SMSA's with fewer than 50,000 inhabitants
○ Places of 25,000 to 50,000 inhabitants outside SMSA's

Standard Metropolitan
Statistical Areas (SMSA's)

U.S. DEPARTMENT OF COMMERCE
BUREAU OF THE CENSUS

1-125.

Wisconsin

LEGEND

- Places of 100,000 or more inhabitants
- Places of 50,000 to 100,000 inhabitants
- SMSA central cities with fewer than 50,000 inhabitants
- Places of 25,000 to 50,000 inhabitants outside SMSA's

Standard Metropolitan Statistical Areas (SMSA's)

U.S. DEPARTMENT OF COMMERCE
BUREAU OF THE CENSUS

1–126.

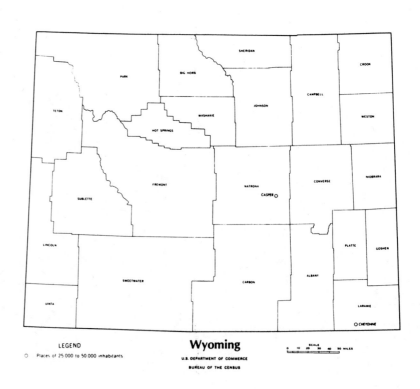

LEGEND

○ Places of 25,000 to 50,000 inhabitants

Wyoming

U.S. DEPARTMENT OF COMMERCE
BUREAU OF THE CENSUS

1–127.

B. GENERAL REFERENCE SYSTEMS

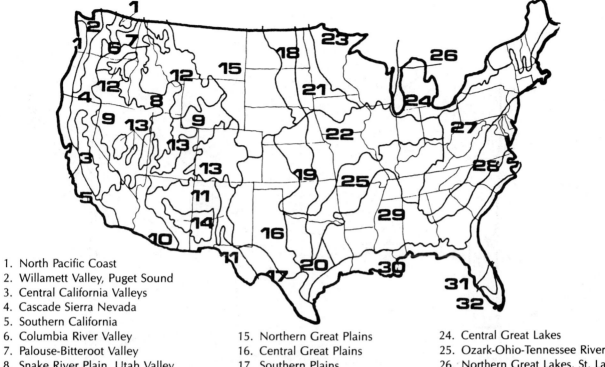

1. North Pacific Coast
2. Willamett Valley, Puget Sound
3. Central California Valleys
4. Cascade Sierra Nevada
5. Southern California
6. Columbia River Valley
7. Palouse-Bitteroot Valley
8. Snake River Plain, Utah Valley
9. Great Basin, Intermontane
10. Southwestern Desert
11. Southern Plateau
12. Northern Rocky Mountains
13. Central Rocky Mountains
14. Southern Rocky Mountains

15. Northern Great Plains
16. Central Great Plains
17. Southern Plains
18. Northern Black Soils
19. Central Black Soils
20. Southern Black Soils
21. Northern Prairies
22. Central Prairies
23. Western Great Lakes

24. Central Great Lakes
25. Ozark-Ohio-Tennessee River Valleys
26. Northern Great Lakes, St. Lawrence
27. Appalachian
28. Piedmont
29. Upper Coastal Plain
30. Swampy Coastal Plain
31. South-Central Florida
32. Subtropical Florida

(From "Landscapes for Living," *USDA Yearbook,* 1972, p. 178)

1-128. Plant-Material Growth Regions

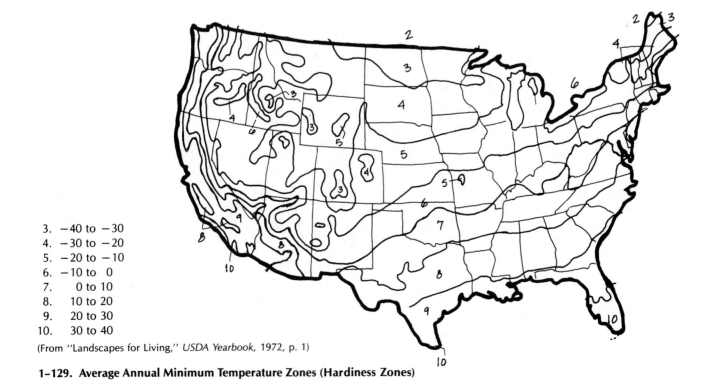

3. −40 to −30
4. −30 to −20
5. −20 to −10
6. −10 to 0
7.   0 to 10
8. 10 to 20
9. 20 to 30
10. 30 to 40

(From "Landscapes for Living," *USDA Yearbook,* 1972, p. 1)

1-129. Average Annual Minimum Temperature Zones (Hardiness Zones)

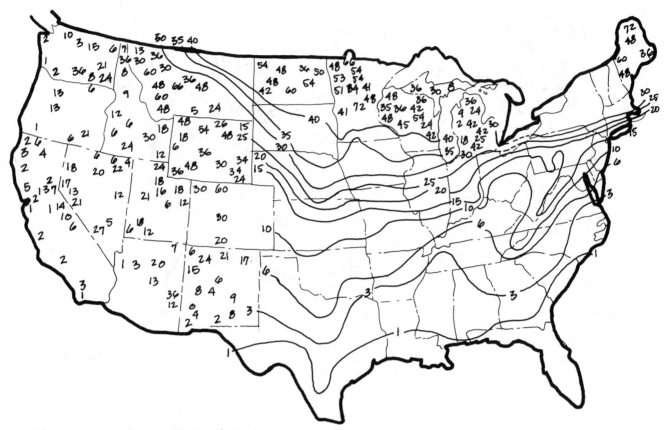

1-130. Average Frost Penetration Depth (Feet)

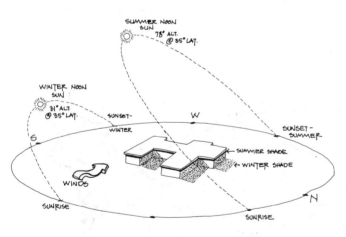

1-131. Sun Angle/Orientation

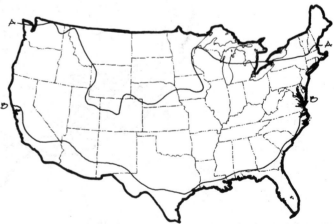

1-132. Range of Termite Damage

B. GENERAL REFERENCE SYSTEMS

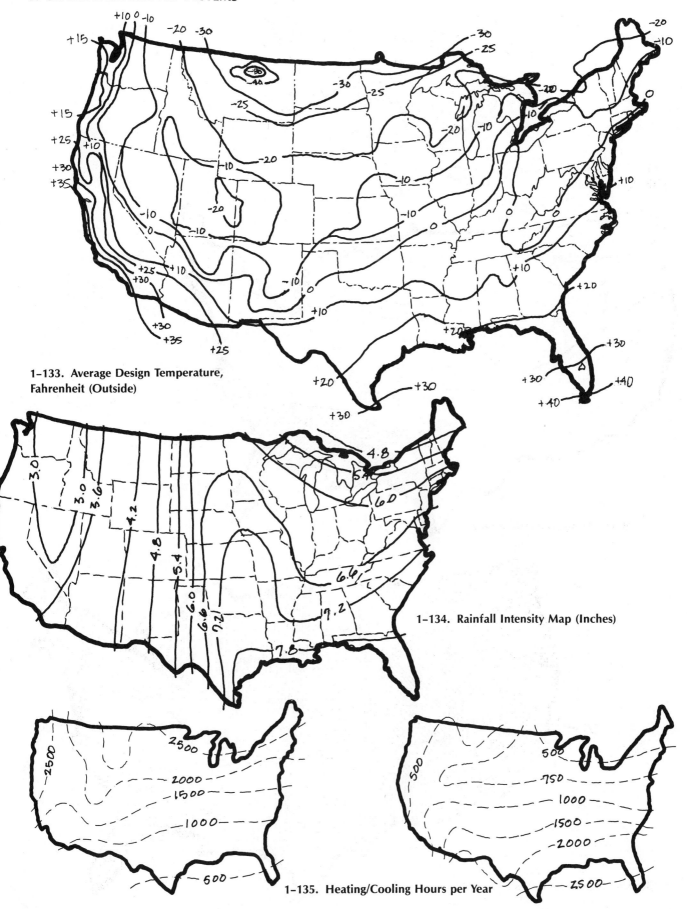

1-133. **Average Design Temperature, Fahrenheit (Outside)**

1-134. **Rainfall Intensity Map (Inches)**

1-135. **Heating/Cooling Hours per Year**

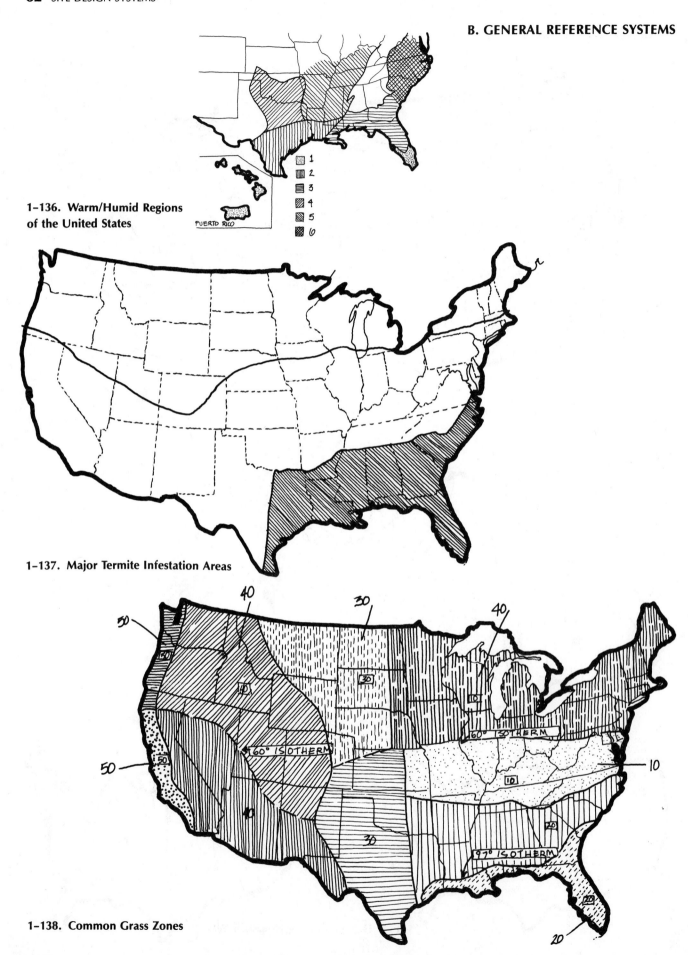

1-136. Warm/Humid Regions of the United States

PUERTO RICO

1
2
3
4
5
6

1-137. Major Termite Infestation Areas

1-138. Common Grass Zones

B. GENERAL REFERENCE SYSTEMS

1–139. United States Time Zones

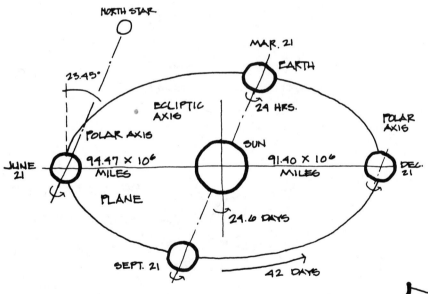

1–140. Earth Motion/Solar Constant

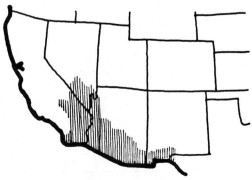

1–141. Dry/Hot Regions of the United States

Human Systems

A. DIMENSIONS: FEMALE

B. DIMENSIONS: MALE
See figures 1–142 to 1–146.

C. REACH LIMITS: SEMIAMBULATORY/ NONAMBULATORY
See figures 1–147 to 1–150.

D. PLEGIA DEFINITIONS
See figures 1–151 to 1–156.

E. FUNCTIONAL HAZARDS: VISUALLY IMPAIRED
See figure 1–157.

F. WALKING CANE FUNCTIONS: VISUALLY IMPAIRED
See figure 1–158.

A. DIMENSIONS:FEMALE
B. DIMENSIONS:MALE

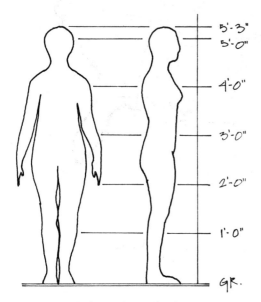

1–142. **Proportions of Female Figure**

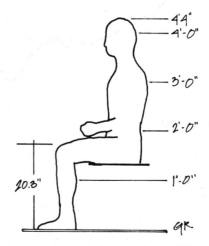

1–143. **Proportions of Seated Figure**

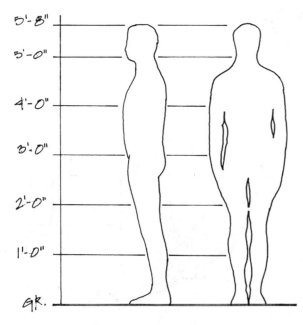

1–144. **Proportions of Male Figure**

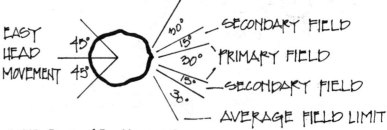

1–145. **Range of Eye Movement**

STANDING - 30°
WALKING - 15°

1–146. **Feet Movement in Average Adult**

C. REACH LIMITS:SEMIAMBULATORY/NONAMBULATORY

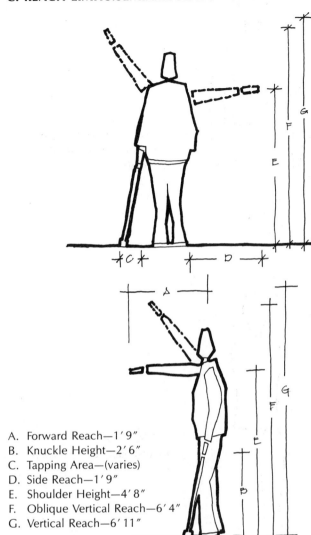

A. Crutch Swing—4′0″
B. Shoulder Height—4′8″
C. Body Crutch Span—10″
D. Body Crutch Swing—3′
E. Standing Crutch Span—3′0″
F. Walking Crutch Swing—3′6″

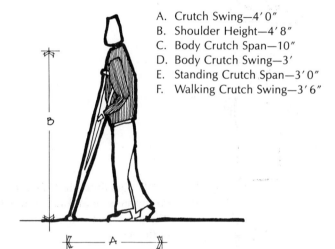

1-148. Space Requirements, Semiambulatory

A. Forward Reach—1′9″
B. Knuckle Height—2′6″
C. Tapping Area—(varies)
D. Side Reach—1′9″
E. Shoulder Height—4′8″
F. Oblique Vertical Reach—6′4″
G. Vertical Reach—6′11″

1-147. Reach Limits, Semiambulatory (Cane)

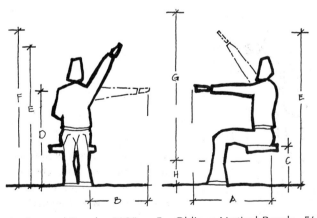

A. Forward Reach—1′9″   E. Oblique Vertical Reach—5′3″
B. Side Reach—1′9″   F. Vertical Reach—5′7″
C. Sitting Height—1′7″   G. Overall Vertical Reach—4′4″
D. Shoulder Height—3′5″   H. Vertical Ground Reach—1′3″

1-149. Reach Limits, Amputee

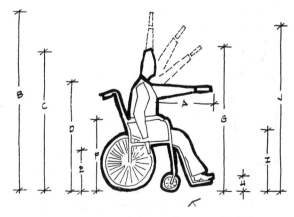

A. Toe Protection—26″   F. Elbow Level—25″
B. Vertical Reach—67″   G. Forward Vertical Reach—55″
C. Head Height—52″   H. Foot Height—5¾″
D. Shoulder Height—41″   I. Knee Level—23″
E. Knuckle Height—15″   J. Oblique Vertical Reach—62¾″

1-150. Reach Limits, Nonambulatory

D. PLEGIA DEFINITIONS

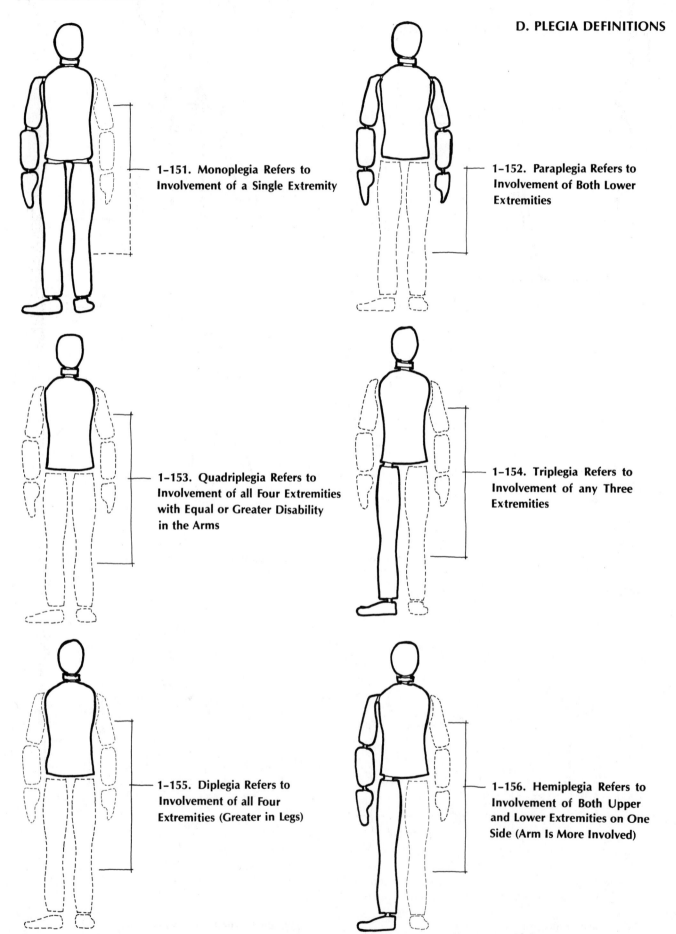

1-151. Monoplegia Refers to Involvement of a Single Extremity

1-152. Paraplegia Refers to Involvement of Both Lower Extremities

1-153. Quadriplegia Refers to Involvement of all Four Extremities with Equal or Greater Disability in the Arms

1-154. Triplegia Refers to Involvement of any Three Extremities

1-155. Diplegia Refers to Involvement of all Four Extremities (Greater in Legs)

1-156. Hemiplegia Refers to Involvement of Both Upper and Lower Extremities on One Side (Arm Is More Involved)

E. FUNCTIONAL HAZARDS:VISUALLY IMPAIRED

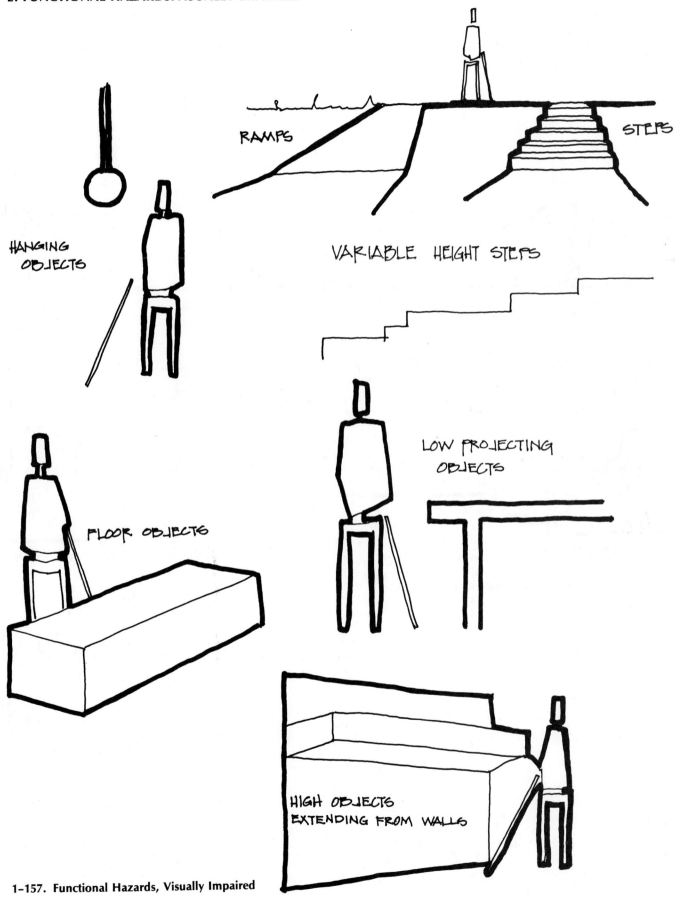

RAMPS

STEPS

HANGING OBJECTS

VARIABLE HEIGHT STEPS

FLOOR OBJECTS

LOW PROJECTING OBJECTS

HIGH OBJECTS EXTENDING FROM WALLS

1–157. Functional Hazards, Visually Impaired

F. WALKING CANE FUNCTIONS: VISUALLY IMPAIRED

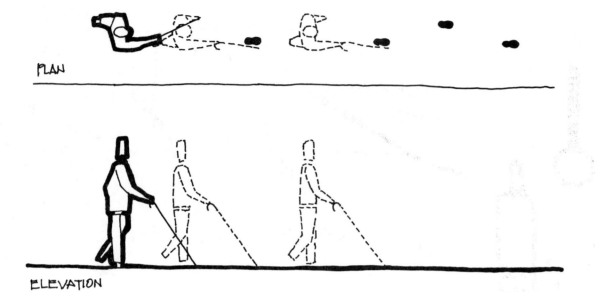

PLAN

ELEVATION

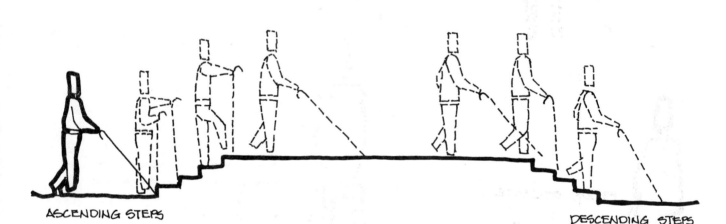

ASCENDING STEPS

DESCENDING STEPS

1-158. Walking Cane Functions, Visually Impaired

2 Recreation Systems

Facility Development Standards ____

A. BADMINTON

Site Space: 1,620 square feet
Site Size: singles = 17′ × 44′
doubles = 20′ × 44′
Orientation: north/south
Service Population: 1 facility per 5,000

B. BASKETBALL

Site Space: youth = 2,400–3,036 square feet
high school = 5,040–7,280
square feet
collegiate = 5,600–7,980 square
feet
Site Size: youth = 46′ × 84′
high school = 50′ × 84′
collegiate = 50′ × 94′
Orientation: north/south
Service Population: 1 facility per 5,000

C. HANDBALL

Site Space: 800–1,000 square feet
Site Size: 20′ × 40′
Orientation: north/south (outside)
Service Population: 1 facility per 10,000

D. ICE HOCKEY

Site Space: 22,000 square feet
Site Size: 85′ × 200′
Orientation: north/south
Service Population: 1 per 100,000

E. TENNIS

Site Space: 7,200 square feet
Site Size: 36′ × 78′
Orientation: north/south
Service Population: 1 per 2,000

F. VOLLEYBALL

Site Space: 4,000 square feet
Site Size: 30′ × 60′
Orientation: north/south
Service Population: 1 per 5,000

G. FOOTBALL

Site Space: 1.5 acres
Site Size: 180′ × 300′
Orientation: north/south
Service Population: 1 per 20,000

H. BASEBALL

Site Space: official = 3.0–3.85 acres
Little League = 1.2 acres
Site Size: official (baseline) = 90′
Little League (baseline) = 60′
Orientation: batter not facing sun
Service Population: 1 per 5,000 (lighted = 1 per
30,000)

I. SOCCER

Site Space: 1.7–2.1 acres
Site Size: 195′–225′ × 330′
Orientation: north/south
Service Population: 1 per 10,000

J. SOFTBALL

Site Space: 1.5–2.0 acres
Site Size: baseline = 60′
Orientation: same as baseball
Service Population: 1 per 5,000

K. ARCHERY RANGE

Site Space: 0.65 acres
Site Size: 300′ (length)
Orientation: archer facing north
Service Population: 1 per 50,000

L. GOLF

Site Space: par 3 = 50–60 acres
                 9 hole = 50 acres minimum
                 18 hole = 110 acres minimum
Site Size: par 3 = 600 yards minimum
                 9 hole = 2,250 yards average
                 18 hole = 6,500 yards average
Orientation: north/south (holes)
Service Population: 9 hole = 1 per 25,000
                 18 holes = 1 per 50,000

M. SWIMMING POOL

Site Space: ½–2 acres
Site Size: teaching = 25 yards
                 competition = 25 meters
Orientation: N/A
Service Population: 1 per 20,000

Community Development Standards

A. FACILITIES

A system of standards for the development of community recreation facilities should be based upon the following criteria:

1. NEIGHBORHOOD PARK/PLAYGROUND

a) Description
(1) This facility is developed for active recreation needs such as field sports, crafts, and team games. It should have scenic qualities (passive areas) and should serve a population of up to 10,000 persons.
(2) Communities should provide at least 1½ acres per 1,000 population. Typical development costs per acre are $45,000. Development costs for an average facility are $325,500. Typical facilities include:
  (a) Parking lot for 10 autos (minimum)
  (b) Playground/tot lot
  (c) Wading pool
  (d) Landscaping
  (e) Shelter

2. COMMUNITY PARK

a) Description
(1) This facility is developed for both active and passive recreation needs. It should have natural qualities such as ponds or lakes and should feature specialized recreation opportunities such as nature trails, botanical gardens, etc.
(2) It should serve a population of 40,000 to 100,000 persons. Communities should provide 3½ acres per 1,000 persons (with a minimum size of 20 acres). Typical development costs per acre are $3,500.

Development costs for an average facility are $2,700,000. Typical facilities include:
  (a) Parking lot for 20 autos (minimum)
  (b) Landscaping
  (c) Softball/baseball (lighted)
  (d) Tennis court
  (e) Basketball court
  (f) Picnic area
  (g) Rest room/shelters

3. METROPOLITAN PARK

a) Description
(1) This facility is developed for its passive qualities and natural scenic beauty. It should have expanded uses such as boating, horseback riding, and camping.
(2) It should serve a regional population and be at least 1,000 acres in size. Typical development costs per acre are $1,500. Development costs for an average facility are $2,200,000. Typical facilities include:
  (a) Parking for 50 autos (minimum)
  (b) Natural areas/landscaping
  (c) Water feature
  (d) Golf course
  (e) Field archery
  (f) Camping units
  (g) Shelters

B. PARK FACILITIES

1. BASEBALL/SOFTBALL

a) Lighting Requirements: Pole Layout
   See figure 2–1.
b) Baseball Diamond Layout
   See figure 2–2.

c) *Little League Diamond Layout*
   See figure 2–3.
d) *Softball Diamond Layout*
   See figure 2–4.
e) *Base Layout: General*
   See figures 2–5 to 2–8.

2. SWIMMING POOL
a) *General Layout*
   See figure 2–9.
b) *Filter System: General*
   See figure 2–10.
c) *Wheelchair Access: Typical*
   See figure 2–11.

3. LAKESIDE/BEACH FACILITIES
a) *Swimming Beach Design*
   See figure 2–12.
b) *Fishing Docks/Piers: Wheelchair Access*
   See figure 2–13.
c) *Outdoor/Beach Shower*
   See figure 2–14.

4. COURT FACILITIES
   See figures 2–15 to 2–72.

5. EXERCISE TRAILS: TYPICAL UNITS
   See figures 2–73 to 2–92.

C. SPECIALIZED PLAY AREAS

1. STANDARDS
   In addition to the standards for the more commonly developed areas, the following are applicable to those special play units designed to accommodate the disabled child:
a) *Motor-Development Unit*
(1) This is an environment designed for the teaching of specific motor skills to a selected group of handicapped children.
(2) The play area should be composed of several interconnected experience units designed to relate a variety of motor experiences/skills.
(3) It should have controlled approaches to each apparatus and tightly controlled inner circulation in order to confront the child with the right type of experience in the proper sequence.
(4) This play area requires supervision at all times.
b) *Therapeutic Play Unit*
(1) This is an environment designed for the general therapeutic value it offers the child.
(2) It should be composed of several interconnected experiences available through creative and abstract apparatus.
(3) Circulation into and away from the apparatus area may be more relaxed, but circulation within the space should be tightly controlled.

(4) The presence of supportive personnel is important for the therapeutic success of the unit.
c) *Free Play Unit*
(1) This is an environment designed to foster experiences encompassing both educational and therapeutic values of a general type.
(2) Circulation should be controlled at individual experience units, with a free evaluation of challenges by the child at his or her own scale.

D. PLAY EXPERIENCE SELECTION

1. LOCOMOTION EQUIPMENT
   The recreational environment created for the handicapped child must contain all the necessary items that fulfill his or her various play needs. Generally, both locomotion and perception experiences should be emphasized, using as many different types of apparatus as are available. Specific locomotion equipment should relate the following experiences:
a) *Gross and Fine Motor Tasks*
(1) Jumping
(2) Running/walking
(3) Throwing/catching
(4) Balancing, dynamic and static
(5) Climbing
(6) Grasping
(7) Bouncing
b) *Health-Related Tasks*
(1) Flexibility
(2) Strength, lifting weight or body
(3) Muscular endurance
c) *Skill-Related Tasks*
(1) Agility
(2) Reaction time
(3) Coordination
   (a) Hand-to-eye
   (b) Foot-to-eye
(4) Pushing/pulling

2. SPECIFIC PERCEPTION EQUIPMENT RELATED TO EXPERIENCES
a) *Perceptual/Motor Oriented*
(1) Laterality
(2) Directionality
(3) Kinesthetic awareness
(4) Motor planning
b) *Spatial Related*
(1) Depth perception
(2) Spatial relationships
(3) Tactile awareness

E. CAMPING FACILITIES
   See figures 2–93 to 2–98.

F. GENERAL RECREATION FACILITIES
   See figures 2–99 to 2–114.

Class	Outfield (ft.)	FLOODLIGHTS		MINIMUM MOUNTING HEIGHT TO BOTTOM FLOODLIGHT CROSSARM (FT.)	
		Type	Class	A and B Poles	C Poles
8-POLE LAYOUT					
Professional and Championship	280	3, 4, or 5	GP	50	60
	240			50	55
Semiprofessional	280	3, 4, or 5	GP	40	55
	240	4, 5, or 6	OI	40	50
Industrial League	280	3, 4, or 5	GP	35	50
	240	4, 5, or 6	OI	35	45
	200	6	O	35	40
6-POLE LAYOUT					
Recreational	200	5	GP	35	40
		4, 5, or 6	OI		
		6	O		

GP—General-purpose lighting
 O—Open lighting
 I—Open eye
Poles: 6 for recreational and 8 for other classes.
 Note: Supplementary corner poles may be installed to carry overhead wire around boundary rather than across playing area. For slow-pitch softball tournament, class is same as industrial league; recreational class same as recreational above.

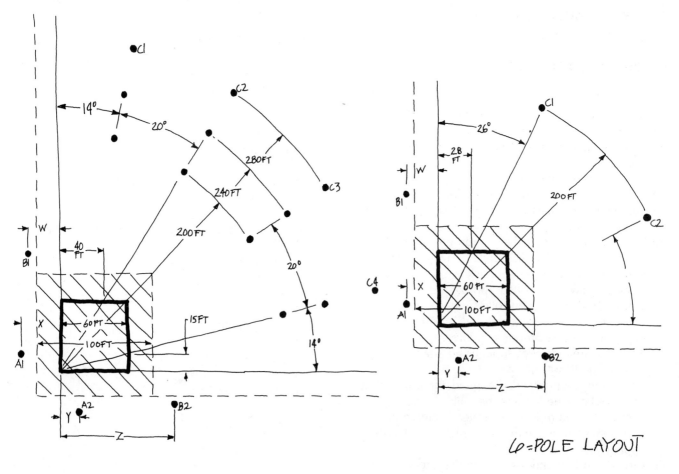

8 = POLE LAYOUT

6 = POLE LAYOUT

2–1. Light Pole Locations—Baseball

B. PARK FACILITIES

Class of Baseball	FLOODLIGHTS		DIMENSION (FEET)				AREA (SQUARE FEET)		MINIMUM MOUNTING HEIGHT TO BOTTOM FLOODLIGHT (FT.)	
	Type	Class	W	X	Y	Z	Infield	Outfield	A and B Poles	C Poles
I	3, 4, or 5	GP	20–30	30–50	5–15	90–110	10,000	24,700	40	50
	4, 5, or 6	O or OI								
II	3, 4, or 5	GP	24–45	35–65	10–25	110–145	15,625	46,600	50	60
	4, 5, or 6	OI								

Lighting recommendations for Junior League Baseball. (a) Class I: baselines 60 feet or less. (b) Class II: baselines 60 ft. and up to 75 ft.

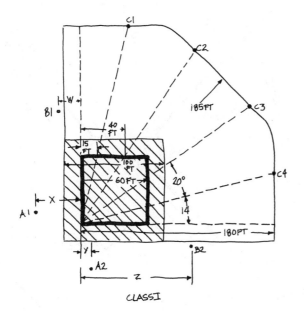

CLASS I

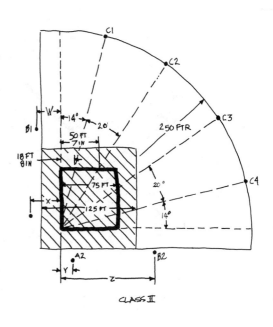

CLASS II

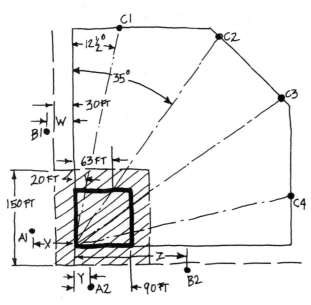

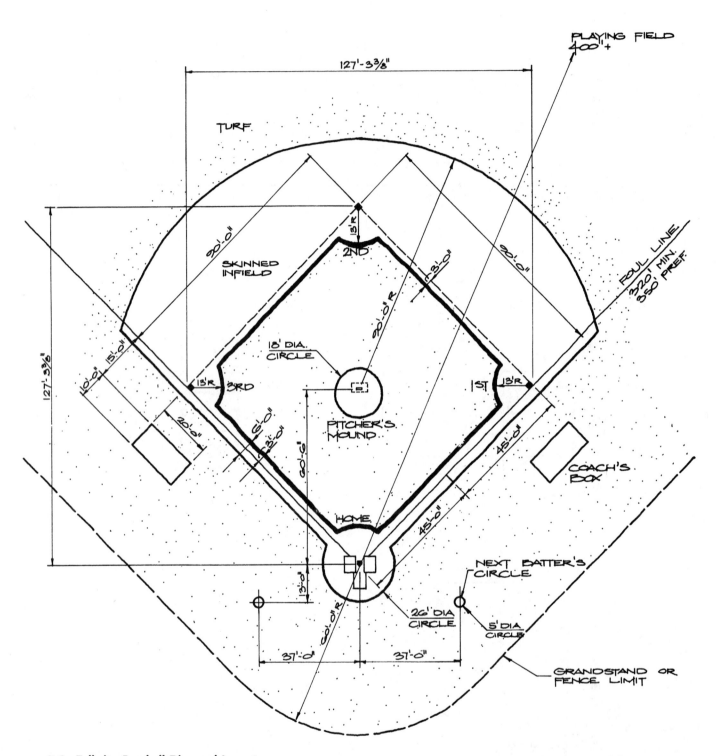

2-2. Full-size Baseball Diamond Layout

B. PARK FACILITIES

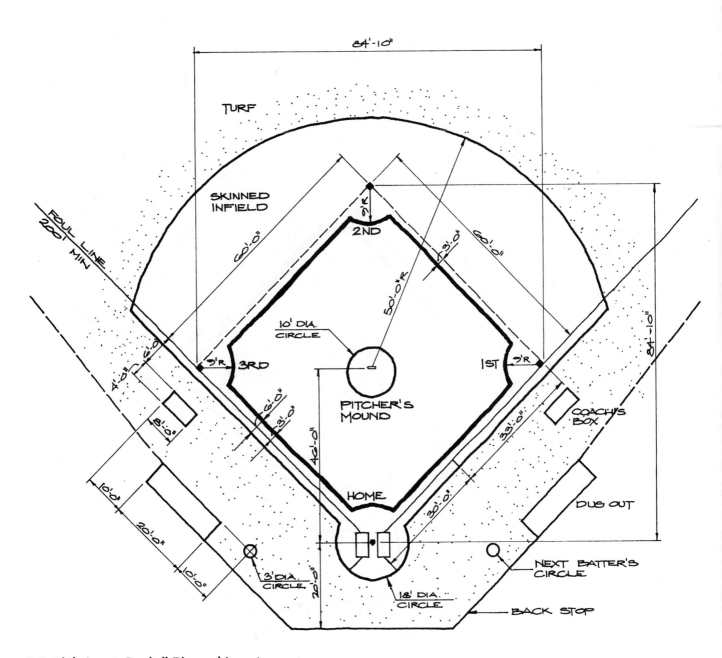

2-3. Little League Baseball Diamond Layout

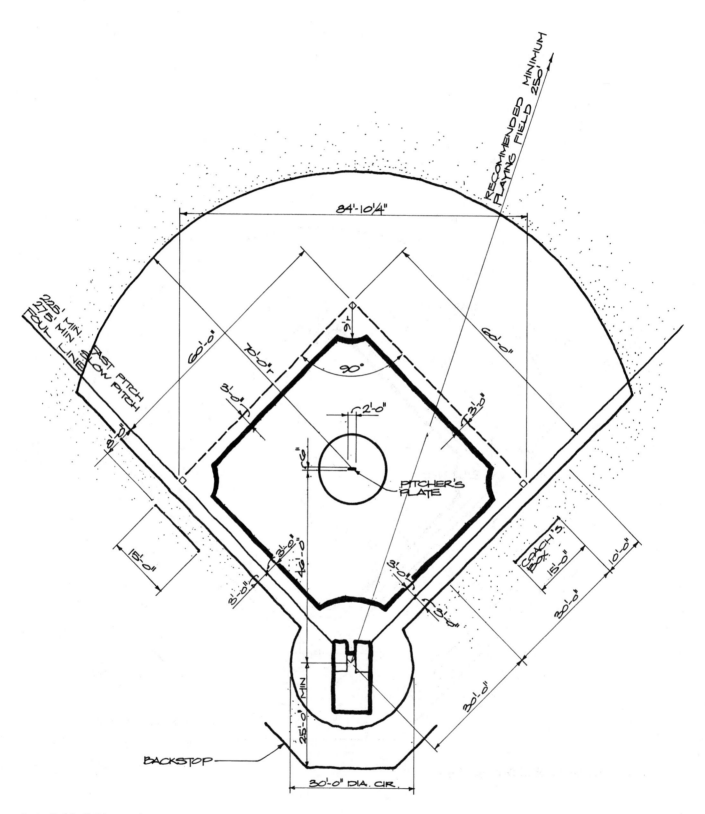

2–4. Softball Diamond

B. PARK FACILITIES

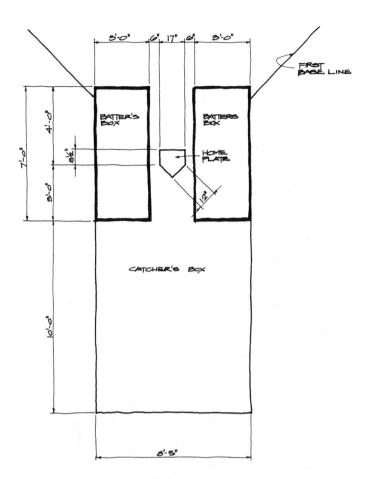

2-5. Home Plate (Softball)

2-7. 1st, 2nd, and 3rd Bases

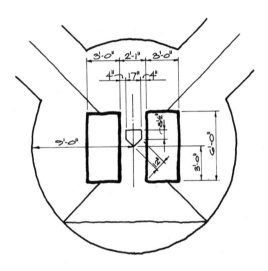

Home Plate: Little League

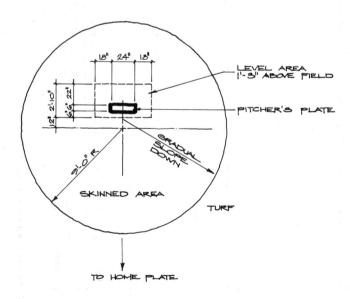

2-6. Pitcher's Mound

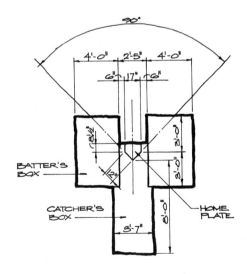

2-8. Home Plate

Recommended Swimming Pool Dimensions

Size	A	B	C	D	E	F	G	H	I	K	L	Length of Spring Board	Overhang	Height of Diving Board Stand
12 × 28	1'6"	7'0"	7'0"	6'6"	6'0"		2'6"	3'0"	4'6"	6'6"	5'0"	0	0	None
12 × 30	1'6"	7'0"	9'0"	6'6"	6'0"		2'6"	3'0"	4'6"	6'6"	5'0"	0	0	None
12 × 32	1'6"	7'0"	9'0"	8'6"	6'0"		3'0"	3'6"	5'0"	7'6"	6'0"	8'0"	1'6"	Deck Level
15 × 30	1'6"	7'0"	8'6"	7'0"	6'0"		3'0"	3'6"	5'0"	7'6"	6'0"	8'0"	1'6"	Deck Level
15 × 32	1'6"	7'0"	8'6"	6'0"	6'0"		3'0"	3'6"	5'0"	7'6"	6'0"	8'0"	1'6"	Deck Level
15 × 35	2'0"	8'0"	10'6"	8'6"	6'0"		3'0"	3'6"	5'0"	8'6"	7'0"	10'0"	2'0"	Deck Level to 12"
16 × 35	2'0"	8'0"	10'6"	8'6"	6'0"		3'0"	3'6"	5'0"	8'6"	7'0"	10'0"	2'0"	Deck Level to 12"
16 × 40	2'0"	8'0"	10'6"	13'6"	6'0"		3'0"	3'6"	5'0"	8'6"	7'0"	10'0"	2'6"	Deck Level to 12"
18 × 38	2'0"	8'0"	12'6"	9'6"	6'0"		3'0"	3'6"	5'0"	8'6"	7'0"	10'0"	3'0"	12" to 18"
18 × 40	3'0"	9'0"	11'6"			16'6"	3'0"	See Note A	5'0"	9'0"	7'6"	12'0"	3'0"	12" to 39"
20 × 40	3'0"	9'0"	11'6"			16'6"	3'0"	See Note A	5'0"	9'0"	7'6"	12'0"	3'0"	12" to 39"

NOTE A: Floor is to slope from 3 ft. to a uniform slope to the 5-ft. depth.
NOTE B: Provide about 30 sq. ft. of floor space for filtration equipment (preferably inside the building).
NOTE C: Slope walks away from pool at 1/4 in. per ft.; provide drains as required.
NOTE D: Provide self-closing, self-latching gates capable of being locked.

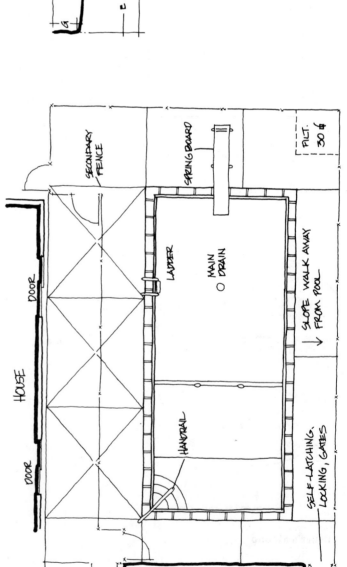

2-9. Swimming Pool: General Layout

B. PARK FACILITIES

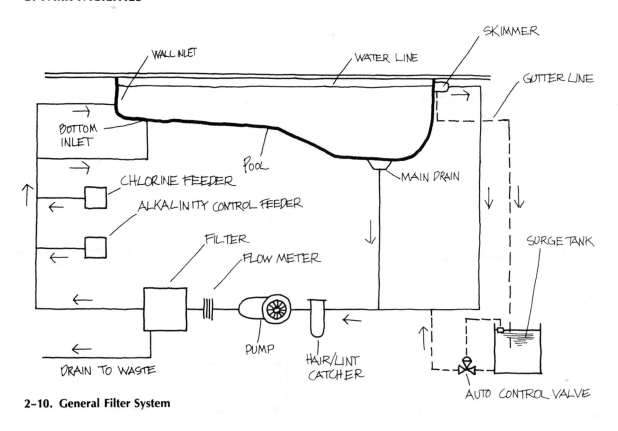

2-10. General Filter System

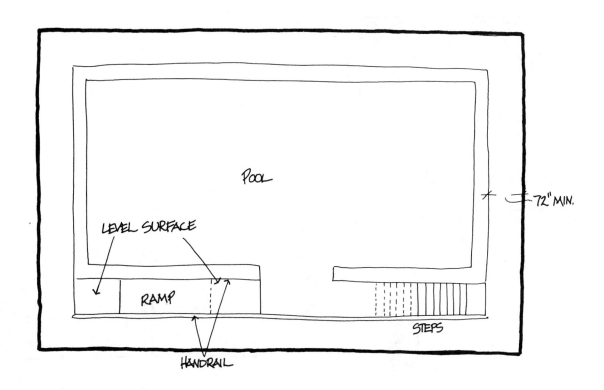

2-11. Swimming Pool: Wheelchair Access

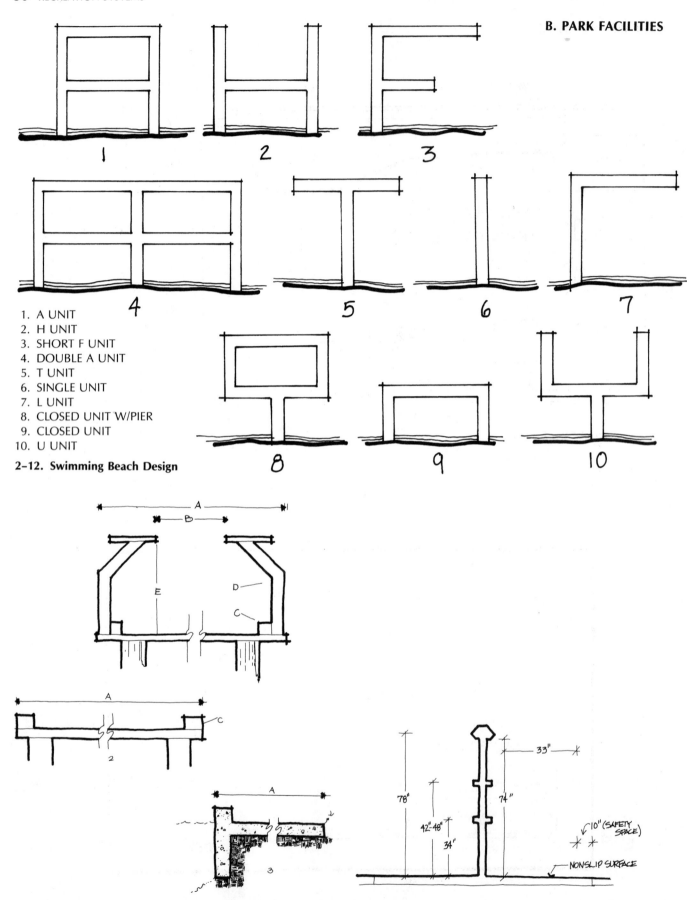

1. A UNIT
2. H UNIT
3. SHORT F UNIT
4. DOUBLE A UNIT
5. T UNIT
6. SINGLE UNIT
7. L UNIT
8. CLOSED UNIT W/PIER
9. CLOSED UNIT
10. U UNIT

2-12. Swimming Beach Design

2-13. Fishing Docks and Piers: Wheelchair Access

2-14. Outdoor/Beach Shower

B. PARK FACILITIES

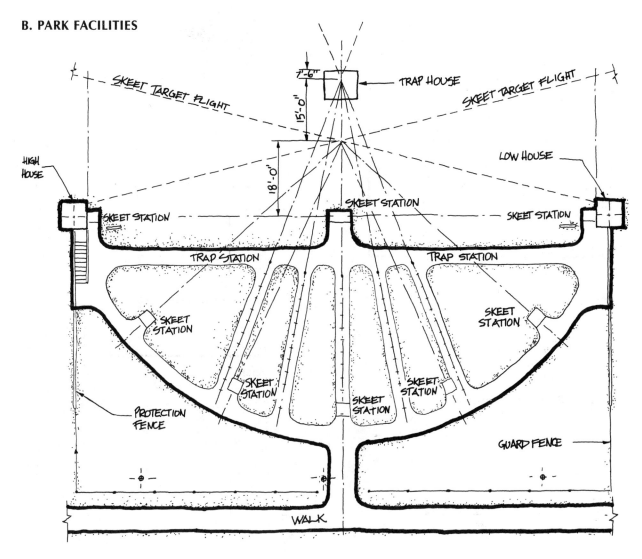

2–15. Skeet/Trap Field: Layout

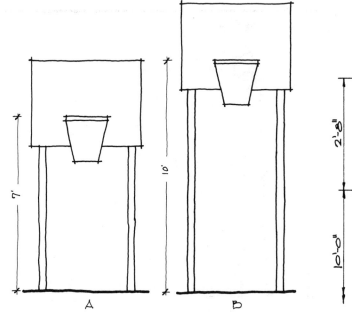

2–16. Basketball Goal: (a) Wheelchair Unit; (b) Nonwheelchair Unit

2–17. Fan-shaped Backboard, Basketball (High School)

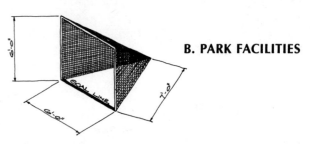

2-21. Goal: Detail

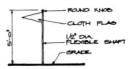

2-22. Flag: Detail

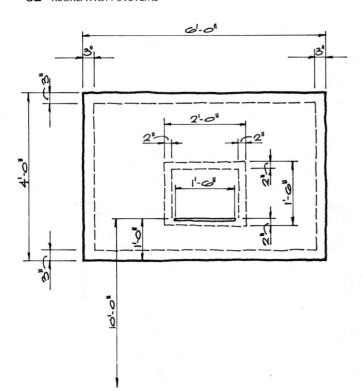

2-18. Rectangular Backboard, Basketball

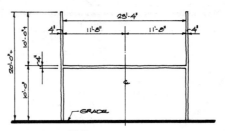

2-23. Football

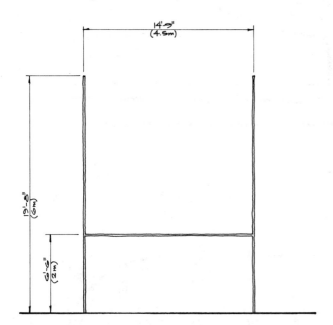

2-19. Camogie Goal

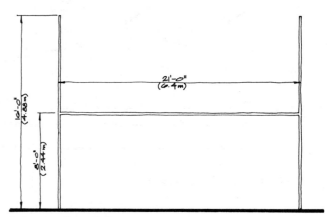

2-24. Hurling Goal

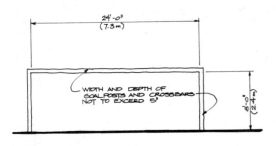

2-20. Goalposts

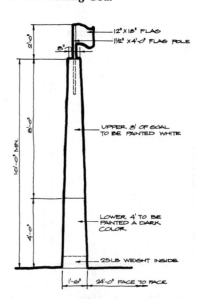

2-25. Polo Goalpost

B. PARK FACILITIES

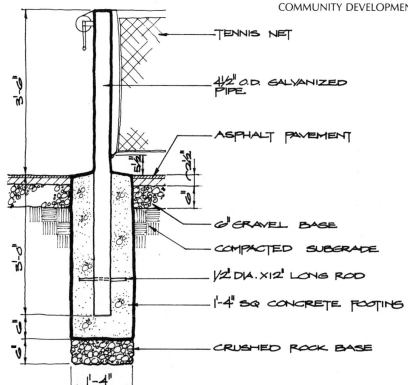

TENNIS NET

4½" O.D. GALVANIZED PIPE.

ASPHALT PAVEMENT

6" GRAVEL BASE

COMPACTED SUBGRADE

½" DIA. X12" LONG ROD

1'-4" SQ CONCRETE FOOTING

CRUSHED ROCK BASE

3'-6"

3'-0"

6"

6"

1'-4"

2-26. Tennis Net Post

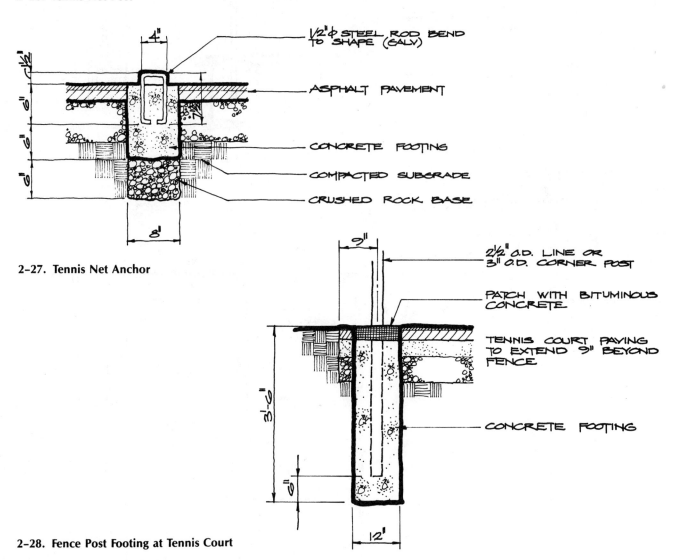

4"

½" Ø STEEL ROD BEND TO SHAPE (GALV)

ASPHALT PAVEMENT

CONCRETE FOOTING

COMPACTED SUBGRADE

CRUSHED ROCK BASE

6"

6"

6"

8"

2-27. Tennis Net Anchor

9"

2½" O.D. LINE OR 3" O.D. CORNER POST

PATCH WITH BITUMINOUS CONCRETE

TENNIS COURT PAVING TO EXTEND 9" BEYOND FENCE

CONCRETE FOOTING

3'-6"

6"

12"

2-28. Fence Post Footing at Tennis Court

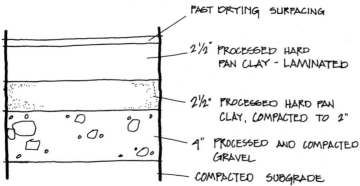

FAST DRYING SURFACING

2½" PROCESSED HARD PAN CLAY - LAMINATED

2½" PROCESSED HARD PAN CLAY, COMPACTED TO 2"

4" PROCESSED AND COMPACTED GRAVEL

COMPACTED SUBGRADE

2-29. Tennis Court Paving: Section

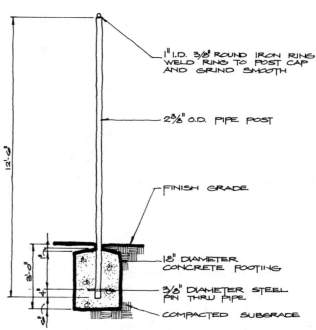

1" I.D. ⅜" ROUND IRON RING WELD RING TO POST CAP AND GRIND SMOOTH

2⅜" O.D. PIPE POST

FINISH GRADE

18" DIAMETER CONCRETE FOOTING

⅜" DIAMETER STEEL PIN THRU PIPE

COMPACTED SUBGRADE

2-31. Tetherball Post

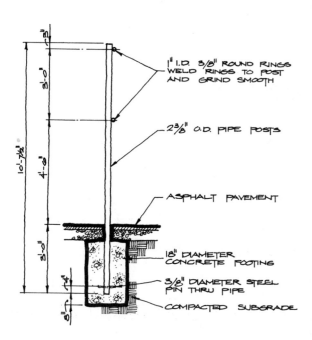

1" I.D. ⅜" ROUND RINGS WELD RINGS TO POST AND GRIND SMOOTH

2⅜" O.D. PIPE POSTS

ASPHALT PAVEMENT

18" DIAMETER CONCRETE FOOTING

⅜" DIAMETER STEEL PIN THRU PIPE

COMPACTED SUBGRADE

2-30. Volleyball Post

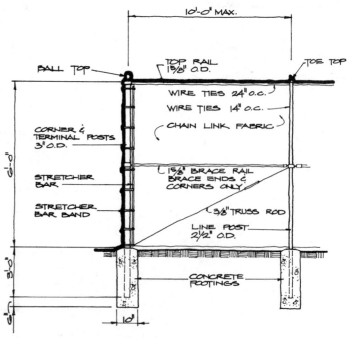

10'-0" MAX.

BALL TOP

TOP RAIL 1⅝" O.D.

TOE TOP

WIRE TIES 24" o.c.

WIRE TIES 14" o.c.

CHAIN LINK FABRIC

CORNER & TERMINAL POSTS 3" O.D.

STRETCHER BAR

STRETCHER BAR BAND

1⅝" BRACE RAIL BRACE ENDS & CORNERS ONLY

⅜" TRUSS ROD

LINE POST 2½" O.D.

CONCRETE FOOTINGS

10"

2-32. Chain Link Fence: Detail

B. PARK FACILITIES

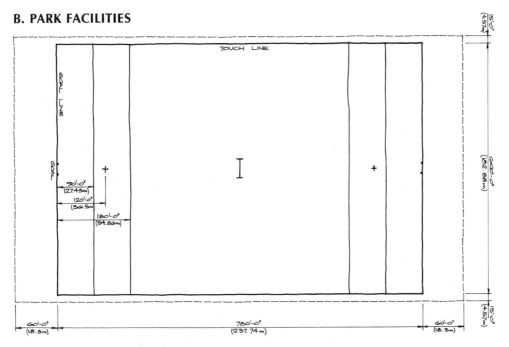

TOUCH LINE

GOAL LINE

GOAL

50'-0"
(27.43m)

120'-0"
(36.5m)

180'-0"
(54.8m)

15'-0"
(4.5m)

600'-0"
(182.88m)

15'-0"
(4.5m)

60'-0"
(18.3m)

780'-0"
(237.74m)

60'-0"
(18.3m)

2-33. Polo Field: Layout

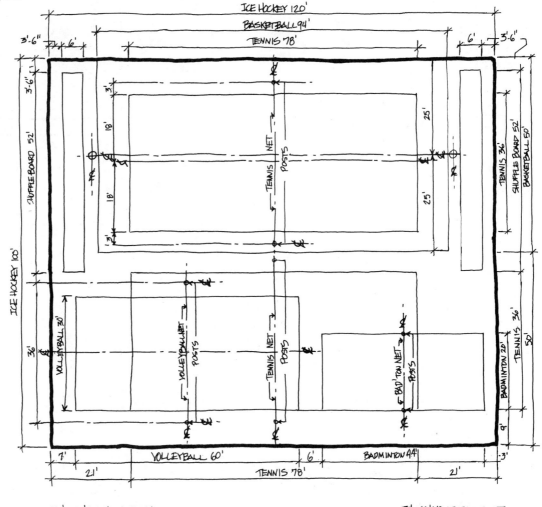

ICE HOCKEY 120'

BASKETBALL 94'

TENNIS 78'

3'-6"   7'x 6'   6'   3'-6"

3'-6"

SHUFFLE BOARD 52'

ICE HOCKEY 100'

3'   18'   18'   3'

TENNIS NET POSTS

25'   25'

SHUFFLE BOARD 50'

BASKETBALL 50'

TENNIS 36'

VOLLEYBALL 30'

3'-6"

VOLLEYBALL NET POSTS

TENNIS NET POSTS

BAD'TON NET POSTS

BADMINTON 20'

TENNIS 36'

50'

9'

7'   VOLLEYBALL 60'   6'   BADMINTON 44'   3'

21'   TENNIS 78'   21'

120'x100' ICE HOCKEY RINK
50'x 94' BASKETBALL COURT
2-36'x 78' TENNIS COURTS

30'x 60' VOLLEYBALL COURT
20'x44' BADMINTON COURT
6'x52' SHUFFLE BOARDS

2-34. Multiuse Recreational Court Area: Plan

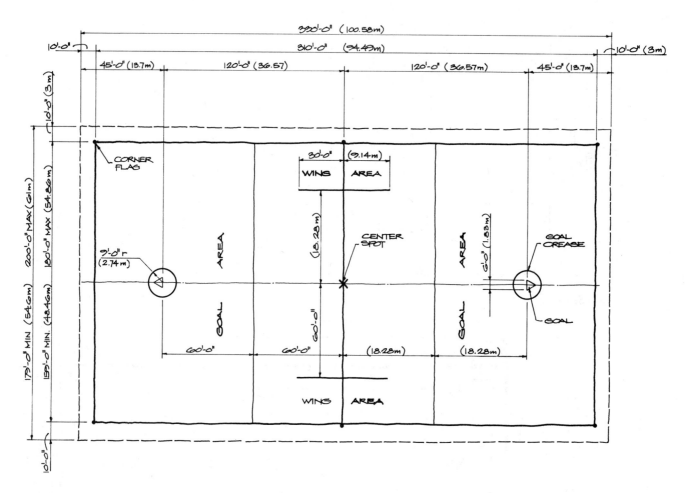

2–35. Lacrosse (Men's)

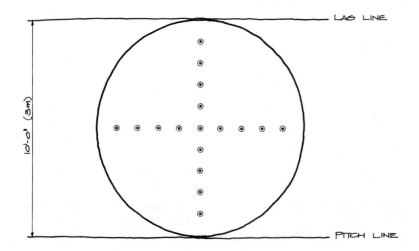

2–36. Marbles

B. PARK FACILITIES

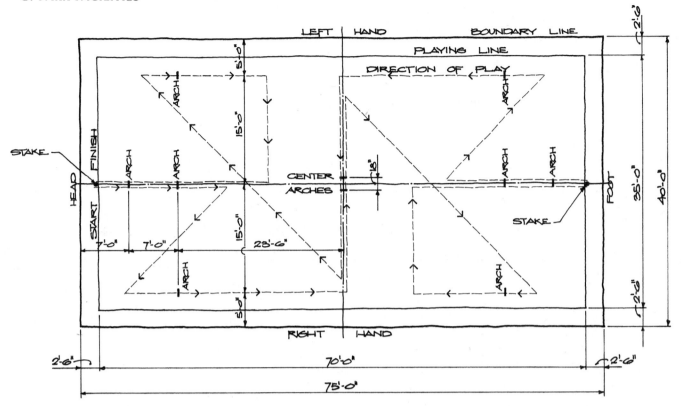

2-37. Croquet

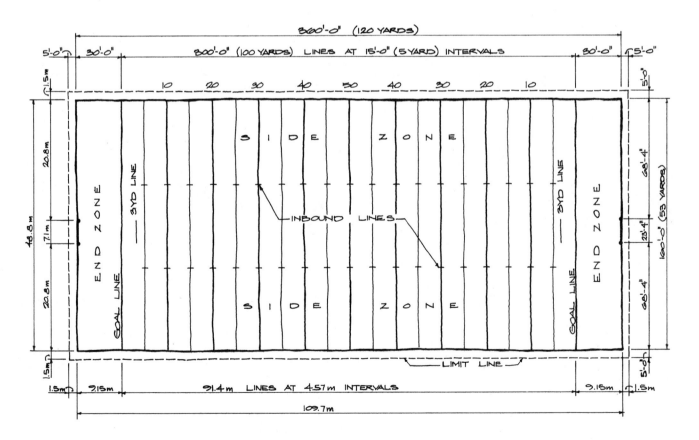

2-38. Eleven-man Football

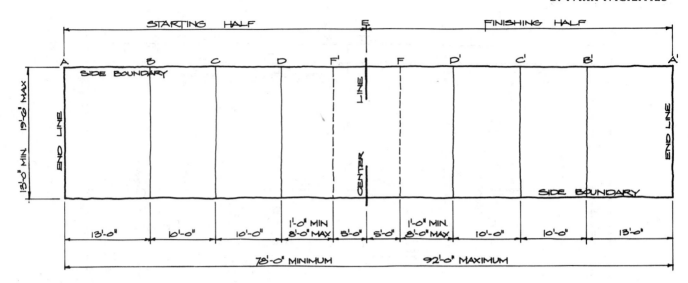

2-39. Boccie: Court Layout

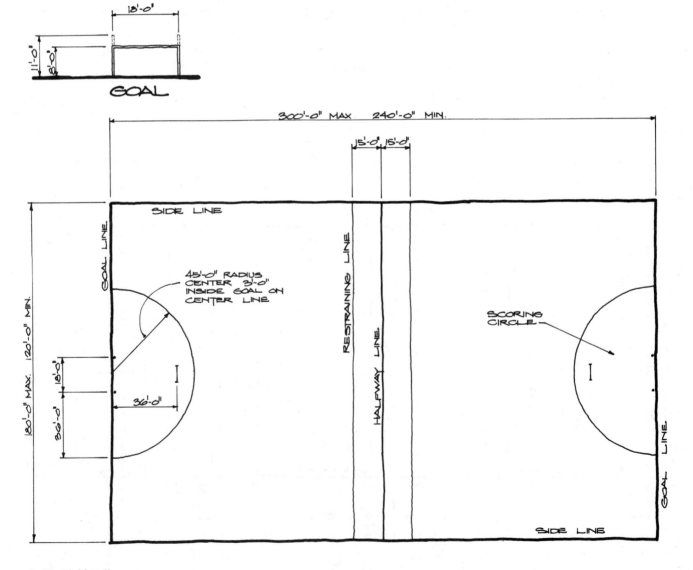

2-40. Field Ball

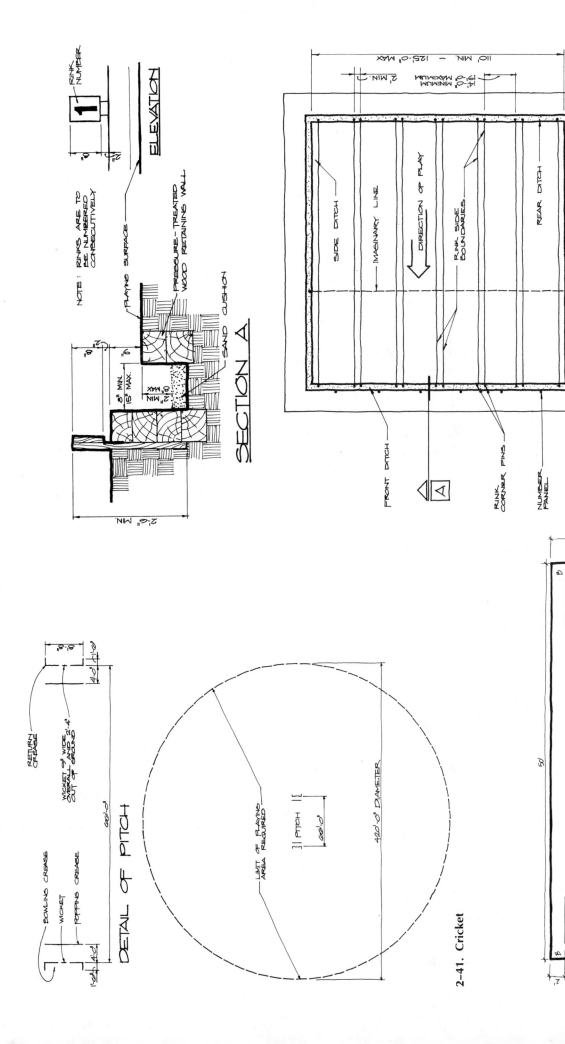

ELEVATION

RINK NUMBER

NOTE : RINKS ARE TO BE NUMBERED CONSECUTIVELY

SECTION A

PLAYING SURFACE

PRESSURE-TREATED WOOD RETAINING WALL

SAND CUSHION

2'-6" MIN.

8" MIN.
15" MAX.

Lawn Bowling: Plan

110' MIN. — 125'-0" MAX

2' MIN.

14'-0"
MINIMUM
MAXIMUM

SIDE DITCH

IMAGINARY LINE

DIRECTION OF PLAY

RINK SIDE BOUNDARIES

REAR DITCH

WALKWAY

81'-0"

110' MIN. - 125'-0" MAX.

FRONT DITCH

A

PSS

RINK CORNER PINS

NUMBER PANEL

2-43. Lawn Bowling: Plan

DETAIL OF PITCH

RETURN CREASE

WICKET 9" WIDE OVERALL AND 2' 4" OUT OF GROUND

BOWLING CREASE

WICKET

POPPING CREASE

66'-0"

420'-0" DIAMETER

LIMIT OF PLAYING AREA REQUIRED

21 PITCH 10
66'-0"

2-41. Cricket

HORSESHOES

STAKE

STAKE

50'

48"

6'

7'

6"

2-42. Horseshoe Court

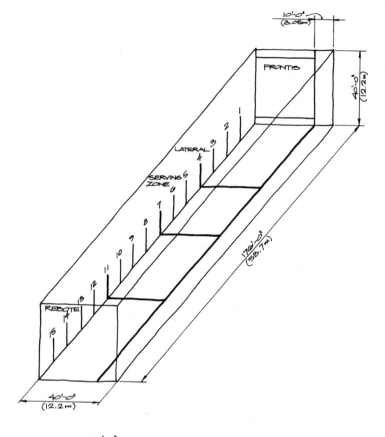

2-44. Pelota Court

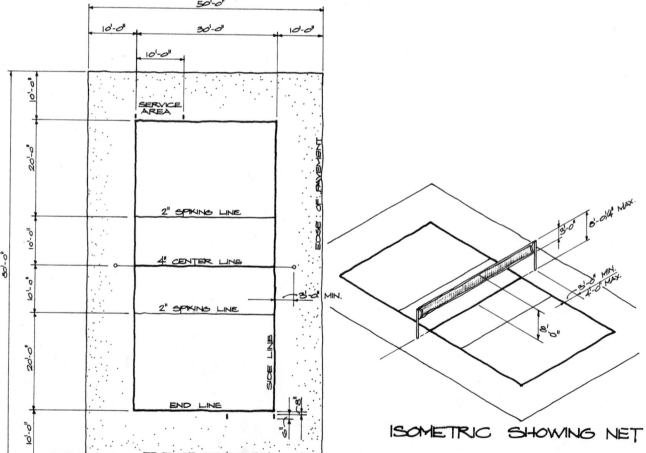

2-45. Volleyball

ISOMETRIC SHOWING NET

B. PARK FACILITIES

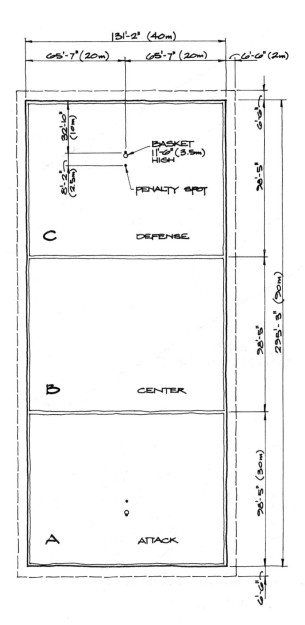

2-46. Korfball Field

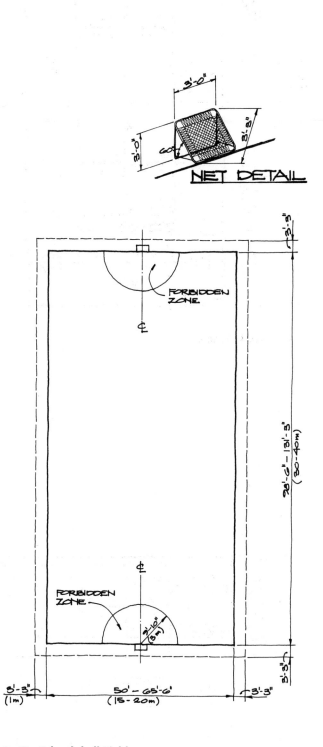

NET DETAIL

2-47. Tchouk-ball Field

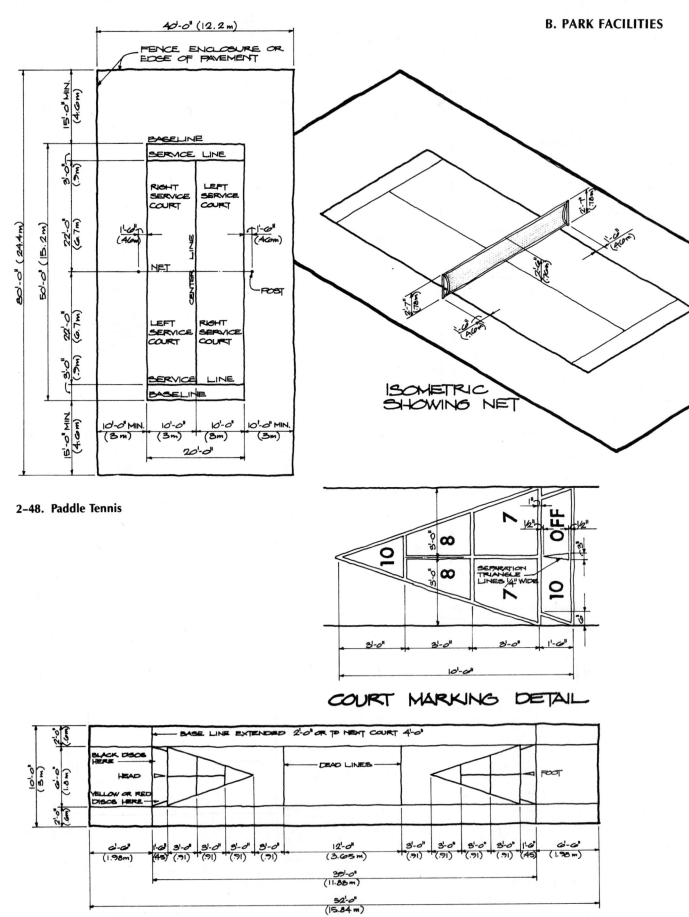

FENCE ENCLOSURE OR EDGE OF PAVEMENT

40'-0" (12.2 m)

15'-0" MIN. (4.6m)

BASELINE

SERVICE LINE

3'-0" (.9m)

RIGHT SERVICE COURT

LEFT SERVICE COURT

80'-0" (24.4m)

50'-0" (15.2 m)

22'-0" (6.7m)

1'-6" (46cm)

1'-6" (46cm)

NET

CENTER LINE

POST

22'-0" (6.7m)

LEFT SERVICE COURT

RIGHT SERVICE COURT

3'-0" (.9m)

SERVICE LINE

BASELINE

15'-0" MIN. (4.6m)

10'-0" MIN. (3 m)

10'-0" (3m)

10'-0" (3m)

10'-0" MIN. (3m)

20'-0"

2-48. Paddle Tennis

ISOMETRIC SHOWING NET

2'-7" (.78m)

1'-0" (46cm)

2'-6" (76cm)

2'-7" (.78m)

1'-6" (46cm)

COURT MARKING DETAIL

10

8

3'-0"

8

3'-0"

7

7

1"

1/2"

OFF

1/2"

3"

10

SEPARATION TRIANGLE LINES 1/4" WIDE

3'-0"

3'-0"

3'-0"

1'-0"

10'-0"

2'-0" (.6m)

10'-0" (3 m)

6'-0" (1.8 m)

2'-0" (.6m)

BASE LINE EXTENDED 2'-0" OR TO NEXT COURT 4'-0"

BLACK DISCS HERE

HEAD

YELLOW OR RED DISCS HERE

DEAD LINES

FOOT

6'-0" (1.98m)

1'-6" (.45)

3'-0" (.91)

3'-0" (.91)

3'-0" (.91)

3'-0" (.91)

12'-0" (3.65 m)

3'-0" (.91)

3'-0" (.91)

3'-0" (.91)

3'-0" (.91)

1'-6" (.45)

6'-0" (1.98 m)

39'-0" (11.88 m)

52'-0" (15.84 m)

2-49. Shuffleboard

B. PARK FACILITIES

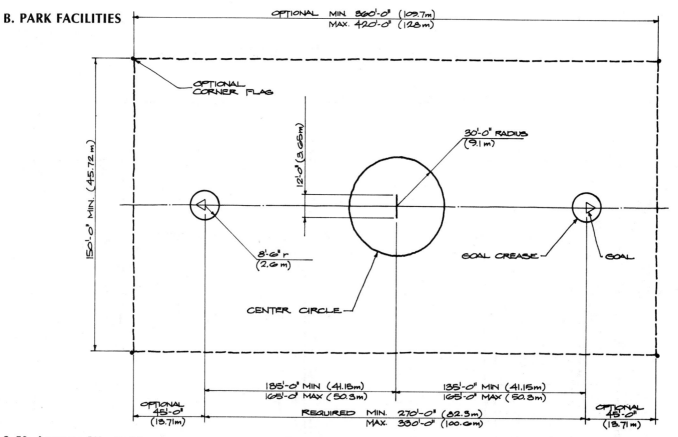

2-50. Lacrosse (Women's)

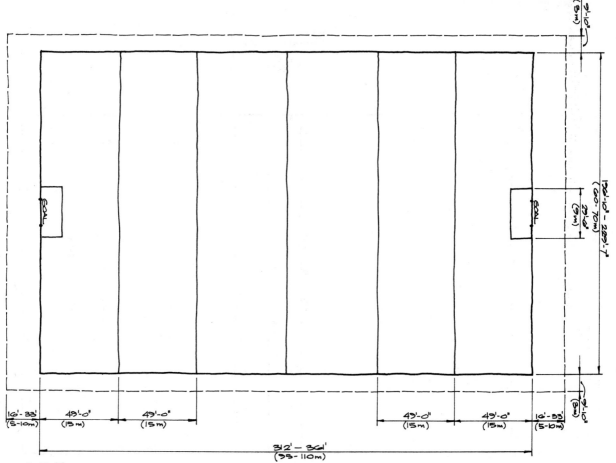

2-51. Camogie Field

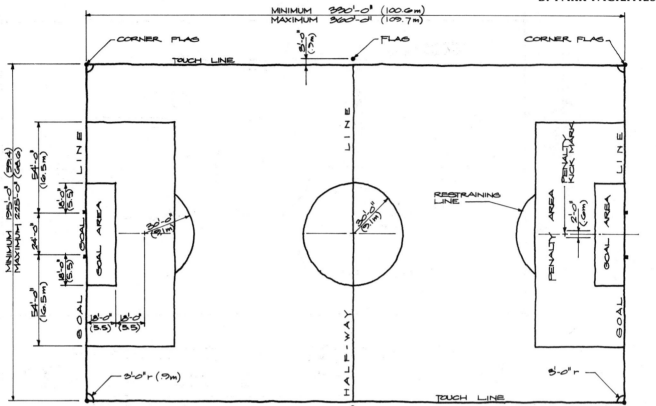

2–52. Soccer (Boys' and Men's)

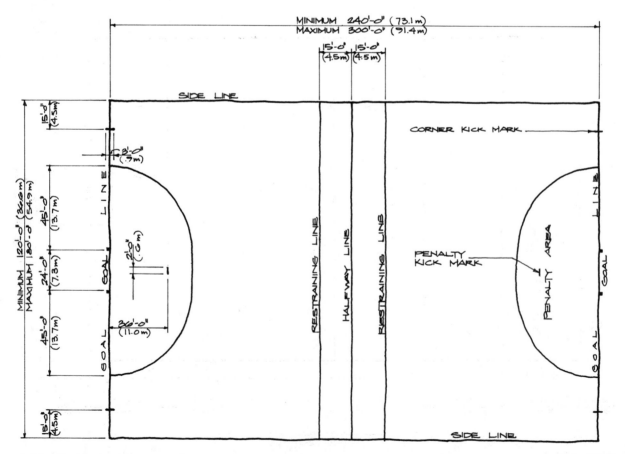

2–53. Soccer (Women's and Girls')

B. PARK FACILITIES

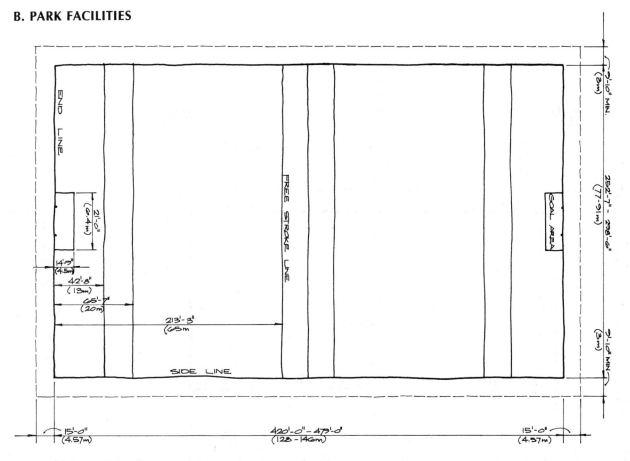

2-54. Hurling Field

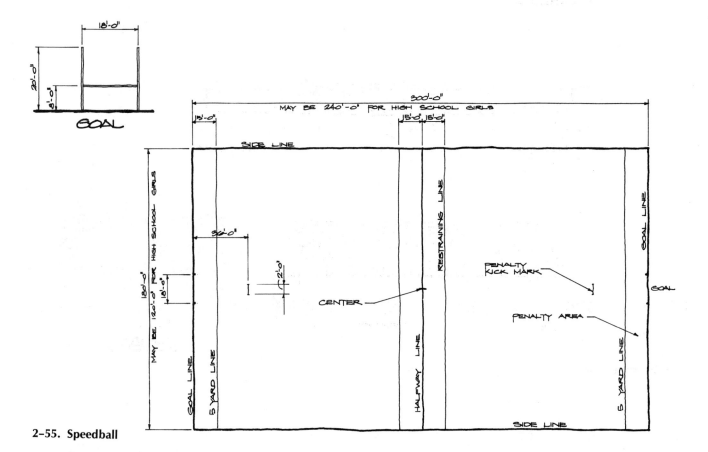

2-55. Speedball

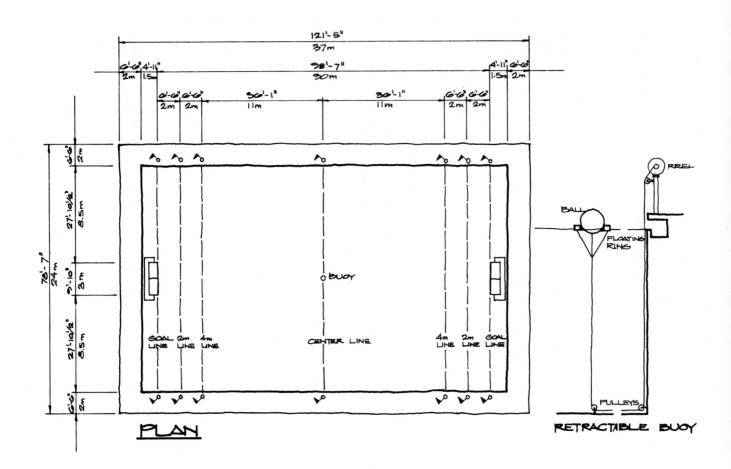

PLAN

RETRACTABLE BUOY

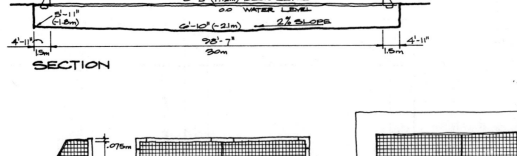

SECTION

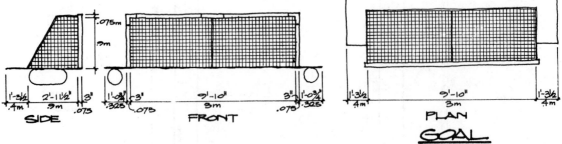

SIDE FRONT PLAN

GOAL

2-56. Water Polo

B. PARK FACILITIES

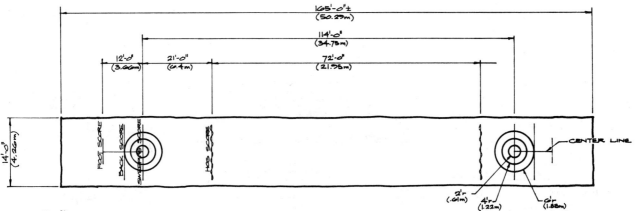

2-57. Curling

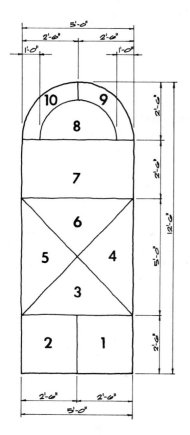

2-58. Hopscotch

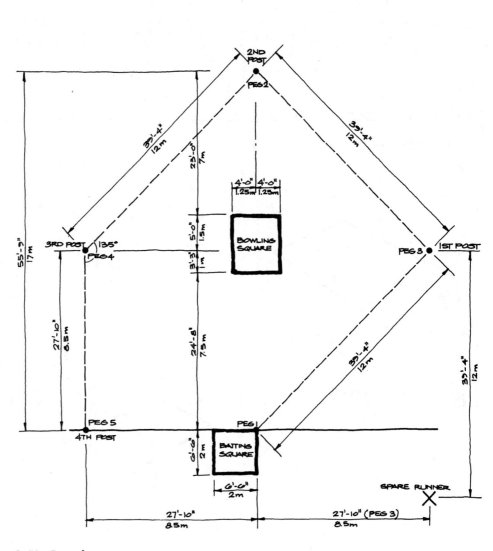

2-59. Rounders

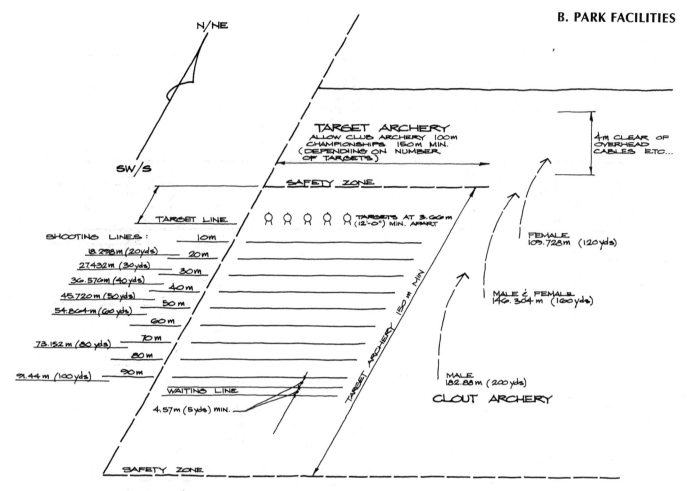

N/NE

SW/S

TARGET ARCHERY
ALLOW CLUB ARCHERY 100m
CHAMPIONSHIPS 150m MIN.
(DEPENDING ON NUMBER
OF TARGETS)

SAFETY ZONE

4m CLEAR OF OVERHEAD CABLES ETC...

TARGET LINE

TARGETS AT 3.66 m
(12'-0") MIN. APART

SHOOTING LINES: 10m
18.298m (20yds) 20m
27.432m (30yds) 30m
36.576m (40yds) 40m
45.720m (50yds) 50m
54.864m (60yds) 60m
                 70m
73.152m (80yds) 80m
91.44m (100yds) 90m

FEMALE
109.728m (120yds)

MALE & FEMALE
146.304m (160yds)

TARGET ARCHERY 150m MIN

WAITING LINE
4.57m (5yds) MIN.

MALE
182.88m (200yds)

CLOUT ARCHERY

SAFETY ZONE

2-60. Target Archery

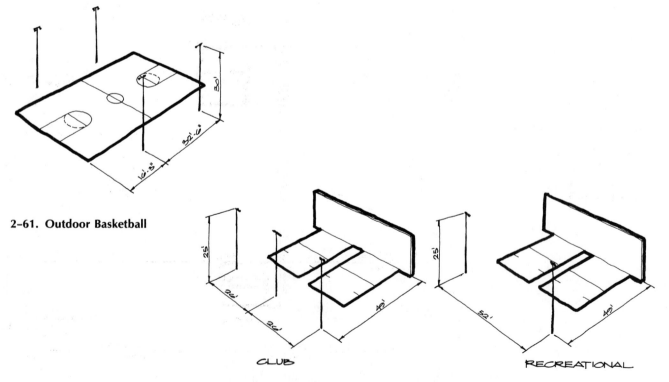

2-61. Outdoor Basketball

CLUB

RECREATIONAL

2-62. Outdoor Handball

B. PARK FACILITIES

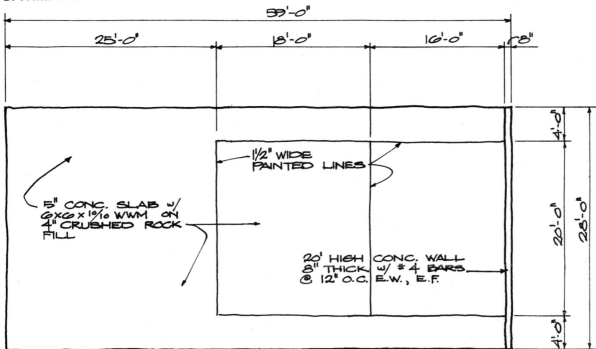

2-63. One-wall Handball Court

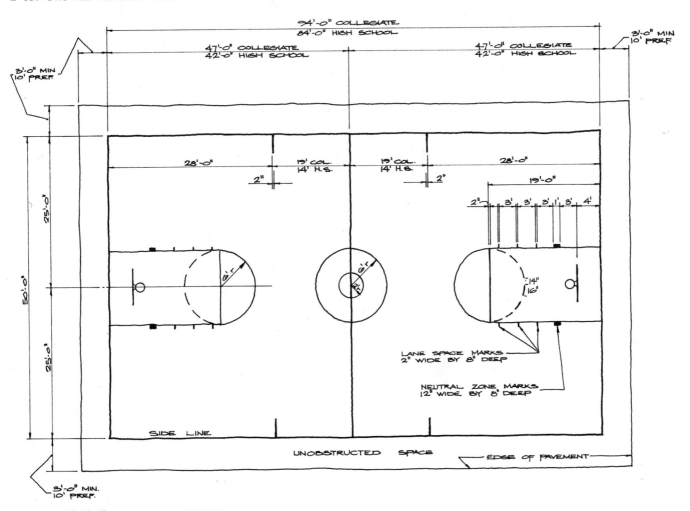

2-64. Basketball Court: Layout (NCAA)

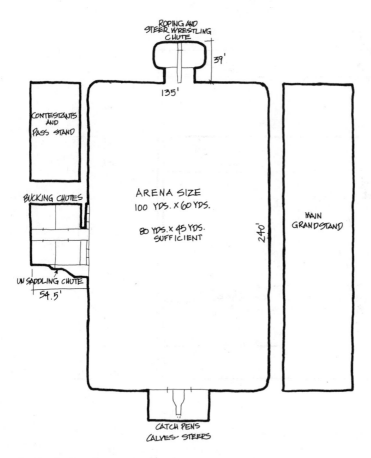

2-65. Rodeo Arena

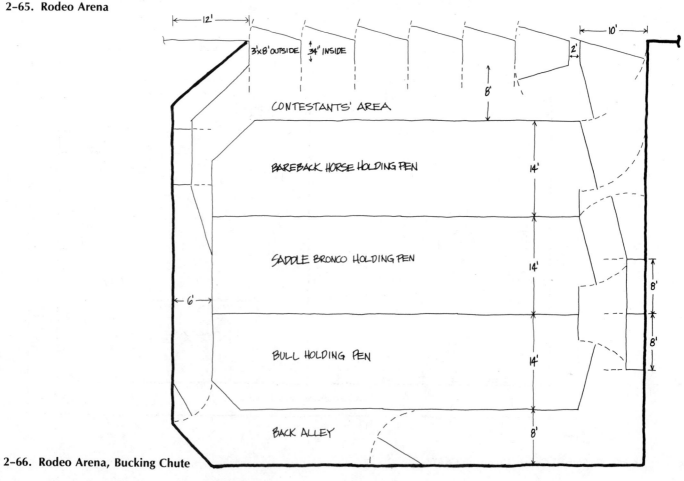

2-66. Rodeo Arena, Bucking Chute

B. PARK FACILITIES

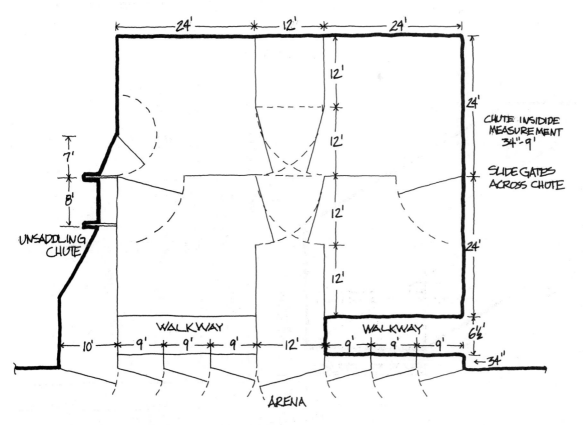

2-67. Rodeo Arena, Roping/Steer Wrestling Chutes

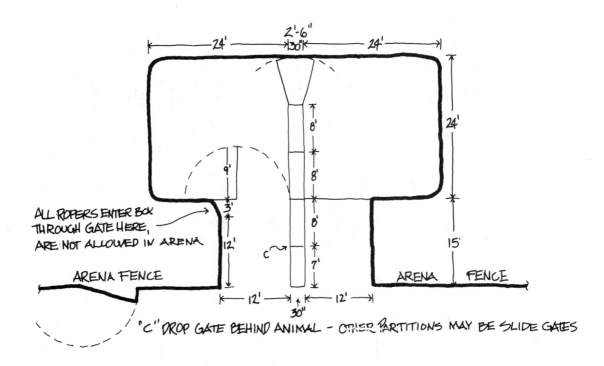

2-68. Rodeo Arena, Riding Chutes

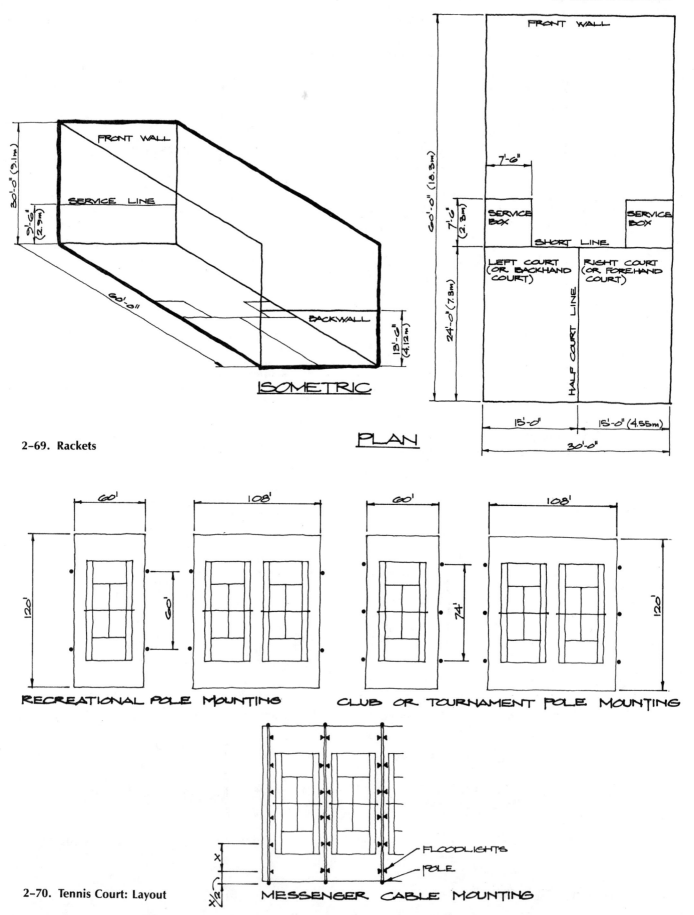

2-69. Rackets

ISOMETRIC

PLAN

FRONT WALL

SERVICE LINE

BACKWALL

30'-0" (9.1m)

7'-6" (2.3m)

15'-6" (4.72m)

60'-0"

FRONT WALL

SERVICE BOX

SERVICE BOX

SHORT LINE

LEFT COURT (OR BACKHAND COURT)

RIGHT COURT (OR FOREHAND COURT)

HALF COURT LINE

60'-0" (18.3m)

7'-6" (2.3m)

24'-0" (7.3m)

7'-6"

15'-0"

15'-0" (4.55m)

30'-0"

RECREATIONAL POLE MOUNTING

CLUB OR TOURNAMENT POLE MOUNTING

60'

108'

120'

60'

60'

108'

74'

120'

MESSENGER CABLE MOUNTING

FLOODLIGHTS

POLE

X

X/2

2-70. Tennis Court: Layout

B. PARK FACILITIES

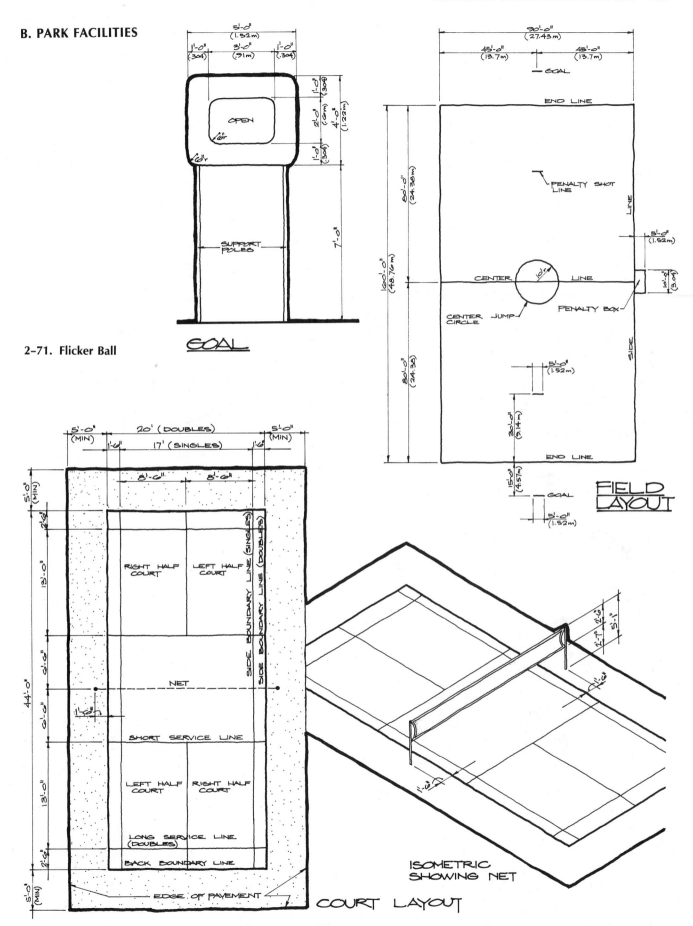

2-71. Flicker Ball

GOAL

FIELD LAYOUT

COURT LAYOUT

ISOMETRIC SHOWING NET

2-72. Badminton Court: Layout

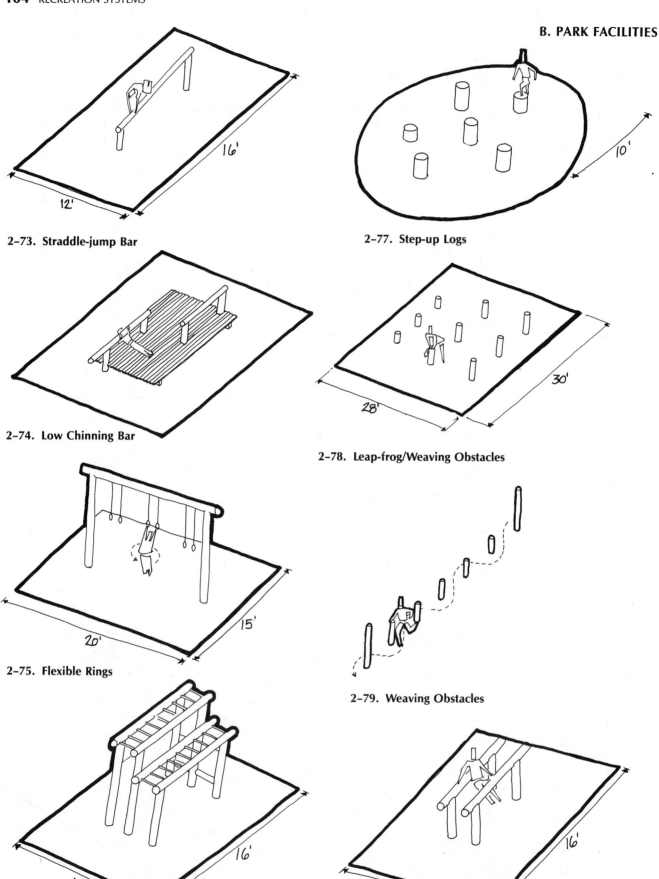

2–73. Straddle-jump Bar

2–77. Step-up Logs

2–74. Low Chinning Bar

2–78. Leap-frog/Weaving Obstacles

2–75. Flexible Rings

2–79. Weaving Obstacles

2–76. Horizontal Ladder

2–80. Parallel Bars

B. PARK FACILITIES

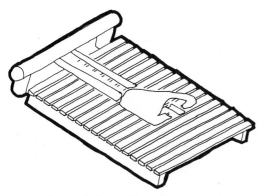

2–81. Sit-up Platform (Type 1)

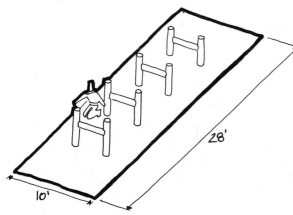

2–82. Jumping Hurdles

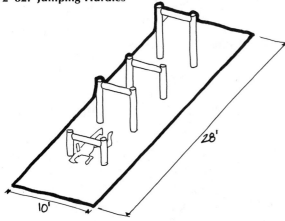

2–83. Crawling Obstacles: Layout

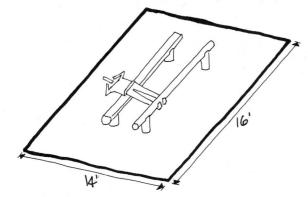

2–84. Sit-up Platform (Type 2)

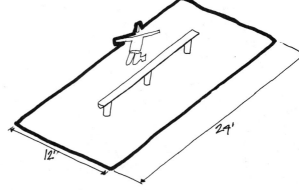

2–85. Straddle-jump Bench

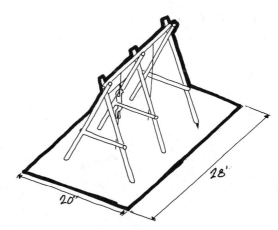

2–86. Climbing Ropes: Layout

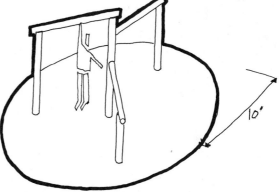

2–87. High Jump: Elevation

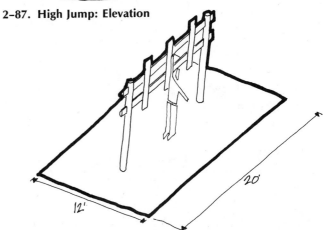

2–88. High-jump Boards

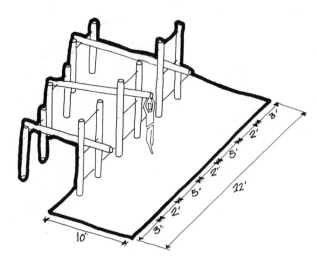

2–89. Weight Bars

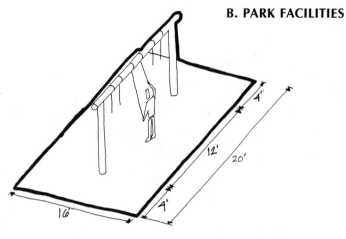

2–91. Arm Exercise

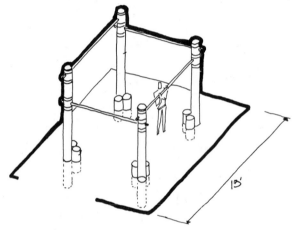

2–90. Chinning Bars

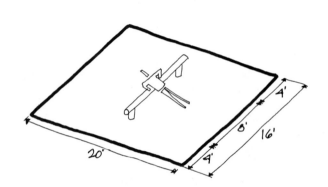

2–92. Push-up Platform

E. CAMPING FACILITIES

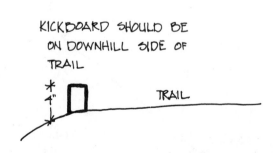

2–93. Camping/Nature Trail: Typical Section

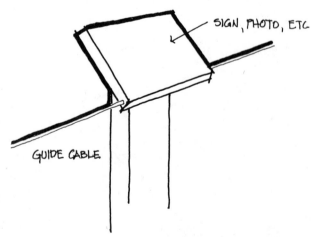

2–94. Interpretive Trail Signage with Guide Cable

E. CAMPING FACILITIES

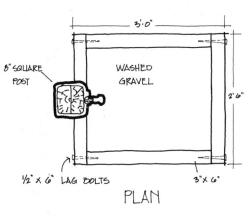

WASHED GRAVEL

8" SQUARE POST

3'-0"

2'-6"

½" x 6" LAG BOLTS

3" x 6"

PLAN

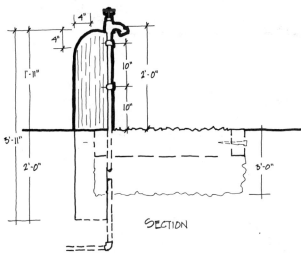

4"

4"

10"

10"

2'-0"

1'-11"

5'-11"

2'-0"

3'-0"

SECTION

2-95. Water Supply Hydrant, Camping Unit

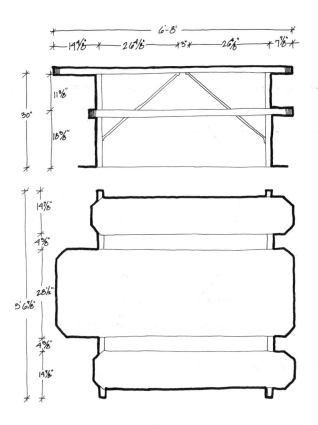

6'-8"

14⅝"   26⅛"   3"   26⅛"   7⅛"

30"

11⅜"

18⅝"

19⅞"

4⅜"

28½"

5'6⅛"

4⅜"

19⅞"

2-97. Wheelchair-accessible Picnic Table

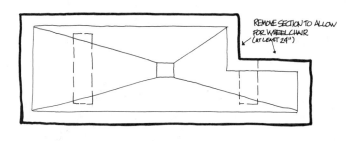

REMOVE SECTION TO ALLOW FOR WHEELCHAIR (AT LEAST 29")

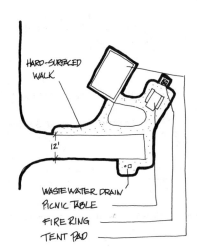

HARD-SURFACED WALK

12'

WASTE WATER DRAIN
PICNIC TABLE
FIRE RING
TENT PAD

2-96. Typical Camping Unit: Layout

30"

2-98. Fish-cleaning Table

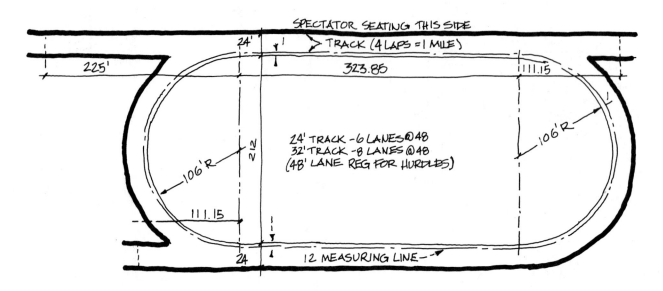

2-99. Quarter-mile Running Track

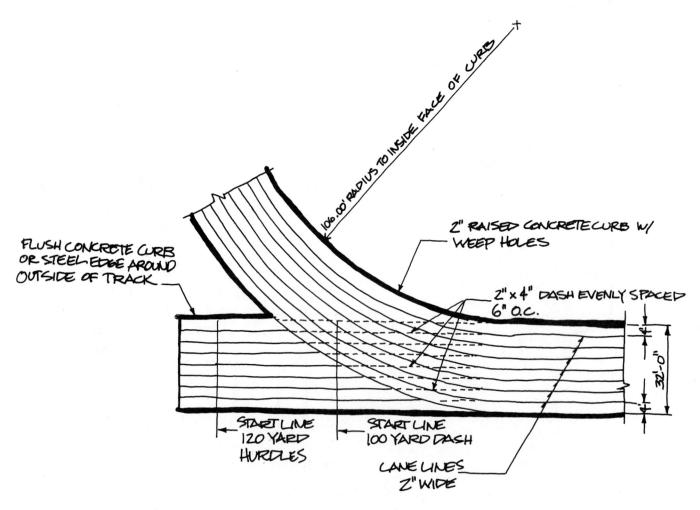

2-100. Quarter-mile Running Track, Lane Marking

F. GENERAL RECREATION FACILITIES

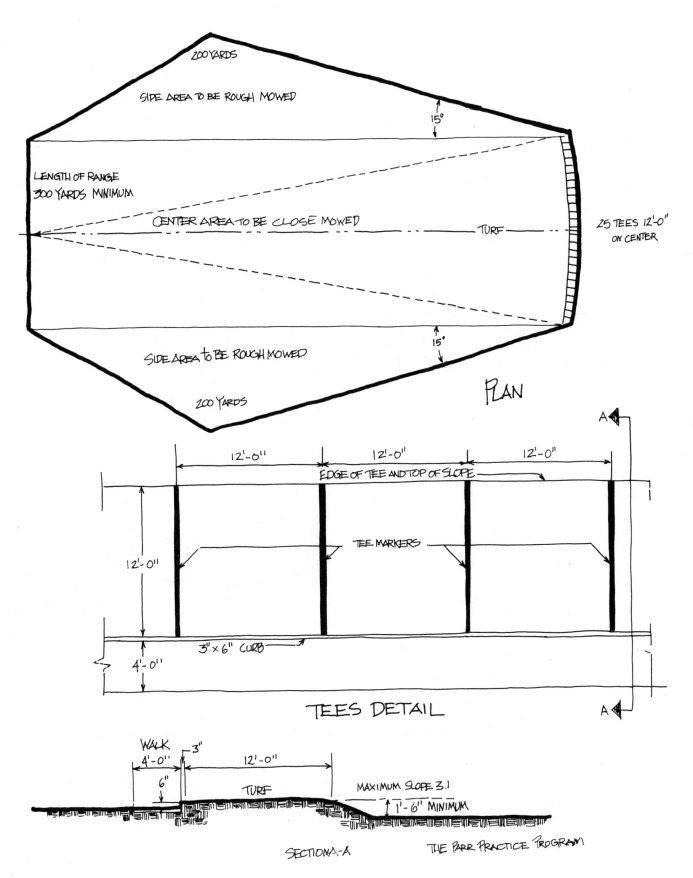

200 YARDS

SIDE AREA TO BE ROUGH MOWED

15°

LENGTH OF RANGE
300 YARDS MINIMUM

CENTER AREA TO BE CLOSE MOWED

TURF

25 TEES 12'-0"
ON CENTER

15°

SIDE AREA TO BE ROUGH MOWED

200 YARDS

PLAN

A

12'-0"   12'-0"   12'-0"

EDGE OF TEE AND TOP OF SLOPE

TEE MARKERS

12'-0"

3" x 6" CURB

4'-0"

TEES DETAIL

A

WALK
4'-0"   3"
6"   12'-0"
TURF   MAXIMUM SLOPE 3.1
1'-6" MINIMUM

SECTION A-A   THE PARR PRACTICE PROGRAM

2-101. Golf Tee

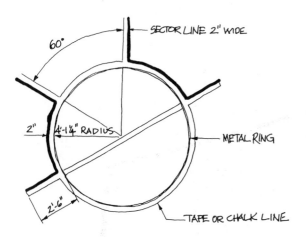

2–102. Discus Throw Circle: Plan

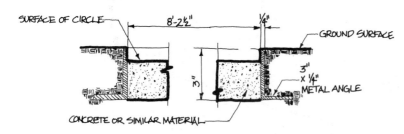

2–103. Discus Throw Circle: Section

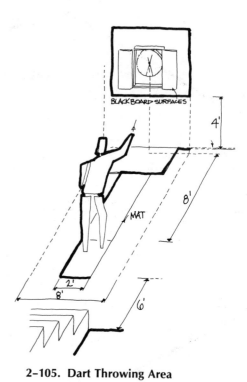

2–105. Dart Throwing Area

2–106. Shot-put Stop Board

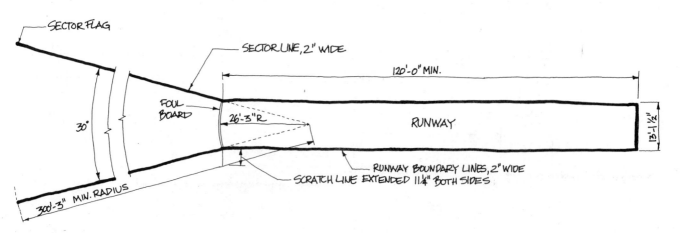

2–104. Javelin Throw: Layout

F. GENERAL RECREATION FACILITIES

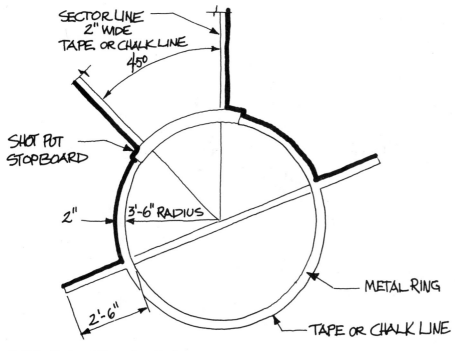

SECTOR LINE
2" WIDE
TAPE OR CHALK LINE
45°

SHOT PUT
STOPBOARD

2"

3'-6" RADIUS

2'-6"

METAL RING

TAPE OR CHALK LINE

2-107. Shot-put Throwing Circle

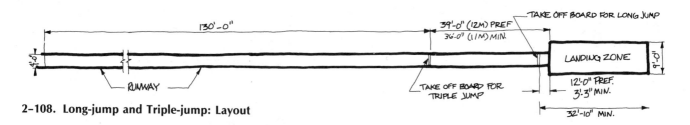

130'-0"

RUNWAY

39'-0" (12M) PREF.
36'-0" (11M) MIN.

TAKE OFF BOARD FOR LONG JUMP

LANDING ZONE

9'-0"

TAKE OFF BOARD FOR
TRIPLE JUMP

12'-0" PREF.
3'-3" MIN.

32'-10" MIN.

2-108. Long-jump and Triple-jump: Layout

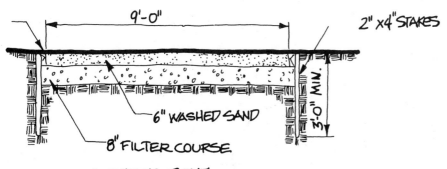

9'-0"

2" x 4" STAKES

3'-0" MIN.

6" WASHED SAND

8" FILTER COURSE.

LANDING ZONE

2-109. Long-jump Landing Area: Section

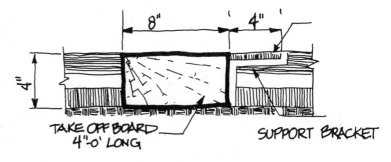

8"

4"

4"

TAKE OFF BOARD
4"-0' LONG

SUPPORT BRACKET

2-110. Long-jump and Triple-jump Takeoff Board: Section

F. GENERAL RECREATION FACILITIES

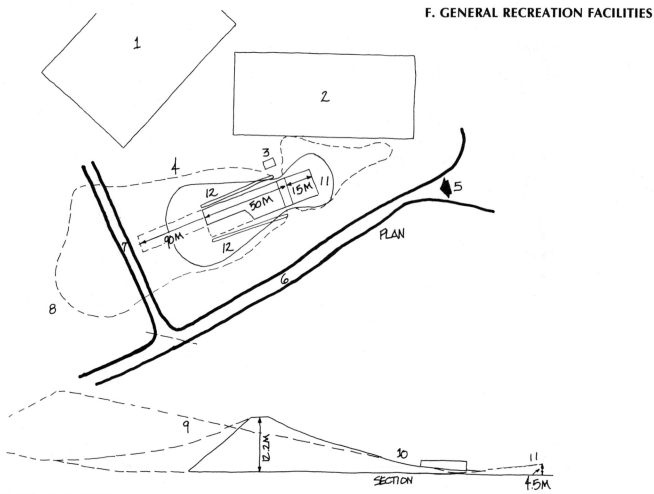

2–111. Typical Ski-jump Area

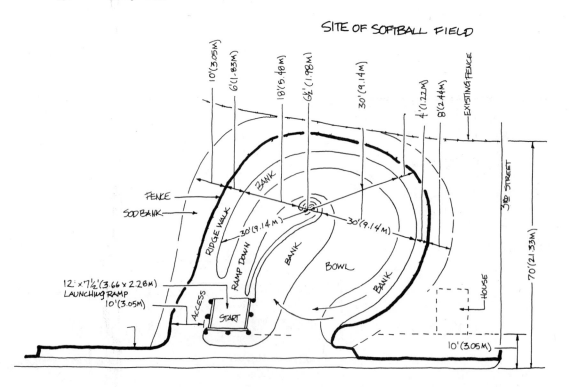

2–112. Skateboard Ramp: General Layout

F. GENERAL RECREATION FACILITIES

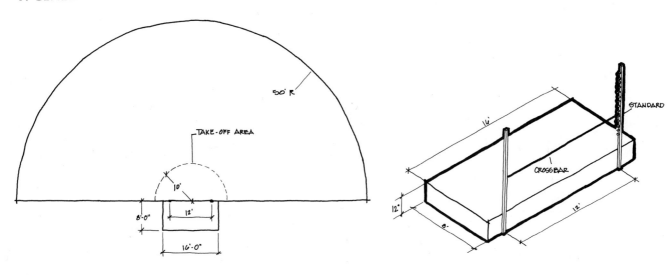

2–113. High-jump Takeoff Area

2–114. High-jump Landing Area

3 Site Modification Systems

Plant Materials _____

A. NATIVE WILDFLOWER SPECIES/MIXES
See table 3–1 and figures 3–1 to 3–9.

Table 3–1. Native Wildflower Species/Mixes

Scientific Name	Common Name	Color
DRY MIXTURE (10–30 in. Rainfall/Year) (Figure 3–1)		
Achillea millefolium	White Yarrow	White
Centaurea cyanus	Cornflower	Blue
Chrysanthemum carinatum	Painted Daisy	White/Yellow/Red/Purple
Coreopsis tinctoria	Plains Coreopsis	Yellow/Maroon
Dianthus barbatus/ D. deltoides	Pinks	Pink/Red/White
Eschscholtzia californica	California Poppy	Yellow/Orange
Gaillardia aristata	Perennial Gaillardia	Yellow/Red
Gaillardia pulchella	Annual Gaillardia	Yellow/Red
Gypsophila elegans	Baby's Breath	White
Linaria maroccana	Spurred Snapdragon	Pink/Yellow/Violet
Linum perenne lewisii	Blue Flax	Blue
Lobularia maritima	Sweet Alyssum	White
Oenothera missouriensis	Dwarf Evening Primrose	Yellow
Papaver rhoeas	Corn Poppy	White/Pink/Red
Penstemon strictus	Penstemon	Blue
Ratibida columnifera	Prairie Coneflower	Yellow/Red
MOIST MIXTURE (Over 30 in. Rainfall/Year) (Figure 3–2)		
Aquilegia caerulea A. vulgaris	Columbine	Yellow/Red/Violet/Blue
Cheiranthus allionii/ C. cheiri	Wallflower	Orange/Pink/Red
Chrysanthemum leucanthemum	Oxeye Daisy	White
Clarkia unguiculata	Clarkia	Pink/Lavender
Coreopsis lanceolata	Lance-leaved Coreopsis	Yellow
Delphinium ajacis	Rocket Larkspur	White/Pink/Blue/Violet
Echinacea purpurea	Purple Coneflower	Purple
Hesperis matronalis	Dame's Rocket	Violet
Iberis umbellata	Candytuft	White/Pink/Violet
Lavatera trimestris	Tree Mallow	White/Pink/Violet
Liatris spicata	Gayfeather	Purple
Linum grandiflorium rubrum	Scarlet Flax	Scarlet

Table 3–1. Continued

Scientific Name	Common Name	Color
Myosotis sylvatica	Forget-Me-Not	Blue
Nemophila menziesii	Baby Blue-eyes	Blue
Rudbeckia hirta	Black-eyed Susan	Yellow
KNEE-HIGH MIXTURE (Less Than 24 in. High)		
Centaurea cyanus (dwarf)	Dwarf Cornflower	Blue
Cheiranthus allionii	Wallflower	Orange
Coreopsis lanceolata	Lance-leaved Coreopsis	Yellow
Coreopsis tinctoria	Plains Coreopsis	Yellow/Maroon
Delphinium ajacis	Rocket Larkspur	White/Pink/Blue/Violet
Dimorphotheca aurantiaca	African Daisy	White/Orange/Salmon
Eschscholtzia californica	California Poppy	Yellow/Orange
Gaillardia aristata	Perennial Gaillardia	Yellow/Red
Gypsophila elegans	Baby's Breath	White
Linum grandiflorium rubrum	Scarlet Flax	Scarlet
Linum perenne lewisii	Blue Flax	Blue
Lobularia maritima	Sweet Alyssum	White
Papaver rhoeas	Corn Poppy	White/Pink/Red
Ratibida columnifera	Prairie Coneflower	Yellow/Red
Rudbeckia hirta	Black-eyed Susan	Yellow
LOW-GROWING MIXTURE (Less Than 16 in. High)		
Centaurea cyanus (dwarf)	Dwarf Cornflower	Blue
Cheiranthus allionii	Wallflower	Orange
Coreopsis lanceolata (dwarf)	Dwarf Lance-leaved Coreopsis	Yellow
Coreopsis tinctoria (dwarf)	Dwarf Plains Coreopsis	Yellow/Maroon
Dimorphotheca aurantiaca	African Daisy	White/Orange/Salmon
Eschscholtzia californica	California Poppy	Yellow/Orange
Gypsophila elegans	Baby's Breath	White

Table 3-1. Continued

Scientific Name	Common Name	Color
Iberis umbellata	Candytuft	White/Pink/Violet
Linaria maroccana	Spurred Snapdragon	Pink/Yellow/Violet
Lobularia maritima	Sweet Alyssum	White
Myosotis sylvatica	Forget-Me-Not	Blue
Oenothera missouriensis	Dwarf Evening Primrose	Yellow
Papaver nudicaule	Iceland Poppy	White/Yellow/Orange
Phacelia campanularia	California Bluebell	Blue
Silene armeria (dwarf)	Dwarf Catchfly	Pink
Viola cornuta	Johnny-Jump-Up	Purple/Yellow/Blue

SHADE MIXTURE

Scientific Name	Common Name	Color
Aquilegia caerulea/ A. vulgaris	Columbine	Yellow/Red/Violet/Blue
Chrysanthemum leucanthemum	Oxeye Daisy	White
Clarkia unguiculata	Clarkia	Pink/Lavender
Coreopsis lanceolata	Lance-leaved Coreopsis	Yellow
Delphinium ajacis	Rocket Larkspur	White/Pink/Blue/Violet
Dianthus barbatus	Pinks	Red
Echinacea purpurea	Purple Coneflower	Purple
Gypsophila elegans	Baby's Breath	White
Hesperis matronalis	Dame's Rocket	Violet
Iberis umbellata	Candytuft	White/Pink/Violet
Linaria maroccana	Spurred Snapdragon	Pink/Yellow/Violet
Mimulus tigrinus	Monkeyflower	Yellow/Red
Myosotis sylvatica	Forget-Me-Not	Blue
Nemophila menziesii	Baby Blue-Eyes	Blue
Papaver rhoeas	Corn Poppy	White/Pink/Red
Viola cornuta	Johnny-Jump-Up	Purple/Yellow/Blue

AGGRESSIVE AMENDMENT (Overseeding/Additives)

Scientific Name	Common Name	Color
Achillea millefolium	White Yarrow	White
Centaurea cyanus	Cornflower	Blue
Cerastium biebersteinii	Snow-in-Summer	White
Cheiranthus allionii	Wallflower	Orange
Cheiranthus cheiri	Wallflower	Orange/Pink/Violet
Cichorium intybus	Chicory	Blue
Cosmos bipinnatus	Cosmos	White/Pink/Crimson
Eschscholtzia californica	California Poppy	Yellow/Orange
Gypsophila elegans	Annual Baby's Breath	White
Gypsophila paniculata	Perennial Baby's Breath	White
Helianthus annuus	Sunflower	Yellow
Hesperis matronalis	Dame's Rocket	Violet
Lathyrus latifolius	Perennial Sweet Pea	Rose/Pink
Linum perenne lewisii	Blue Flax	Blue
Lotus corniculatus	Bird's-foot Trefoil	Yellow
Oenothera hooken	Tall Evening Primrose	Yellow
Rudbeckia hirta	Black-eyed Susan	Yellow
Sanguisorba minor	Small Burnet	Green

Table 3-1. Continued

Scientific Name	Common Name	Color
MIDWEST MIXTURE (Figure 3-3)		
Achillea filipendulina	Gold Yarrow	Gold
Achillea millefolium	White Yarrow	White
Aquilegia caerulea	Columbine	Yellow/Red/Violet/Blue
Campanula rotundifolia/C. carpatica	Harebell/Bellflower	Lavender/Blue
Centaurea cyanus	Cornflower	Blue
Cerastium biebersteinii	Snow-in-Summer	White
Cheiranthus allionii/ C. cheiri	Wallflower	Orange/Pink/Red
Chrysanthemum leucanthemum	Oxeye Daisy	White
Delphinium ajacis	Rocket Larkspur	White/Pink/Blue/Violet
Dianthus barbatus/ D. deltoides	Pinks	Pink/Red/White
Eschscholtzia californica	California Poppy	Yellow/Orange
Gaillardia aristata	Perennial Gaillardia	Yellow/Red
Gypsophila elegans	Baby's Breath	White
Hesperis matronalis	Dame's Rocket	Violet
Linum perenne lewisii	Blue Flax	Blue
Lupinus perennis	Perennial Lupine	Blue
Myosotis sylvatica	Forget-Me-Not	Blue
Oenothera missouriensis	Dwarf Evening Primrose	Yellow
Penstemon strictus	Penstemon	Blue
Rudbeckia hirta	Black-eyed Susan	Yellow
Silene armeria	Catchfly	Pink
NORTHEAST MIXTURE (Figure 3-4)		
Achillea filipendulina	Gold Yarrow	Gold
Achillea millefolium	White Yarrow	White
Aster novae-angliae	New England Aster	Violet
Centaurea cyanus	Cornflower	Blue
Cheiranthus allionii/ C. cheiri	Wallflower	Orange/Pink/Red
Chrysanthemum leucanthemum	Oxeye Daisy	White
Coreopsis lanceolata	Lance-leaved Coreopsis	Yellow
Delphinium ajacis	Rocket Larkspur	White/Pink/Blue/Violet
Dianthus barbatus/ D. deltoides	Pinks	Pink/Red/White
Digitalis purpurea	Foxglove	Purple/Cream
Echinacea purpurea	Purple Coneflower	Purple
Gypsophila elegans	Baby's Breath	White
Hesperis matronalis	Dame's Rocket	Violet
Ipomopsis rubra	Gilia	White/Red/Coral
Liatris spicata	Gayfeather	Purple
Linaria maroccana	Spurred Snapdragon	Pink/Yellow/Violet
Linum grandiflorum rubrum	Scarlet Flax	Scarlet
Lupinus perennis	Perennial Lupine	Blue
Oenothera missouriensis	Dwarf Evening Primrose	Yellow
Papaver rhoeas	Corn Poppy	White/Pink/Red
Rudbeckia hirta	Black-eyed Susan	Yellow
Silene armeria	Catchfly	Pink

Table 3–1. Continued

Scientific Name	Common Name	Color
NORTHWEST MIXTURE (Below 7,000 ft.) (Figure 3–5)		
Aquilegia caerulea	Columbine	Yellow/Red/Violet/Blue
Chieranthus allionii/ C. cheiri	Wallflower	Orange/Pink/Red
Chrysanthemum leucanthemum	Oxeye Daisy	White
Clarkia unguiculata	Clarkia	Pink/Lavender
Collinsia heterphylla	Chinese Houses	White/Violet
Coreopsis lanceolata	Lance-leaved Coreopsis	Yellow
Delphinium ajacis	Rocket Larkspur	White/Pink/Blue/Violet
Dianthus barbatus/ D. deltoides	Pinks	Pink/Red/White
Eschscholtzia californica	California Poppy	Yellow/Orange
Gilia tricolor	Bird's Eyes	Lavender/White
Hesperis matronalis	Dame's Rocket	Violet
Liatris spicata	Gayfeather	Purple
Linaria maroccana	Spurred Snapdragon	Pink/Yellow/Violet
Linum grandiflorium rubrum	Scarlet Flax	Scarlet
Lobularia maritima	Sweet Alyssum	White
Mirabilis jalapa	Four-O'Clock	Red/Pink/Yellow/White
Nemophila maculata	Five-Spot	White/Purple
Nemophila menziesii	Baby Blue-Eyes	Blue
Papaver rhoeas	Corn Poppy	White/Pink/Red
Rudbeckia hirta	Black-eyed Susan	Yellow
Silene armeria	Catchfly	Pink

Scientific Name	Common Name	Color
SOUTHEAST MIXTURE (Figure 3–6)		
Centaurea cyanus	Cornflower	Blue
Cheiranthus allionii/ C. cheiri	Wallflower	Orange/Pink/Red
Coreopsis lanceolata	Lance-leaved Coreopsis	Yellow
Coreopsis tinctoria	Plains Coreopsis	Yellow/Maroon
Delphinium ajacis	Rocket Larkspur	White/Pink/Blue/Violet
Echinacea purpurea	Purple Coneflower	Purple
Eschscholtzia californica	California Poppy	Yellow/Orange
Gaillardia pulchella	Annual Gaillardia	Yellow/Red
Gilia tricolor	Bird's Eyes	Lavender/White
Gypsophila elegans	Baby's Breath	White
Hesperis matronalis	Dame's Rocket	Violet
Ipomopsis rubra	Gilia	White/Red/Coral
Lavatera trimestris	Tree Mallow	White/Pink/Violet
Liatris spicata	Gayfeather	Purple
Linum grandiflorium rubrum	Scarlet Flax	Scarlet
Lobularia maritima	Sweet Alyssum	White
Lupinus perennis	Perennial Lupine	Blue
Mirabilis jalapa	Four-O'Clock	Red/Pink/Yellow/White
Nemophila menziesii	Baby Blue-Eyes	Blue
Papaver rhoeas	Corn Poppy	White/Pink/Red
Rudbeckia hirta	Black-eyed Susan	Yellow

Table 3–1. Continued

Scientific Name	Common Name	Color
SOUTHWEST MIXTURE (Below 7,000 ft.) (Figure 3–7)		
Achillea filipendulina	Gold Yarrow	Gold
Achillea millefolium	White Yarrow	White
Centaurea cyanus	Cornflower	Blue
Clarkia unguiculata	Clarkia	Pink/Lavender
Coreopsis tinctoria	Plains Coreopsis	Yellow/Maroon
Dimorphotheca africana	African Daisy	White/Orange/Salmon
Eschscholtzia californica	California Poppy	Yellow/Orange
Gaillardia pulchella	Annual Gaillardia	Yellow/Red
Gilia tricolor	Bird's Eyes	Lavender/White
Gypsophila elegans	Baby's Breath	White
Layia platyglossa	Tidytips	Yellow/White
Linaria maroccana	Spurred Snapdragon	Pink/Yellow/Violet
Linum grandiflorium rubrum	Scarlet Flax	Scarlet
Linum perenne lewisii	Blue Flax	Blue
Lobularia maritima	Sweet Alyssum	White
Machaeranthera tanacetifolia	Prairie Aster	Violet
Mirabilis jalapa	Four-O'Clock	Red/Pink/Yellow/White
Nemophila maculata	Five-Spot	White/Purple
Nemophila menziesii	Baby Blue-Eyes	Blue
Papaver rhoeas	Corn Poppy	White/Pink/Red
Penstemon spp.	Penstemon	Lavender/Blue/Purple
Ratibida columnifera	Prairie Coneflower	Yellow/Red

Scientific Name	Common Name	Color
TEXAS/OKLAHOMA MIXTURE (Figure 3–8)		
Achillea filipendulina	Gold Yarrow	Gold
Achillea millefolium	White Yarrow	White
Centaurea cyanus	Cornflower	Blue
Cheiranthus allionii/ C. cheiri	Wallflower	Orange/Pink/Red
Chrysanthemum carinatum	Painted Daisy	White/Yellow/Red/Purple
Coreopsis lanceolata	Lance-leaved Coreopsis	Yellow
Coreopsis tinctoria	Plains Coreopsis	Yellow/Maroon
Dianthus barbatus/ D. deltoides	Pinks	Pink/Red/White
Dimorphotheca africana	African Daisy	White/Orange/Salmon
Echinacea purpurea	Purple Coneflower	Purple
Gaillardia aristata	Perennial Gaillardia	Yellow/Red
Gaillardia pulchella	Annual Gaillardia	Yellow/Red
Gypsophila elegans	Baby's Breath	White
Iberis umbellata	Candytuft	White/Pink/Violet
Linum grandiflorium rubrum	Scarlet Flax	Scarlet
Linum perenne lewisii	Blue Flax	Blue
Lobularia maritima	Sweet Alyssum	White
Lupinus texensis	Texas Bluebonnet	Blue
Mirabilis jalapa	Four-O'Clock	Red/Pink/Yellow/White
Nemophila menziesii	Baby Blue-Eyes	Blue

Table 3–1. Continued

Scientific Name	Common Name	Color
Oenothera missour-iensis	Dwarf Evening Primrose	Yellow
Papaver rhoeas	Corn Poppy	White/Red/Pink
Ratibida columni-fera	Prairie Coneflower	Yellow/Red
Rudbeckia hirta	Black-eyed Susan	Yellow

WESTERN MIXTURE (Below 7,000 ft.) (Figure 3–9)

Scientific Name	Common Name	Color
Achillea filipendu-lina	Gold Yarrow	Gold
Achillea millefolium	White Yarrow	White
Centaurea cyanus	Cornflower	Blue
Cerastium bieber-steinii	Snow-in-Summer	White
Chrysanthemum carinatum	Painted Daisy	White/Yellow/Red/ Purple
Clarkia unguiculata	Clarkia	Pink/Lavender
Coreopsis tinctoria	Plains Coreopsis	Yellow/Maroon
Dianthus barbatus/ D. deltoides	Pinks	Pink/Red/White
Dimorphotheca afri-cana	African Daisy	White/Orange/ Salmon
Eschscholtzia califor-nica	California Poppy	Yellow/Orange
Gaillardia aristata	Perennial Gaillardia	Yellow/Red
Gaillardia pulchella	Annual Gaillardia	Yellow/Red
Gypsophila elegans	Baby's Breath	White
Iberis umbellata	Candytuft	White/Pink/Violet
Linaria maroccana	Spurred Snapdragon	Pink/Yellow/Violet
Linum grandiflorium rubrum	Scarlet Flax	Scarlet
Linum perenne lew-isii	Blue Flax	Blue
Lobularia maritima	Sweet Alyssum	White
Lupinus perennis	Perennial Lupine	Blue
Machaeranthera tanacetifolia	Prairie Aster	Violet
Oenothera missour-iensis	Dwarf Evening Primrose	Yellow
Papaver rhoeas	Corn Poppy	White/Pink/Red
Penstemon strictus	Penstemon	Blue
Ratibida columni-fera	Prairie Coneflower	Yellow/Red

GULF COAST/CARIBBEAN MIXTURE (Includes Southern Texas and Southern Florida)

Scientific Name	Common Name	Color
Asparagus densiflo-rus sprengen	Asparagus sprengen	White
Centaurea cyanus	Cornflower	Blue
Cheiranthus allionii/ C. cheiri	Wallflower	Orange/Pink/Red
Coreopsis lanceolata	Lance-leaved Cor-eopsis	Yellow
Cosmos bipinnatus	Cosmos	White/Pink/Crimson
Dimorphoteca afri-cana	African Daisy	White/Orange/ Salmon
Gaillardia pulchella	Annual Gaillardia	Yellow/Red
Gypsophila elegans	Baby's Breath	White
Liatris spicata	Gayfeather	Purple
Linaria maroccana	Spurred Snapdragon	Pink/Yellow/Violet
Linum grandiflorium rubrum	Scarlet Flax	Scarlet
Linum perenne lew-isii	Blue Flax	Blue

Table 3–1. Continued

Scientific Name	Common Name	Color
Lobularia maritima	Sweet Alyssum	White
Mirabilis jalapa	Four-O'Clock	Red/Pink/Yellow/ White
Rudbeckia hirta	Black-eyed Susan	Yellow
Silene armeria	Catchfly	Pink
Thunbergia alata	Black-eyed Susan Vine	Yellow-Orange

B. NORTH AMERICAN FOREST AREAS
See figures 3–10 to 3–18.

C. NORTH AMERICAN GRASSLAND AREAS
See figures 3–19 and 3–20.

D. REFERENCE GUIDES FOR PLANTING IMPLEMENTATION
See tables 3–2 to 3–12.

Table 3–2. Diameter of Planting Ball for Shade Trees (Recommended)

Caliper* (in.)	Minimum Diameter	Minimum Depth
1½–1½	18″ (45.72 cm)	13.5″ (34.29 cm)
1½–1¾	20″ (50.80 cm)	13.3″ (33.78 cm)
1¾–2	22″ (55.88 cm)	14.7″ (37.34 cm)
2 –2½	24″ (60.96 cm)	16.0″ (40.64 cm)
2½–3	28″ (71.12 cm)	18.7″ (47.50 cm)
3 –3½	32″ (81.28 cm)	19.2″ (48.77 cm)
3½–4	38″ (96.52 cm)	22.8″ (57.91 cm)
4 –4½	42″ (106.68 cm)	25.2″ (64.00 cm)
4½–5	46″ (116.84 cm)	27.6″ (70.10 cm)
5 –5½	54″ (137.16 cm)	32.4″ (82.30 cm)

*Horicultural determination

Table 3–3. Bare Root Trees: Spread of Roots for Planting

Caliper* (in.)	Height	Root Spread
½– ¾	5– 6′ (1.53–1.83 m)	12″ (30.48 cm)
¾–1	6– 8′ (1.83–2.44 m)	16″ (40.64 cm)
1 –1¼	7– 9′ (2.13–2.74 m)	18″ (45.72 cm)
1¼–1½	8–10′ (2.44–3.05 m)	20″ (50.80 cm)
1½–1¾	10–12′ (3.05–3.66 m)	22″ (55.88 cm)
1¾–2	10–12′ (3.05–3.66 m)	24″ (60.96 cm)
2 –2½	12–14′ (3.66–4.27 m)	28″ (71.12 cm)
2½–3	12–14′ (3.66–4.27 m)	32″ (81.28 cm)
3 –3½	14–16′ (4.27–4.88 m)	38″ (96.52 cm)

*Horticultural determination

Table 3–4. Height Relationship to Caliper

Caliper* (in.)	Height
½– ¾	5– 6′ (1.53–1.83 m)
¾–1	6– 8′ (1.83–2.44 m)
1 –1½	7– 9′ (2.13–2.74 m)
1½–1¾	10–12′ (3.05–3.66 m)
1¾–2	10–12′ (3.05–3.66 m)
2 –2½	12–14′ (3.66–4.27 m)
2½–3	12–14′ (3.66–4.27 m)
3 –3½	14–16′ (4.27–4.88 m)
3½–4	14–16′ (4.27–4.88 m)
4 –5	16–18′ (4.88–5.49 m)
5 –6	18′ (5.49 m) and up

*Horticultural determination

Table 3–5. Planting Pit Requirements: B & B Stock

Height of Shrub* (in.)	Size of Pit (Diameter)**
18/24″	16 × 10″ (40.64 × 25.40 cm)
24/36″	18 × 12″ (45.72 × 30.48 cm)
36/48″	20 × 14″ (50.8 × 35.56 cm)

Caliper of Tree*	Size of Pit (Diameter)**
1 –1½″	34 × 21″ (86.36 × 53.34 cm)
1½–2″	36 × 22″ (91.44 × 55.88 cm)
2 –2½″	40 × 25″ (101.6 × 63.5 cm)
2½–3″	44 × 26″ (111.76 × 66.04 cm)
3 –4″	52 × 30″ (132.08 × 76.2 cm)
4 –5″	56 × 32″ (142.24 × 81.28 cm)

*Horticultural determination
**To determine pit volume in cubic feet: (3.14) (diameter in inches²) ÷ 4 × depth in inches × 1,728 = volume

Table 3–6. Container Stock: Volume of Soil

Size (Gal.)	Volume (cu.ft.)
1	0.13
2	0.27
5	0.67
7	0.94

Table 3–7. Groundcover Planting

Spacing of Plants	Multiplier*
4″ (10.16 cm) on center	9.10
6″ (15.24 cm) o.c.	4.00
9″ (22.86 cm) o.c.	1.77
12″ (30.48 cm) o.c.	1.00
18″ (45.72 cm) o.c.	.45
24″ (60.96 cm) o.c.	.25

*Square feet of planting area × multiplier = number of plants required.

Table 3–8. Planting Ball Volumes and Weights

Ball Size	Volume** (cu. ft.)	Weight* (lbs.)
18 × 14″	1.81	155–200
20 × 15″	2.39	203–263
22 × 15″	2.89	246–318
24 × 16″	2.64	310–400
28 × 18″	5.62	477–618
32 × 20″	9.30	741–1,023
38 × 22″	14.43	1,111–1,587
42 × 27″	12.95	1,610–2,084
46 × 28″	26.92	2,218–2,691
54 × 33″	38.20	3,255–4,210

*Weight range depending on soil density
**Volume of planting ball = (ball diameter in feet)³ × ball depth in feet × 2/3

Table 3–9. Planting Container Volumes and Weights

Container Size (gal.)	Volume (cu. ft.)	Weight (lbs.)
1	.13	12–14
2	.27	24–29
5	.67	60–73
7	.94	85–103

Table 3–10. Plants per Linear Foot of Hedge (Estimate)

Plant Spacing	Plants per Linear Foot	Plants per 10 Linear Feet
10″ (25.40 cm)	1.20	12.0
12″ (30.48 cm)	1.00	10.0
15″ (38.10 cm)	.80	8.0
18″ (45.72 cm)	.67	6.7
24″ (60.96 cm)	.50	5.0
30″ (76.20 cm)	.40	4.0
3′ (0.91 m)	.33	3.3
4′ (1.22 m)	.25	2.5
5′ (1.53 m)	.20	2.0

Table 3–11. Minimum Grades for Surface Drainage

Use	Ratio Horizontal to Vertical	Slope
Patio	1″(2.54 cm) in 10′(3.06 m)	.8%
Open Lawn, Well-Drained	1″(2.54 cm) in 8′(2.44 m)	1%
Open Lawn, Heavy Soil	1″(2.54 cm) in 4′(1.22 m)	2%
Around Building Foundations and Areas Requiring Good Drainage	1″(2.54 cm) in 2′(0.61 m)	5%

Table 3–12. Tree and Shrub Planting Requirements: Time Factors*

a. Staking out plants = 25/hr.
b. Digging planting pit, average soil = 20 cu. ft./hr.
c. Placing tree in planting pit

Weight of Plant (lbs.)	No. per Hour
50–100	12.5
100–200	12.5
200–300	6.25
300–400	4.37
400–500	3.12

d. Backfilling planting pit, average soil = 28.75 cu. ft./hr.
e. Pruning tree of dead or injured wood

Size (Caliper)	No. per Hour
1″	11.87
2″	6.25
Over 2″	5.25

f. Prune shrubs of dead or injured wood

Size (Height)	No. per Hour
To 3′	24.37
3′–6′	11.87
Over 6′	6.25

g. Wrapping tree with burlap

Size (Caliper)	No. per Hour
1″–2″	18.75
2″–4″	6.25
4″–6″	4.37

h. Guying tree (three wooden stakes)

Size (Caliper)	No. per Hour
Up to 3″	3.12
3″–6″	1.75
6″ and up	1.12

i. Planting ground cover plants

Size of Pot	No. per Hour
2¼″	75
3″	50
4″	35

j. Planting container plants

Size	No. per Hour
1 qt.	12.5
1 gal.	7.5
2 gal.	5.6
5 gal.	3.1

k. Lawn sodding

Function	No. per Hour
Hand-place Sod	438.75 sq. ft.
Roll rod w/Hand Roller	3,999.28 sq. ft.

l. Soil tilling

Table 3–12. Continued

Depth of Till	Area per Hour
4″ (by Hand)	67.5 sq. ft.
6″ (by Hand)	50.63 sq. ft.
4″ (w/Rototiller)	798.75 sq. ft.
6″ (w/Rototiller)	601.87 sq. ft.

m. Lawn seeding

Function	Area per Hour
Hand Broadcast	0.201 acres
Push Spreader	0.459 acres
800 gal. Hydroseeder	1.799 acres
1,500 gal. Hydroseeder	4.65 acres

n. Lawn mowing

Equipment	Minutes per 1,000 sq. ft.
25″ Power Motor	3
58″ Power Motor	1
7′ Power Motor	½

o. Edge and trim

Operation	Minutes per 100 Linear Ft.
Hand Trim Along Walks	25–30
Power Trimmer	8–10
Around Shrubs	
By Hand	45–60
Power Trimmer	30–40

*All figures regarding time are averaged for semiskilled laborers working an 8-hour day in medium soils.

E. LANDSCAPE ILLUMINATION

1. Trunk Lights (Down): Use on the most vertical trunk of a multitrunk specimen. This fixture is placed on the trunk of the tree to produce shadow patterns directly under the tree.
2. Moonlight Units
   a. Incandescent (150 W): Use in small gardens and on small trees. Accents the body of a tree.
   b. Mercury Vapor (175 W): Less expensive to operate than incandescent unit. Use for broad washes of light for very large landscape jobs.
   c. Accent Trunk Light: Best unit for color and color patterns. Same basics as 1, but poor color pattern obtained when mercury vapor units are used.
3. Accent Light: Accent with color and/or with raw light (raw light is more popular). Use for sculpture, rocks, water, or small area of special interest. Size of subject will determine size of light unit. Distance from subject determines strength of accent required.
   a. Statue Spot—smallest unit (can be used with any color).

b. Par Units—use for broad areas. Cheap light source. Many sizes available.

See figure 3–21.

F. PLANT MATERIAL FOR THE VISUALLY IMPAIRED

Ornamental plant materials are used to decorate and enhance the exterior environments. From time to time, however, these vegetative elements function as environmental stimulators, especially for the visually impaired facility user. The list of plant materials in table 3–13 is presented to provide the site designer with a palette of planting design components that will extend the environmental perception of both the partially sighted and the totally blind.

Table 3-13. Plant Material for the Visually Impaired

Abbreviations: **1** Visual Characteristics (for the partially sighted); **2** Tactual Characteristics; **3** Odoriferous Characteristics; *SC* Summer Color; *T* Texture; *FC* Fall Color; *BC* Bloom Color; *BT* Bark Texture; *LT* Leaf Texture; *FT* Fruit Texture; *BS* Bloom Scent; *PS* Plant Scent; *H* Height; *F* Form

Scientific/Common Names	Characteristics
ROCKY MOUNTAINS (Wyoming, Idaho, Vermont, Colorado)	
GROUND COVERS	
Achillea tomentosa (Wolly Yarrow)	**1** (H) 8–10′, (SC) grayish, (T) fine, (BC) Yellow **2** (LT) medium-fuzzy **3** no distinguishing characteristics
Alyssum saxatile (Golden Tuft)	**1** (H) 8–10′, (SC) green, (T) medium, (BC) yellow **2** no distinguishing characteristics **3** no distinguishing characteristics
Arabis alpina (Alpine Rockcress)	**1** (H) 6″, (SC) green, (BC) white **2** no distinguishing characteristics **3** (BS) very fragrant
Convallaria majalis (Lily of the Valley)	**1** (H) 5–6″, (SC) green, (T) medium, (BC) white **2** (LT) medium **3** no distinguishing characteristics
Dianthus deltoides (Maiden Pink)	**1** (H) 5–6″, (F) mat, (SC) green, (T) fine, (BC) red to white **2** no distinguishing characteristics **3** no distinguishing characteristics
Euphorbia sp. (Spurge)	**1** (H) 1′, (BC) yellow **2** (BT) Semirough, hairy, (LT) slick and thick, (FT) smooth **3** (BS) fragrant
Phlox subulata (Moss Phlox)	**1** (H) 6–8″, (SC) green, (T) medium, (BC) pink to white **2** (LT) medium, (FT) mealy smooth berry **3** no distinguishing characteristics

Table 3-13. Continued

Scientific/Common Names	Characteristics
Sedum sp. (Stonecrop)	**1** (H) 1–15″, (F) spreading, (SC) greens, (T) fine, (FC) varies **2** (BT) smooth, (LT) smooth **3** no distinguishing characteristics
Vinca minor (Periwinkle)	**1** (H) 6–8″, (F) training, (SC) dark green, (T) medium **2** (BT) smooth, (LT) rolled and smooth **3** no distinguishing characteristics
SHRUBS	
Caragana microphylla (Peashrub)	**1** (H) 5′, (F) V-shaped, (SC) yellow-green, (T) fine, (BC) yellow **2** (BT) slightly winged on young, spines on older, (FT) Pea pod **3** no distinguishing characteristics
Cornus canadensis (Creeping Dogwood)	**1** (H) 6–12′, (F) weeping, (SC) evergreen, (BC) white **2** (BT) forms woody base, (LT) whorled and slightly pubescent **3** no distinguishable characteristics
Cornus stolonifera (Dogwood)	**1** (H) 5′, (F) upright-spreading, (SC) yellow **2** (LT) roughish **3** no distinguishing characteristics
Forsythia suspensa (Weeping Forsythia)	**1** (H) 3–6′, (F) weeping, (SC) light green, (T) fine, (FC) yellowish **2** (BT) square-round, rough, (LT) slick **3** no distinguishing characteristics
Lonicera tatarica (Tatarian Honeysuckle)	**1** (H) 10′, (F) rounded, (SC) bluish green, (T) medium **2** (BT) medium, shaggy, (LT) medium **3** (BS) fragrant
Rhododendron lapponicum (Lapland Rhododendron)	**1** (H) 4′, (F) upright, (SC) green, (T) coarse **2** (LT) thick and leathery **3** no distinguishing characteristics
Spiraea vanhouttei (Vanhoutte Spirea)	**1** (H) 6–10′, (F) arching, round, (SC) green, (T) medium-fine **2** (BT) varies, (LT) flattened, needlelike **3** no distinguishing characteristics
Taxum cuspidata (Japanese Yew)	**1** (H) 4–8′, (SC) dark green, (T) fine **2** (LT) spiny **3** no distinguishing characteristics
Trees	
Betula papyrifera (Paper Birch)	**1** (H) 60′, (F) upright, (SC) light green, (T) fine, (FC) yellow **2** (BT) smooth, peels into paper, (LT) double-serrated **3** no distinguishing characteristics
Elaeagnus angustifolia (Oleaster)	**1** (H) 25′, (F) upright, (SC) silver-gray, (T) fine **2** (BT) shaggy, (LT) roughish-coarse **3** (BS) fragrant
Malus baccata (Siberian Crab)	**1** (H) 15–25′, (F) roundish, (SC) green, (T) medium, (FL) reddish

Table 3–13. Continued

Scientific/Common Names	Characteristics
	2 (*BT*) medium-rough, (*LT*) roughish, (*FT*) round
	3 (*BS*) somewhat fragrant
Populus tremuloides (American Aspen)	1 (*H*) 50', (*F*) upright, (*SC*) green, (*T*) medium
	2 (*BT*) peels, smooth, (*LT*) roughish
	3 no distinguishing characteristics

SOUTH (South Carolina, Alabama, Mississippi, Louisiana, Georgia, East Texas, North Florida)

GROUND COVERS

Scientific/Common Names	Characteristics
Aspidistra elatior (Castiron Plant)	1 (*H*) 6–12", (*F*) clumplike, (*SC*) medium green, (*T*) coarse
	2 (*LT*) smooth rolled edges
	3 no distinguishing characteristics
Hedera helix (English Ivy)	1 (*H*) 20', (*F*) climber, (*SC*) dark green, (*T*) medium
	2 (*BT*) semirough, hairy, (*LT*) slick, thick, (*FT*) smooth and egg shaped
	3 no distinguishing characteristics
Hypericum calycinum (St. Johnswort)	1 (*H*) 1', (*F*) dense mass, (*SC*) bluish green, (*T*) medium to fine, (*FC*) yellowish, (*BC*) yellow
	2 (*BT*) slick with bumpy rings, (*LT*) slick and waxy smooth edges, (*FT*) flowers are feathery
	3 no distinguishable characteristics
Liriope muscari (Monkey Grass)	1 (*H*) 12", (*F*) dense clumps
	2 (*LT*) slick, pointed
	3 no distinguishing characteristics

SHRUBS

Scientific/Common Names	Characteristics
Aucuba japonica (Japanese Aucuba)	1 (*H*) 3–6', (*F*) upright, (*T*) coarse
	2 (*BT*) twigs very slick, flat edged
	3 no distinguishing characteristics
Berberis julianae (Barberry)	1 (*H*) 4–6', (*SC*) green, (*T*) medium-fine, (*BC*) yellow
	2 (*BT*) slightly bumpy thorns, (*LT*) sharp-pointed, slick and smooth, (*FT*) slightly thorny
	3 (*BS*) fragrant
Buddleia davidii (Butterfly Bush)	1 (*H*) 3–8', (*F*) open, (*SC*) bright green, (*T*) medium coarse, (*FC*) green, (*BC*) white to red
	2 (*BT*) rough, (*LT*) fuzzy
	3 (*BS*) odor like cut grass
Buxus sempervirens (Boxwood)	1 (*H*) 2–3', (*F*) compact, upright, (*SC*) dark green, (*T*) fine, dense
	2 (*BT*) rough, (*LT*) smooth
	3 no distinguishing characteristics
Euonymus alatus (Winged Euonymus)	1 (*H*) 7', (*SC*) green (*T*) medium-coarse, (*FC*) rose red, (*BC*) light yellow
	2 (*BT*) corky and winged, (*LT*) waxy/smooth above, waxy/slick below, (*FT*) smooth and waxy

Table 3–13. Continued

Scientific/Common Names	Characteristics
	3 no distinguishing characteristics
Exochorda racemosa (Pearlbush)	1 (*H*) 6–8', (*F*) spreading, (*SC*) bluish-green, (*T*) medium to fine, (*FC*) bluish green, (*BC*) white
	2 (*BT*) smooth and waxy, (*LT*) waxy/smooth above, fuzzy below, (*FT*) waxy and hard
	3 no distinguishing characteristics
Forsythia sp. (Forsythia)	1 (*H*) 4–8', (*F*) erect to weeping, (*SC*) yellow green to green, (*T*) medium to fine, (*FC*) yellow green, (*BC*) yellow
	2 (*BT*) square-round, rough, (*LT*), slick
	3 no distinguishing characteristics
Hydrangea arborescens grandiflora (Hills-of-Snow)	1 (*H*) 4', (*F*) round to erect oval, (*SC*) bright green, (*T*) coarse, (*FC*) yellow-tan, (*BC*) white
	2 (*IBT*) papery, (*LT*) hairy, but slick
	3 (*BS*) sweet
Ilex cornuta (Chinese Holly)	1 (*H*) 6–8', (*F*) upright, round, (*SC*) deep, dark green, (*T*) medium coarse, (*BC*) white
	2 (*BT*) waxy with spines, (*LT*) smooth and pointed, (*FT*) round, waxy
	3 fruit has unpleasant odor
Jasminum floridum (Florida Jasmine)	1 (*H*) 3–10', (*F*) weeping-round, (*SC*) green, (*T*) medium (*BC*) yellow
	2 (*BT*) smooth-waxy and bumpy, (*LT*) smooth-waxy, flowers smooth
	3 no distinguishing characteristics
Pinus mugo (Mugo Pine)	1 (*H*) 3–5', (*F*) round, (*SC*) bright green, (*T*) medium
	2 (*BT*) bumpy and roughish, (*LT*) slick and prickly
	3 no distinguishing characteristics
Rhododendron sp. (Azalea)	1 (*H*) 4–8', (*F*) open, (*SC*) dark green, (*T*) medium coarse, (*BC*) varies
	2 (*BT*) smooth, (*LT*) rough and waxy
	3 no distinguishing characteristics
Weigela florida (Weigela)	1 (*H*) 4–10', (*F*) arching, (*SC*) green, (*T*) medium to coarse, (*BC*) red, pink, white
	2 (*BT*) slightly waxy, (*LT*) very slick, (*FT*) hard, bottle shaped
	3 (*BS*) fragrant

TREES

Scientific/Common Names	Characteristics
Acer rubrum (Red Maple)	1 (*H*) 70–75', (*F*) ovalish, (*SC*) green, (*T*) medium, (*FC*) red, (*BC*) red
	2 (*BT*) knotted, (*LT*) slick above, fuzzy below, (*FT*) winged
	3 no distinguishing characteristics
Albizia julibrissin (Mimosa)	1 (*H*) 20–40', (*F*) flat-topped, (*SC*) light green, (*T*) fine, (*BC*) pink to white
	2 (*BT*) knotted, (*LT*) flat on one side, (*FT*) long, papery
	3 no distinguishing characteristics

Table 3–13. Continued

Scientific/Common Names	Characteristics
Betula nigra (River Birch)	**1** (H) 40–60', (F) irregular, (SC) deep, shiny green, (T) fine, (FC) yellow **2** (BT) papery, (LT) smooth above, fuzzy below, (FT) long, fuzzy, and waxy **3** no distinguishing characteristics
Cercis canadensis (Eastern Redbud)	**1** (H) 15–20', (F) spreading, flat-top, (SC) green, (T) medium coarse, (FC) yellow, (BC) purple to white **2** (BT) roughish, (LT) waxy above, smooth below, (FT) pods, waxy and flexible **3** no distinguishing characteristics
Cornus florida (Flowering Dogwood)	**1** (H) 15–25', (F) spreading, horizontal, (SC) dull green, (T) medium, (FC) rose, (BC) white to pink **2** (BT) flakes and soft, (LT) smooth above, veined below, (FT) egg-shaped **3** no distinguishing characteristics
Magnolia grandiflora (Southern Magnolia)	**1** (H) 60–80', (F) roundish, (SC) dark green, (T) coarse, (BC) white **2** (BT) smooth with tiny bumps, (LT) leathery above, fuzzy below **3** (BS) very strong fragrance
Pinus strobus (White Pine)	**1** (H) 50–70', (F) pyramidal, (SC) green, (T) fine **2** (BT) sticky, smooth, (LT) needles, wiry, (FT) cone, rough **3** no distinguishing characteristics
VINES *Campsis radicans* (Trumpet Creeper)	**1** (H) 40', (F) climbing, (SC) bright green, (T) medium-smooth **2** (BT) smooth, slick, bumpy, (LT) smooth above, rough below **3** no distinguishing characteristics
Celastrus scandens (American Bittersweet)	**1** (H) 30', (F) twining, (SC) dark green, (T) medium-coarse, (FC) yellowish, (BC) yellow **2** (BT) shaggy, (LT) smooth above, serrated, (FT) coarse outside, smooth waxy inside
Gelsemium sempervirens (Carolina Jesmine)	**1** (H) 15', (F) twines, (SC) green, (T) medium, (FC) bronze, (BC) yellow **2** (BT) fuzzy, (LT) smooth-slick, (Ft) flowers waxy **3** (BS) fragrant
Lonicera japonica (Common Honeysuckle)	**1** (H) 15–20', (F) twining, (SC) deep green, (T) medium coarse, (FC) blue green, (BC) white, pink, yellow **2** (BT) twigs slick, branches papery, (LT) slick above, veined below **3** (BS) fragrant
Polygonum aubertii (Silver Lace Vine)	**1** (H) 15–20', (F) twining, (SC) light green, (T) medium, (FC) bright green, (BC) greenish white **2** (BT) smooth, (LT) smooth **3** no distinguishing characteristics

Table 3–13. Continued

Scientific/Common Names	Characteristics
Vitis labrusca (Fox Grape)	**1** (H) 15–20', (F) tendrils, (SC) green, (T) coarse, (FC) yellowish **2** (BT) slick with flat areas, (LT) smooth and slick, (FT) round, slick **3** no distinguishing characteristics

LOW PLAINS (Kansas, Missouri, Oklahoma)

GROUND COVERS *Campsis radicans* (Trumpet Creeper)	**1** (H) varies, (F) twining, (SC) bright green, (T) medium, (FC) deep green, (BC) orange **2** (BT) smooth, slick, bumpy, (LT) smooth above, rough below **3** no distinguishing characteristics
Clematis paniculata (Clematis)	**1** (H) varies, (F) climbs, (SC) bright green, (T) medium, (BC) white **2** no distinguishing characteristics **3** (BS) fragrant
Euonymus fortunei vegetus (Wintercreeper)	**1** (H) varies, (F) climbs, (SC) bright to dark green, (T) medium, (BC) greenish **2** (BT) warty, (LT) leathery, coarsely toothed **3** no distinguishing characteristics
Hedera helix (English Ivy)	**1** (H) varies, (F) climbing, trailing, (SC) dark green, (T) medium **2** (BT) semirough, hairy (LT) slick and thick, (FT) smooth and egg shaped **3** (BS) fragrant
Lonicera sempervirens (Trumpet Honeysuckle)	**1** (H) varies, (F), twining, (SC) bluish green, (T) medium-coarse, (FC) blue-green, (BC) scarlet **2** (BT) medium, (LT) medium **3** (BS) fragrant
Vinca sp. (Periwinkle)	**1** (H) 6", (F) spreading, (SC) dark green, (T) fine, (BC) varies **2** (BT) prism shaped, (LT) rolled and smooth **3** no distinguishing characteristics
SHRUBS *Berberis sp.* (Barberry)	**1** (H) 3–6', (F) upright, (SC) green, (T) fine, (FC) red, (BC) yellow **2** (BT) thorny, (FT) round-hard **3** fragrant
Kolkwitzia amabillis (Beauty Bush)	**1** (H) 6–8', (F) round, (SC) gray-green, (T) medium, (FC) gray-green, (BC) pink (FC) deep green, (BC) orange **2** (BT) smooth-slick, bumpy, (LT) smooth above, rough below **3** no distinguishing characteristics
Prunus glandulosa (Cherry Bush Cherry)	**1** (H) 3–4', (F) round, (SC) green, (T) medium, (FC) green, (BC) pink to white **2** (BT) medium, (LT) semismooth **3** fragrant
TREES *Celtis occidentalis* (Hackberry)	**1** (H) 50–70', (F) open, (SC) light green, (T) medium, (FC) light-yellow

Table 3–13. Continued

Scientific/Common Names	Characteristics
	2 (BT) corky ridges, (LT) smooth and veined below **3** no distinguishing characteristics
Cercis canadensis (Eastern Redbud)	**1** (H) 10–20', (F) horizontal, (SC) green, (T) medium-coarse, (FC) yellow-brown, (BC) pink **2** (BT) roughish, (LT) waxy above, veined below, (FT) egg shaped **3** no distinguishing characteristics
Elaeagnus angustifolia (Oleaster)	**1** (H) 15–25', (F) irregular, (SC) silver-green, (T) fine, (FC) gray-green **2** (BT) shaggy, (LT) roughish coarse **3** (BS) fragrant
Malus sp. (Crab Apple)	**1** (H) 15–25', (F) round, spreading, (T) medium, (FC) green, (BC) pink **2** (BT) varies, (LT) varies, (FT) round **3** (BS) fragrant
Pinus sp. (Pines)	**1** (H) varies, (F) pyramidal, (SC) varies, (T) varies **2** (BT) varies, (LT) varies, pointed, (FT) varies, cones
Populus deltoides (Cottonwood)	**1** (H) 80', (F) spreads, (SC) yellow-green, (T) coarse, (FC) yellow **2** (BT) buds sticky, (LT) toothed, (FT) cottony filament **3** no distinguishing characteristics
VINES Caragana arborescens (Siberian Peashrub)	**1** (H) 65–10', (F) upright, round, (SC) light green, (T) medium-fine, (FC) yellow-green, (BC) yellow **2** (BT) slightly winged on young, spiny, (FT) pea-pod **3** no distinguishing characteristics
Celastrus scandens (American Bittersweet)	**1** (H) 30', (F) twining, (SC) dark green, (T) medium-coarse, (FC) yellowish, (BC) yellow **2** (BT) shaggy, (LT) smooth above, serrated, (FT) coarse outside, smooth waxy inside **3** no distinguishing characteristics
Chaenomeles lagenaria (Flowering Quince)	**1** (H) 5–6', (F) upright, (SC) glossy, reddish-green, (T) medium-fine, (FC) dull green **2** (BT) sometimes warty, (LT) serrated, (FT) semismooth **3** (BS) fragrant
Cornus stolonifera (Redosier Dogwood)	**1** (H) 6–8', (F) upright, (SC) bright green, (T) medium-coarse, (FC) reddish, (BC) white **2** (LT) concaved **3** (BS) fragrant
Cotoneaster acutifolia (Peking Cotoneaster)	**1** (H) 5–7', (SC) dark green, (T) medium-fine, (FC) dark green, (BC) pink **2** (LT) pubescent below, (FT) round berries **3** no distinguishing characteristics

Table 3–13. Continued

Scientific/Common Names	Characteristics
Euonymus alatus (Winged Euonymus)	**1** (H) 4–8', (F) roundish, (SC) green, (T) medium-coarse, (FC) red, (BC) yellow **2** (BT) corky and winged, (LT) smooth, leathery, (FT) round semismooth and waxy **3** no distinguishing characteristics
Forsythia suspensa (Forsythia)	**1** (H) 5–6', (F) weeping, (SC) yellow-green, (T) medium, (FC) yellow-green, (BC) yellow **2** (BT) semismooth, (LT) semismooth **3** (BC) fragrant
Gelsemium sempervirens (Carolina Jesmine)	**1** (H) 15', (F) twines, (SC) green, (T) medium, (FC) bronze, (BC) yellow **2** (BT) fuzzy, (LT) smooth, slick, (FT) flowers waxy **3** (BS) fragrant
Hydrangea paniculata (Panicle Hydrangea)	**1** (H) 6–8', (F) upright, (SC) bright green, (T) coarse, (FC) yellow, (BC) white to blue **2** (Bt) slightly pubescent when young, (LT) pointed and slightly pubescent **3** no distinguishing characteristics
Juniperus sp. (Juniper)	**1** (H) varies, (F) varies, (SC) varies, (T) medium-fine **2** (BT) shaggy, (LT) sticky and prickly, (FT) rounded **3** no distinguishing characteristics
Ligustrum amurense (Amur Privet)	**1** (H) 8–10', (F) upright, spreading, (SC) deep green, (T) fine, (FC) deep green, (BC) white **2** (BT) slightly pubescent, (LT) rounded **3** no distinguishing characteristics
Lonicera japonica (Common Honeysuckle)	**1** (H) 15–20', (F) twining, (SC) deep green, (T) medium coarse, (FC) blue green, (BC) white, pink, yellow **2** (BT) twigs slick, branches papery, (LT) slick above, veined below **3** (BS) fragrant
Lonicera morrowii (Morrow Honeysuckle)	**1** (H) 5–6', (F) spreading, (SC) bluish green, (T) medium, (FC) blue-green, (BC) white **2** (BT) smooth, (LT) pubescent on veins **3** (BS) fragrant
Mahonia aquifolium (Oregon Grape)	**1** (H) 3–5', (F) upright, irregular, (SC) bluish green, (T) medium, (FC) bronze, (BC) yellow **2** (BT) medium-coarse, (LT) spiny, (FT) rounded **3** no distinguishing characteristics
Philadelphus coronarius (Mock Orange)	**1** (H) 8–10', (F) upright, (SC) deep green, (T) medium, (FC) yellow-green, (BC) white **2** (BT) peels, (LT) pubescent on veins below **3** (BS) fragrant

Table 3–13. Continued

Scientific/Common Names	Characteristics
Pinus mugo (Mugho Pine)	1 (*H*) 3–10', (*F*) round, (*SC*) bright green, (*T*) medium 2 (*BT*) sometimes scaly, (*LT*) long, twisted, sharply pointed 3 no distinguishing characteristics
Polygonum aubertti (Silver Lace Vine)	1 (*H*) 15–20', (*F*) twining, (*SC*) light green, (*T*) medium, (*FC*) bright green, (*BC*) greenish white 2 (*BT*) smooth, (*LT*) smooth 3 no distinguishing characteristics
Pyracantha coccinea (Firethorn)	1 (*H*) 5–7', (*F*) horizontal, (*SC*) dark green, (*T*) fine, (*BC*) white 2 (*BT*) roughish, (*LT*) smooth, (*FT*) round 3 no distinguishing characteristics
Rhus aromatica (Fragrant Sumac)	1 (*H*) 3–6', (*F*) upright, (*SC*) dull red, (*T*) medium, (*FC*) scarlet, (*BC*) yellow 2 (*BT*) pubescent when young, (*FT*) Hairy 3 (*PS*) ill-scented
Symphoricarpos orbiculatus (Coral Berry)	1 (*H*) 2–3', (*SC*) grayish-green, (*T*) fine, (*FC*) grayish, (*BC*) white 2 (*LT*) pubescent below, (*FT*) round berries 3 no distinguishing characteristics
Tamarix odessana (Tamarisk)	1 (*H*) 6–12', (*F*) upright, (*SC*) bright green, (*T*) very fine, (*FC*) bright green, (*BC*) pink 2 (*BT*) slick but ringed, (*LT*) soft 3 no distinguishing characteristics

EASTERN MOUNTAIN (West Virginia, Tennessee, North Carolina, Kentucky, Arkansas, Southern Missouri)

GROUND COVERS

Arctostaphylos uvauris (Red Bearberry)	1 (*H*) 6–10', (*F*) trailing, (*SC*) dark green, (*T*) medium to coarse, (*BC*) white to pink 2 (*LT*) medium, (*FT*) mealy smooth berry 3 no distinguishing characteristics
Hedera helix (English Ivy)	1 (*H*) 6–8', (*F*) spreading, (*SC*) dark green, (*T*) medium to coarse 2 (*BT*) semirough hairy, (*LT*) slick and thick, (*FT*) smooth and egg shaped 3 (*BS*) fragrant
Liriope spicata (Creeping Lilyturf)	1 (*H*) 3", (*F*) mat, (*SC*) green, (*BC*) purple 2 (*LT*) grasslike 3 no distinguishing characteristics
Lonicera japonica (Common Honeysuckle)	1 (*H*) 15–20', (*F*) climbing, (*SC*) deep green, (*T*) medium-coarse, (*FC*) blue-green 2 (*BT*) twigs slick, branches papery, (*LT*) slick above, veined below 3 (*BS*) fragrant
Mahonia repens (Dwarf Holly Grape	1 (*H*) 10", (*F*) mat spreading, (*SC*) dull blue-green, (*BC*) yellow 2 (*LT*) toothed and bristled 3 no distinguishing characteristics (evergreen)

Table 3–13. Continued

Scientific/Common Names	Characteristics
Sedum acre (Goldmoss Stonecrop)	1 (*H*) 4", (*F*) mat forming, (*SC*) green, (*T*) fine, (*BC*) yellow 2 (*LT*) triangular, (*FT*) wide, semirough 3 no distinguishing characteristics
Thymus serpyllum (Creeping Thyme)	1 (*H*) 3", (*F*) mat, (*SC*) green, (*BC*) purple 2 no distinguishing characteristics 3 (*PS*) fragrant when crushed
Vaccinium vitis-idaea (Cowberry)	1 (*H*) 12", (*F*) mat forming, (*SC*) glossy green, (*FC*) reddish, (*BC*) pink 2 (*LT*) bristle topped 3 no distinguishing characteristics

SHRUBS

Abelia grandiflora (Glossy Abelia)	1 (*H*) 4–7', (*F*) round, (*SC*) rich green, (*BC*) pinkish 2 (*BT*) young branches downy, (*LT*) hairy 3 (*BS*) fragrant
Aucuba japonica (Aucuba)	1 (*H*) 3–6', (*F*) upright, (*SC*) green, (*T*) coarse 2 (*BT*) twigs very slick, flat edged, (*LT*) thick and smooth above, waxy below, (*FT*) slick 3 no distinguishing characteristics
Berberis julianae (Winterberry)	1 (*H*) 4–6', (*F*) compact, (*SC*) green, (*T*) medium-fine, (*BC*) yellow 2 (*BT*) thorny, (*LT*) sharp pointed, slick and smooth, (*FT*) slightly thorny 3 (*BS*) fragrant
Buxus sempervirens (Boxwood)	1 (*H*) 3–12', (*F*) rounded, (*SC*) dark green, (*T*) fine 2 (*BT*) rough, (*LT*) smooth 3 no distinguishing characteristics
Chaenomeles japonica (Flowering Quince)	1 (*H*) 2–3', (*F*) spreading, (*SC*) lustrous green, (*BC*) white to red 2 (*BT*) thorny to warty, (*LT*) serrated, (*FT*) semismooth 3 no distinguishing characteristics
Cotoneaster divaricata (Spreading Cotoneaster)	1 (*H*) 3–6', (*F*) arching, (*T*) medium-fine, (*BC*) pink 2 no distinguishing characteristics 3 no distinguishing characteristics
Elaeagnus pungens (Thorny Elaeagnus)	1 (*H*) 6–12', (*F*) spreading, (*SC*) dark green, (*T*) medium-coarse, (*BC*) silvery 2 (*BT*) spiny, (*LT*) scaly, (*FT*) scaly 3 (*BS*) fragrant
Euonymus alatus (Winged Euonumus)	1 (*H*) 6–10', (*F*) horizontal, roundish, (*SC*) green, (*T*) medium-coarse 2 (*BT*) corky and winged, (*LT*) waxy and smooth-slick, (*FT*) smooth-waxy 3 no distinguishing characteristics
Ilex cornuta (Chinese Holly)	1 (*H*) 6–20', (*F*) upright-round, (*SC*) dark green, (*T*) medium-coarse 2 (*BT*) waxy with spines, (*LT*) spiny but smooth, (*FT*) round waxy 3 (*PS*) unpleasant (evergreen)

Table 3–13. Continued

Scientific/Common Names	Characteristics
Jasminum floridum (Snowy Jasmine)	1 (*H*) 3–6′, (*F*) mounded-weeping, (*SC*) glossy green, (*BC*) yellow 2 (*BT*) smooth-slick, waxy-bumpy, (*LT*) smooth-slick 3 no distinguishing characteristics
Kolkwitzia amabilis (Beauty Bush)	1 (*H*) 4–10′, (*F*) upright, (*SC*) light green to bluish gray, (*T*) medium to fine 2 (*LT*) slightly toothed, hairy, (*FT*) covered with bristles 3 no distinguishing characteristics
Ligustrum japonicum (Japanese Privet)	1 (*H*) 5–15′, (*F*) arching, (*SC*) dark green, (*T*) medium, (*BC*) white 2 (*BT*) slightly pubescent, (*LT*) rounded 3 no distinguishing characteristics
Lonicera maackii (Amur Honeysuckle)	1 (*H*) 8–15′, (*F*) arching, (*SC*) dark green, (*T*) medium, (*BC*) white 2 (*BT*) pubescent on veins 3 (*BS*) fragrant
Mahonia bealei (Leatherleaf Mahonia)	1 (*H*) 3–10′, (*F*) oval roundish, (*SC*) bluish green, (*T*) coarse, (*BC*) yellow 2 (*LT*) spiny 3 no distinguishing characteristics
Philadelphus coronarius (Mock Orange)	1 (*H*) 5–9′, (*F*) upright, (*SC*) medium green, (*T*) medium-coarse, (*FC*) yellowish, (*BC*) white 2 (*BT*) shaggy-medium, (*LT*) medium-rough 3 (*BS*) fragrant
Pinus mugo (Mugho Pine)	1 (*H*) 2–8′, (*F*) rounded, (*SC*) bright green, (*T*) medium 2 (*BT*) bumpy and rough, (*LT*) slick and prickly 3 no distinguishing characteristics
Pyracantha coccinea (Firethorn)	1 (*H*) 7–15′, (*F*) semiupright, spreading, (*SC*) green, (*T*) fine 2 (*BT*) sometimes roughish, (*LT*) smooth, (*FT*) rough 3 no distinguishing characteristics
Rhododendron sp. (Azalea)	1 (*H*) 2–10′, (*F*) upright-broad, (*SC*) green, (*T*) medium-coarse, (*BC*) varies 2 (*LT*) medium 3 no distinguishing characteristics
Spiraea thunbergii (Spirea)	1 (*H*) 3–6′, (*F*) arching, (*T*) fine, (*BC*) white 2 (*BS*) fragrant 3 no distinguishing characteristics
Viburnum carlesii (Fragrant Viburnum)	1 (*H*) 4–6′, (*SC*) dull green, (*T*) medium to coarse, (*FC*) reddish, (*BC*) pink to white 2 (*LT*) irregularly toothed 3 (*BS*) fragrant
Viburnum rhytidophyllum (Leatherleaf Viburnum)	1 (*H*) 8–20′, (*F*) upright, (*SC*) green, (*T*) coarse, (*BC*) white 2 (*LT*) wrinkled 3 no distinguishing characteristics

Table 3–13. Continued

Scientific/Common Names	Characteristics
TREES	
Acer rubrum (Red Maple)	1 (*H*) 70–75′, (*F*) ovalish, (*SC*) green, (*T*) medium, (*FC*) red 2 (*BT*) very smooth and slick, (*LT*) slick above, fuzzy below, (*FT*) winged 3 no distinguishing characteristics
Betula nigra (River Birch)	1 (*H*) 40–60′, (*F*) oval to upright, (*SC*) shiny green, (*T*) fine, (*FC*) yellow 2 (*BT*) papery, (*LT*) smooth above, fuzzy below, (*FT*) long, fuzzy, but waxy 3 no distinguishing characteristics
Cercis canadensis (Redbud)	1 (*H*) 15–20′, (*F*) spreading, flat-topped, (*SC*) green, (*T*) medium-coarse, (*FC*) yellow, (*BC*) purple to white 2 (*BT*) roughish, (*LT*) waxy above, smooth below, (*FT*) egg shaped 3 no distinguishing characteristics
Cornus florida (Flowering Dogwood)	1 (*H*) 15–20′, (*F*) spreading, horizontal, (*SC*) dull green, (*T*) medium-coarse, (*FC*) rose, (*BC*) white to pink 2 (*BT*) loose, rough, (*LT*) smooth 3 (*BS*) fragrant
Liriodendron tulipifera (Tulip Tree)	1 (*H*) 50–70′, (*F*) oval, (*SC*) light to yellowish green, (*T*) coarse, (*FC*) yellow, (*BC*) yellow to orange 2 (*BT*) smoothish, (*LT*) flexible, smooth edged, (*FT*) hard, waxy 3 (*BS*) fragrant
Pinus strobus (White Pine)	1 (*H*) 50–70′, (*F*) pyramidal, (*SC*) green, (*T*) fine 2 (*BT*) sticky smooth, (*LT*) wiry needles 3 no distinguishing characteristics
Quercus alba (White Oak)	1 (*H*) 60–80′, (*F*) rounded, (*SC*) deep green, (*T*) medium-coarse, (*FC*) purplish, red 2 (*BT*) rough, flaky, (*LT*) lobed 3 no distinguishing characteristics

EAST (Maine, Vermont, New Hampshire, Connecticut, Rhode Island, Massachusetts)

GROUND COVERS

Arctostaphylos uva-uris (Bearberry)	1 (*H*) 6″, (*F*) spreading, (*SC*) dark green, (*T*) medium-coarse, (*BC*) white to pink 2 (*LT*) medium, (*FT*) nearly smooth berry 3 no distinguishing characteristics
Cornus canadensis (Creeping Dogwood)	1 (*H*) 6″, (*F*) creeping, forms a mat, (*SC*) green, (*BC*) white 2 (*BT*) forms wooly base, (*LT*) whorled and slightly pubescent 3 no distinguishing characteristics
Celastrus scandens (American Bittersweet)	1 (*H*) 30′, (*F*) twining, (*SC*) green 2 (*BT*) shaggy, (*FT*) coarse outside, smooth inside 3 no distinguishing characteristics

Table 3–13. Continued

Scientific/Common Names	Characteristics
Parthenocissus tri-cuspidata (Boston Ivy)	**1** (*H*) 45′, (*F*) climbing, (*SC*) dark green, (*T*) medium, (*FC*) red **2** (*LT*) semismooth, veined **3** no distinguishing characteristics
Xanthorhiza simpli-cissima (Yellow-root)	**1** (*H*) 24″, (*F*) mat forming, (*SC*) green, (*FC*) orange-yellow **2** (*LT*) sharply lobed and toothed **3** no distinguishing characteristics
SHRUBS *Caragana arbores-cens* (Siberian Peashrubs)	**1** (*H*) 10′, (*F*) upright, (*SC*) yellow green, (*T*) very fine, (*BC*) yellow **2** (*BT*) sometimes forms spines, (*FT*) pea-like pod **3** no distinguishing characteristics
Chaenomeles japon-ica (Flowering Quince)	**1** (*H*) 4–5′, (*F*) low spreading, (*SC*) green, (*BC*) orange **2** (*BT*) sometimes warty, (*LT*) serrated, (*FT*) semismooth **3** no distinguishing characteristics
Euonymus alatus (Burning Bush)	**1** (*H*) 2–4′, (*F*) horizontal branching, (*SC*) dark green, (*T*) medium, (*FC*) red **2** (*BT*) corky winged, (*LT*) smooth, leathery, (*FT*) round and semismooth and waxy **3** no distinguishing characteristics
Euonymus alatus compactus (Dwarf Winged Euony-mus)	**1** (*H*) 4′, (*F*) dense rounded, (*SC*) green, (*T*) medium, (*FC*) red, (*BC*) green **2** (*BT*) corky winged, (*LT*) sharply serrated **3** no distinguishing characteristics
Philadelphus lemo-inei (Lemoine Mock Orange)	**1** (*H*) 4–5′, (*F*) round, (*SC*) green, (*T*) fine, (*BC*) white **2** (*BT*) older branches peel in flakes **3** (*BS*) very fragrant
Rhododendron sp. (Rhododendron)	**1** (*H*) 12′, (*F*) upright, (*SC*) dark green, (*T*) medium-coarse, (*BC*) varies **2** (*LT*) medium-sticky, (*FT*) round **3** no distinguishing characteristics
Rhus typhina (Stag's-horn Su-mac)	**1** (*H*) 15′, (*F*) stiff-upright, (*T*) medium to coarse **2** (*BT*) branchlets densely hairy, (*LT*) buds hairy **3** no distinguishing characteristics
Syringa persica (Per-sian Lilac)	**1** (*H*) 8′, (*F*) bushy-arching, (*T*) medium-fine, (*BC*) Lilac **2** (*BT*) very slender, medium smooth **3** (*BS*) very fragrant
Taxus cuspidata (Japanese Yew)	**1** (*H*) 10′, (*F*) spreading-upright, (*SC*) dark green, (*T*) fine **2** (*LT*) leaves ending in an abrupt spur, (*FT*) fleshy fruit **3** no distinguishing characteristics
Viburnum opulus nanum (Dwarf Cranberry Bush)	**1** (*H*) 2′, (*F*) low dense, (*SC*) medium green, (*FC*) red, (*BC*) white **2** (*BT*) very smooth, (*LT*) slightly pubescent **3** no distinguishing characteristics

Table 3–13. Continued

Scientific/Common Names	Characteristics
Weigela florida (Weigela)	**1** (*H*) 6–8′, (*F*) upright-spreading, (*BC*) pink **2** (*BT*) branchlets have hairy strips **3** (*BS*) fragrant
TREES (Small) *Amelanchier laevis* (Allegheny Service-berry)	**1** (*H*) 25′, (*F*) upright-spreading, (*SC*) pur-plish, (*BC*) white **2** (*LT*) serrated, (*FT*) bloomy **3** no distinguishing characteristics
Betula papyrifera (Paper Birch)	**1** (*H*) 60′, (*F*) upright, (*SC*) light green, (*T*) fine, (*FC*) yellow **2** (*BT*) peels into papery layers, (*LT*) double serrated veins, pubescent, (*FT*) nutlets **3** no distinguishing characteristics
Cornus alternifolia (Pagoda Dogwood)	**1** (*H*) 15–20′, (*F*) horizontal-branching, (*T*) medium (*FC*) yellow **2** (*BT*) medium, (*LT*) appressed, pubescent below, (*FT*) globular **3** (*BS*) fragrant
Celtis occidentalis (Hackberry)	**1** (*H*) 40′, (*F*) upright, (*SC*) green, (*T*) me-dium coarse, (*FC*) yellow **2** (*BT*) corky ridge, (*LT*) smooth and veined below **3** no distinguishing characteristics
Crataegus sp. (Haw-thorne)	**1** (*H*) 15′, (*F*) upright, (*SC*) green, (*T*) me-dium, (*FC*) reddish, (*BC*) white **2** (*BT*) thorny **3** no distinguishing characteristics
Elaeagnus angusti-folia (Oleaster)	**1** (*H*) 25′, (*F*) upright, (*SC*) silvery-gray, (*T*) fine, (*BC*) silvery-yellow **2** (*BT*) shaggy, (*LT*) roundish coarse **3** (*BS*) fragrant
Malus sp. (Crab Ap-ple)	**1** (*H*) 15–25′, (*F*) roundish, (*SC*) green, (*T*) medium, (*FC*) varies, (*BC*) varies **2** (*BT*) varies, (*LT*) smooth, (*FT*) round, smooth **3** no distinguishing characteristics
Rhus galbra (Smooth Sumac)	**1** (*H*) 12′, (*F*) upright, (*SC*) medium green, (*T*) medium-coarse, (*FC*) red, (*BC*) green-ish **2** (*BT*) hairy, (*LT*) coarse and hairy **3** no distinguishing characteristics
Sambucus sp. (Elder)	**1** (*H*) 8′, (*F*) upright, (*SC*) green to yellow-ish, (*T*) coarse **2** (*BT*) serrated, (*LT*) drupes **3** no distinguishing characteristics
Syringa chinensis (Chinese Lilac)	**1** (*H*) 8′, (*F*) compact-upright, (*SC*) green, (*T*) medium, (*FC*) varies, (*BC*) lilac **2** (*BT*) medium, (*LT*) medium **3** (*BS*) *fragrant*
TREES (Large) *Abies balsamea* (Bal-sam Fir)	**1** (*H*) 60′, (*F*) pyramidal, (*SC*) green, (*T*) medium-fine **2** (*FT*) roughish but fragile cone **3** no distinguishing characteristics

Table 3–13. Continued

Scientific/Common Names	Characteristics
Acer ginnala (Amur Maple)	**1** (*H*) 15′, (*F*) upright, (*SC*) green, (*T*) coarse, (*FC*) reddish, (*BC*) yellow **2** (*BT*) medium, (*LT*) double serrated, (*FT*) winged **3** (*BS*) fragrant
Picea abies (Norway Spruce)	**1** (*H*) 70′, (*F*) pyramidal, (*SC*) dark green, (*T*) medium-fine **2** (*BT*) branches semismooth with pubescents, (*LT*) smooth, but sharp pointed, (*FT*) slightly jagged **3** no distinguishing characteristics
Aesculus glabra (Ohio Buckeye)	**1** (*H*) 30′, (*F*) round, (*SC*) green, (*T*) coarse, (*FC*) yellow, (*BC*) yellow-white **2** (*BT*) medium, (*LT*) finely toothed, (*FT*) prickly outside, smooth inside **3** no distinguishing characteristics
Populus deltoides (Cottonwood)	**1** (*H*) 80′, (*F*) spreading, (*SC*) green, (*T*) medium, (*FC*) yellow **2** (*BT*) rough sticky, (*LT*) toothed, (*FT*) cottony filament **3** no distinguishing characteristics

SOUTHWEST (New Mexico, Arizona, Nevada, West Texas)

GROUND COVERS AND SMALL SHRUBS

Ceratostigma plumbaginoides (Blue Leadwort)	**1** (*H*) 12″, (*F*) spreading, (*SC*) dark green, (*T*) fine, (*FC*) bronze red, (*BC*) blue **2** (*LT*) hairy margins **3** no distinguishing characteristics
Cotoneaster horizontalis (Rock Cotoneaster)	**1** (*H*) 2′, (*F*) spreading, (*SC*) green, (*T*) semifine, (*BC*) pink-white **2** (*BT*) pubescent branches, (*LT*) lightly hairy below, (*FT*) smooth ovoid **3** no distinguishing characteristics
Dichondra repens (Dichondra)	**1** (*H*) low, (*F*) grasslike, (*SC*) medium green, (*T*) fine, (*FC*) yellowish **2** no distinguishing characteristics **3** no distinguishing characteristics
Hedera helix (English Ivy)	**1** (*H*) 6–8′, (*F*) spreading, (*SC*) dark green, (*T*) medium-coarse **2** (*BT*) slightly shaggy, (*LT*) medium-smooth **3** no distinguishing characteristics
Juniperus sp. (Junipers)	**1** (*H*) 18–20′, (*F*) varies, (*T*) fine **2** (*LT*) sticky **3** no distinguishing characteristics
Liriope spicata (Creeping Lilyturf)	**1** (*H*) 10″, (*F*) spreading, grasslike, (*SC*) medium green, (*T*) medium-fine, (*FC*) tends to get off-color **2** (*LT*) fine, grasslike **3** no distinguishing characteristics
Vinca major (Periwinkle)	**1** (*H*) 12″, (*F*) spreading, (*SC*) medium green, (*T*) medium, (*BC*) blue (varies) **2** (*BT*) smooth, (*LT*) smooth **3** (*BC*) some fragrant

Table 3–13. Continued

Scientific/Common Names	Characteristics
SHRUBS	
Abelia grandiflora (Abelia)	**1** (*H*) 4–5′, (*F*) round, (*SC*) rich green, (*BC*) white-pink **2** (*BT*) young branches downy, (*LT*) hairy **3** (*BC*) fragrant
Berberis thunbergii (Japanese Barberry)	**1** (*H*) 4–6′, (*F*) roundish, (*SC*) green, (*T*) medium-fine, (*FC*) orange-red **2** (*BT*) thorny, (*LT*) smooth, veined, (*FT*) round, smooth **3** no distinguishing characteristics
Buddleia alternifolia (Butterfly Bush)	**1** (*H*) 4–6′, (*F*) upright-arching, (*SC*) gray-green, (*T*) fine (*BC*) lilac **2** (*BT*) scaly-pubescent, (*LT*) medium-smooth
Chaenomeles japonica (Japanese Quince)	**1** (*H*) 4–6′, (*F*) open-spreading, (*SC*) green, (*T*) medium-fine, (*FC*) green-bronze, (*BC*) orange-red **2** (*BT*) sometimes warty, (*LT*) serrated, (*FT*) semismooth **3** no distinguishing characteristics
Cornus alba (Siberian Dogwood)	**1** (*H*) 4–6′, (*F*) upright-spreading, (*FC*) red twigs and reddish leaf, (*BC*) yellow-white **2** (*LT*) roughish-pubescent **3** no distinguishing characteristics
Cortaderia selloana (Pampas Grass)	**1** (*H*) 3–6′, (*F*) grasslike, (*SC*) green to brown, (*T*) very fine, (*FC*) brown, (*BC*) cream to pink **2** (*LT*) rough and sharp **3** no distinguishing characteristics
Elaeagnus pungens (Fruitland Elaeagnus)	**1** (*H*) 6′, (*SC*) silver gray, (*T*) medium, (*BC*) white **2** (*BT*) spiny and scaly, (*LT*) leathery, (*FT*) covered with small scales **3** (*BS*) very fragrant
Ilex vomitoria "nana" (Dwarf Yaupon)	**1** (*H*) 2′, (*F*) round spreading, (*SC*) green, (*T*) medium **2** (*BT*) semismooth, (*FT*) smooth-round **3** no distinguishing characteristics
Jasminum floridum (Showy Jasmine)	**1** (*H*) 2–3′, (*F*) unruly spread, (*SC*) green, (*T*) medium, (*BC*) yellow **2** (*BT*) angled branches, (*LT*) medium **3** (*BS*) fragrant (semi)
Ligustrum ovalifolium (California Privet)	**1** (*H*) 10–12′, (*F*) upright, (*SC*) medium green, (*T*) medium **2** (*BT*) pubescent, (*LT*) smooth **3** no distinguishing characteristics
Nandina domestica (Nandina)	**1** (*H*) 4–6′, (*F*) upright, (*SC*) medium green, (*T*) medium, (*FC*) red **2** (*BT*) roughish, cavelike, (*LT*) smooth **3** no distinguishing characteristics
Pyracantha coccinea (Firethorn)	**1** (*H*) 8–10′, (*F*) semiupright, (*SC*) green, (*T*) fine, (*BC*) white **2** (*BT*) sometimes roughish, (*LT*) smooth, (*FT*) sometimes crinkly **3** no distinguishing characteristics

Table 3–13. Continued

Scientific/Common Names	Characteristics
SMALL TREES	
Albizia julibrissin (Mimosa)	**1** (H) 15–20′, (F) low-flat, topped, (SC) light green, (T) fine, (BC) white to pink **2** (BT) medium, (LT) smooth, (FT) long seed pods **3** (BS) fragrant
Prunus persica (Flowering Peach)	**1** (H) 15–20′, (F) compact, well-rounded, (SC) green, (T) medium, (BC) white to pink to red **2** (BT) medium, (LT) semicoarse, serrated (FT) thick fleshed **3** (BS) fragrant
Sophora japonica (Japanese Pagoda Tree)	**1** (H) 20′, (F) rounded, (SC) dark green, (T) fine, (FC) yellowish, (BC) white **2** (LT) glossy above, pubescent below **3** no distinguishing characteristics
Vitex agnus-castus (Chasle Tree)	**1** (H) 15′, (SC) light green, (T) coarse, (BC) blue **2** (BT) medium, (LT) medium **3** (PS) aromatic
LARGE TREES	
Acer saccharinum (Sugar Maple)	**1** (H) 50′, (F) upright-rounded, (SC) silvery-green-gray, (T) medium, (FC) yellow, (BC) light yellow-green **2** (BT) smooth, (LT) lobed, (FT) winged fruit **3** no distinguishing characteristics
Cedrus sp. (Cedars)	**1** (H) 25–30′, (F) varies, (SC) gray-green, (T) fine **2** (LT) scalelike **3** no distinguishing characteristics
Cupressus arizonica (Arizona Cypress)	**1** (H) 25–30′, (F) pyramidal, (SC) gray-green, (T) fine **2** (LT) scalelike **3** no distinguishing characteristics
Diospyros virginiana (Persimmon)	**1** (H) 30′, (SC) green, (T) medium-coarse, (FC) yellow **2** (BT) medium, (LT) leathery **3** no distinguishing characteristics
Gleditsia triacanthos inermis (Thornless Honey Locust)	**1** (H) 50′, (F) rounded, (SC) dark green, (T) fine, (FC) yellowish **2** (BT) roughish, (LT) fine-smoothed, (FT) forms interesting pealike pod **3** no distinguishing characteristics
HIGH PLAINS (South Dakota, North Dakota, Montana)	
GROUND COVERS	
Celastrus scandens (American Bittersweet)	**1** (H) 20′, (F) climbing, (SC) deep green, (T) medium, (FC) yellow **2** (BT) rough, (LT) smooth above, serrated below, (FT) rough outside, waxy inside **3** no distinguishing characteristics
Lonicera sempervirens (Trumpet Honeysuckle)	**1** (H) 15′, (F) climbing, (SC) medium green, (T) coarse, (FC) red **2** (BT) twigs slick-papery, (LT) slick above, veined below **3** (BS) fragrant

Table 3–13. Continued

Scientific/Common Names	Characteristics
Parthenocissus inserta (Virginia Creeper)	**1** (H) 30′, (F) climbing, (SC) dark green, (T) coarse, (FC) red **2** (BT) roughish, (LT) pubescent below, (FT) round **3** no distinguishing characteristics
Vitis riparia (Wild Grape)	**1** (H) 35′, (F) climbing, (SC) dark to medium green, (T) coarse, (FC) yellowish, (FC) blue to violet **2** (BT) shreads, (LT) large irregular teeth, (FT) round and fleshy **3** no distinguishing characteristics
SHRUBS	
Berberis thunbergii (Japanese Barberry)	**1** (H) 3′, (F) low-compact, (SC) glossy green, (T) fine, (FC) red, (BC) yellow **2** (BT) spiny-thorny, (LT) smooth-veined, (FT) smooth-crinkly when old **3** no distinguishing characteristics
Caragana arborescens (Siberian Peashrub)	**1** (H) 12′, (F) upright, (SC) green, (T) medium fine, (BC) yellow **2** (BT) slightly winged on young, spiny on old, (FT) pea pod **3** no distinguishing characteristics
Cotoneaster acutifolius (Peking Cotoneaster)	**1** (H) 5′, (F) upright-spreading, (SC) dark glossy green, (T) medium, (FC) red, (BC) pink **2** (BT) pubescent, (LT) pubescent below, (FT) elliptical-smooth **3** no distinguishing characteristics
Elaeagnus commutata (Silver Berry)	**1** (H) 6–8′, (F) upright-spreading, (SC) silver-green, (T) medium, (BC) silver-yellow **2** (BT) scaly, (LT) scales **3** (BS) fragrant
Lonicera clavey (Clavey's Honeysuckle)	**1** (H) 3′, (F) rounded, (SC) dull green, (T) medium, (BC) pale yellow **2** (BT) medium, (LT) medium, (FT) rounded **3** (BS) very fragrant
Philadelphus coronarius (Mock Orange)	**1** (H) 8′, (F) upright, (SC) medium green, (T) coarse, (FC) yellowish, (BC) white **2** (BT) medium, (LT) medium-rough **3** (BS) fragrant
Physocarpus opulifolius nanus (Dwarf Nine Bark)	**1** (H) 4′, (F) compact-spreading, (SC) light green, (T) medium-fine, (FC) bronzing, (BC) greenish white **2** (BT) shaggy, (LT) medium **3** no distinguishing characteristics
Pinus mugo (Mugho Pine)	**1** (H) 3–4′, (F) compact-globe, (SC) bright green, (T) medium-fine **2** (BT) bumpy and roundish, (LT) slick and prickly **3** no distinguishing characteristics
Pinus strobus (White Pine)	**1** (H) 80′, (F) pyramidal, (SC) bluish green, (T) medium **2** (BT) roughish-fissured, (LT) sharp, but flexible **3** no distinguishing characteristics

Table 3-13. Continued

Scientific/Common Names	Characteristics
Pinus sylvestris (Scotch Pine)	1 (H) 75', (F) pyramidal, (SC) blue-green, (T) medium-fine 2 (BT) roughish-fissured base, (FT) small roughish 3 no distinguishing characteristics
Prunus besseyi (Sand Cherry)	1 (H) 4', (F), varies, (SC) glossy green, (T) medium, (FC) reddish, (BC) white 2 (BT) medium, (LT) thick, (FT) round 3 no distinguishing characteristics
Prunus japonica (Korean Bush Cherry)	1 (H) 4', (F) compact-rounded, (SC) dull green, (T) medium, (BC) pink to white 2 (BT) medium, (LT) sharply serrated, (FT) rounded 3 no distinguishing characteristics
Prunus tenella (Russian Almond)	1 (H) 3', (F) upright-spreading, (SC) green, (T) medium, (FC) yellowish, (BC) pink 2 (BT) roundish, (LT) stiff, (FT) small-hard 3 no distinguishing characteristics
Rhamnus cathartica (Common Buckthorn)	1 (H) 12', (F) upright, (SC) dull green, (T) medium-coarse 2 (BT) stout spines, scales, (LT) serrates and veins, (FT) round 3 no distinguishing characteristics
Rhus trilobata (Fragrant Sumac)	1 (H) 5', (F) upright, (SC) green, (T) medium, (FC) varies 2 (FT) hairy 3 (PS) ill-scented
Salix purpurea nana (Dwarf Arctic Willow)	1 (H) 4', (F) compact, (SC) blue-green, (T) medium 2 (BT) long-erect, (LT) finely serrated 3 no distinguishing characteristics
Spiraea sp. (Spiraea)	1 (H) 4-8', (F) varies, (SC) varies, (T) fine, (BC) white 2 no distinguishing characteristics 2 (BS) fragrant
Tsuga canadensis (Canada Hemlock)	1 (H) 75', (F) pyramidal, (SC) green, (T) very fine 2 (BT) pubescent branchlets, (LT) feathery, (FT) scaly-ovoid cones 3 no distinguishing characteristics
Viburnum opulus (Snowball)	1 (H) 4', (F) compact, (SC) medium green, (FC) reddish, (BC) white 2 (BT) very smooth, (LT) slightly pubescent below 3 no distinguishing characteristics

PACIFIC NORTHWEST (Washington, Oregon, North California)

GROUND COVERS

Scientific/Common Names	Characteristics
Ajuga reptans (Carpet Bugle) (Ajuga)	1 (H) 8-10", (F) spreading, (SC) bronzish green, (T) medium, (BC) blue 2 no distinguishing characteristics 3 no distinguishing characteristics
Alyssum saxatile (Goldentuft Alyssum)	1 (H) 10", (F) spreading, (SC) grayish, (BC) yellow 2 (LT) toothed, (FT) round 3 no distinguishing characteristics

Table 3-13. Continued

Scientific/Common Names	Characteristics
Arctostaphylos uva-ursi (Bearberry)	1 (H) 10", (F) spreading, (SC) dark green, (BC) pink 2 (LT) medium, (FT) smooth berry 3 no distinguishing characteristics
Convallaria majalis (Lily of the Valley)	1 (H) 18", (F) spreading, (BC) white 2 (BT) slender, (LT) oblong smooth, (FT) rounded smooth 3 (BS) fragrant
Euonymus fortunei (Wintercreeper)	1 (H) 18", (F) spreading, (SC) dark green, (T) medium, (FC) purple-green, (BC) pink 2 (BT) warty, (LT) serrated 3 no distinguishing characteristics
Juniperus sp. (Junipers)	1 (H) 18-20", (F) varies, (T) fine 2 (LT) sticky 3 no distinguishing characteristics
Nepeta mussinii (Persian Nepeta)	1 (H) 10-18", (F) spreading, (SC) green, (BC) violet 2 (BT) slightly pubescent, (LT) softly wooly 3 no distinguishing characteristics
Phlox subulata (Moss Phlox)	1 (H) 6", (F) spreading mat, (SC) green, (T) fine, (BC) purple 2 (BT) slightly pubescent 3 no distinguishing characteristics
Vinca sp. (Periwinkle)	1 (H) 6-8", (F) trailing, (SC) dark green, (T) fine, (BC) blue 2 (BT) smooth, (LT) smooth 3 no distinguishing characteristics

LOW SHRUBS

Scientific/Common Names	Characteristics
Juniperus sp. (Junipers)	1 (H) 24-30", (F) spreading, (SC) varies, (T) fine 2 (LT) sticky 3 no distinguishing characteristics
Paeonia officinalis (Peony)	1 (H) 18", (F) round, (SC) green, (BC) varies 2 no distinguishing characteristics 3 (BS) fragrant
Picea abies nidiformis (Birdnest Spruce)	1 (H) 18", (F) spreading, (SC) dark green, (T) medium to fine 2 (BT) slightly pubescent, (LT) pointed 3 no distinguishing characteristics
Potentilla fruticosa (Bush Cinquefoil)	1 (H) 3-4', (F) round, (SC) green to gray, (BC) yellow 2 (BT) loosely shredding, (LT) silky 3 (BS) somewhat fragrant
Spiraea bumalda (Anthony Waterer)	1 (H) 3', (F) rounded, (SC) light green, (T) medium to fine, (BC) crimson 2 (BT) semismooth, (LT) semirough 3 no distinguishing characteristics
Symphoricarpos albus (Snowberry)	1 (H) 3", (F) round, (SC) light green, (T) medium, (BC) pink 2 (BT) fine-medium, (LT) pubescent below, (FT) fine 3 no distinguishing characteristics
Viburnum opulus (Cranberry Bush)	1 (H) 2', (F) round, (SC) medium green, (FC) red, (BC) white

Table 3–13. Continued

Scientific/Common Names	Characteristics
	2 (*BT*) smooth, (*LT*) slightly pubescent
	3 no distinguishing characteristics
Yucca filamentosa (Yucca)	**1** (*H*) 3–5′, (*F*) rounded, (*SC*) green, (*T*) coarse, (*BC*) white
	2 (*BT*) fuzzy, (*LT*) hairy, sharp pointed
	3 (*BS*) faint odor
TALL SHRUBS AND SMALL TREES	
Lonicera tatarica (Tartarian Honeysuckle)	**1** (*H*) 10′, (*F*) rounded, (*SC*) bluish green, (*T*) medium, (*BC*) white to pink
	2 no distinguishing characteristics
	3 (*BS*) fragrant
Philadelphus gordonianus (Gordon Mock Orange)	**1** (*H*) 12′, (*F*) upright, (*SC*) deep green, (*T*) medium, (*BC*) white
	2 (*BT*) peels, (*LT*) pubescent on veins below
	3 (*BS*) fragrant
Prunus triloba (Flowering Plum)	**1** (*H*) 10′, (*F*) oval, (*SC*) green, (*T*) medium to coarse, (*BC*) pink
	2 (*BT*) medium, (*LT*) coarse, (*FT*) medium
	3 (*BS*) fragrant
Rhus typhina (Stag's-horn Sumac)	**1** (*H*) 15′, (*F*) irregular, (*SC*) dull green, (*T*) fine to medium, (*FC*) green
	2 (*BT*) hairy, (*LT*) medium to coarse,
	3 no distinguishing characteristics
Syringa sp. (Lilac)	**1** (*H*) 6–10′, (*F*) oval-round, (*SC*) green, (*T*) medium
	2 (*BT*) medium, (*LT*) medium
	3 (*BS*) fragrant
Tamarix sp. (Tamarisks)	**1** (*H*) 6–12′, (*F*) upright, oval, (*SC*) bright green, (*T*) fine, (*BC*) pinkish
	2 (*BT*) slick, (*LT*) soft, grasslike, (*FT*) feathery
	3 no distinguishing characteristics
TREES	
Betula pendula (White Birch)	**1** (*H*) 50–75′, (*F*) rounded, (*SC*) light green, (*T*) fine
	2 (*BT*) papery, (*LT*) smooth above, fuzzy below
	3 no distinguishing characteristics
Cornus florida (Flowering Dogwood)	**1** (*H*) 10–20′, (*F*) oval to round, (*SC*) dull green, (*T*) medium to coarse, (*FC*) rose, (*BC*) white
	2 (*BT*) flakes, soft, (*LT*) smooth above, veined below, (*FT*) egg shaped
	3 no distinguishing characteristics
Malus sp. (Crab Apple)	**1** (*H*) 10–20′, (*F*) rounded, (*SC*) dark green, (*T*) medium
	2 (*BT*) smoothish, (*LT*) flexible, (*FT*) hard, waxy
	3 (*BS*) fragrant

Table 3–13. Continued

Scientific/Common Names	Characteristics
Phellodendron amurense (Amur Cork Tree)	**1** (*H*) 30–50′, (*F*) V shaped, (*SC*) green, (*T*) medium
	2 (*BT*) corky, (*LT*) hairy
	3 no distinguishing characteristics
Prunus subcordata (Klamath Plum)	**1** (*H*) 10–20′, (*F*) oval, (*SC*) green, (*T*) medium, (*BC*) white
	2 (*BT*) spiny, (*LT*) sharp and thick, (*FT*) fleshy
	3 (*BS*) fragrant
Robinia pseudoacacia (Umbrella Blacklocust)	**1** (*H*) 30–50′, (*F*) round, (*SC*) bluish green, (*T*) medium to fine, (*BC*) white
	2 (*BT*) prickly
	3 (*BS*) fragrant
Sorbus aucuparia (Mountain Ash)	**1** (*H*) 50′, (*F*) oval, (*SC*) light green, (*T*) medium
	2 (*BT*) pubescent when young, (*LT*) sharp serrated
	3 no distinguishing characteristics
VINES	
Campsis radicans (Trumpet Vine)	**1** (*H*) 40′, (*F*) climbing, (*SC*) bright green, (*T*) medium-smooth, (*FC*) deep green, (*BC*) orange
	2 (*BT*) smooth-slick-bumpy, (*LT*) smooth above, rough below
	3 no distinguishing characteristics
Celastrus scandens (American Bittersweet)	**1** (*H*) 30′, (*F*) twining, (*SC*) dark green, (*T*) medium-coarse, (*FC*) yellowish, (*BC*) yellow
	2 (*BT*) shaggy, (*LT*) smooth above, serrated below, (*FT*) coarse outside, smooth waxy inside
	3 no distinguishing characteristics
Clematis sp. (Clematis)	**1** (*H*) 35′, (*F*) clinging, (*SC*) dark green, (*BC*) white
	2 no distinguishing characteristics
	3 no distinguishing characteristics
Euonymus fortunei vegetus (Wintercreeper)	**1** (*H*) 10′, (*F*) shrubby vine, (*SC*) green, (*T*) medium
	2 (*BT*) warty, (*LT*) leathery, coarse toothed
	3 no distinguishing characteristics
Parthenocissus quinquefolia (Virginia Creeper)	**1** (*H*) 30–40′, (*F*) climbing, (*SC*) dark green, (*T*) coarse, (*FC*) red
	2 (*BT*) roughish, (*LT*) roughish above, pubescent below
	3 no distinguishing characteristics

G. PLANTING IMPLEMENTATION DETAILS
See figures 3–22 to 3–39.

A. NATIVE WILDFLOWER SPECIES/MIXES

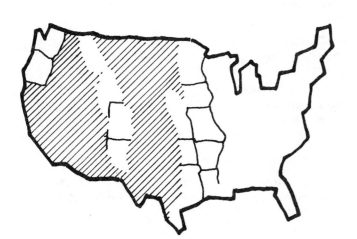

3-1. Dry Mixture (10–30 Inches Rainfall/Year)

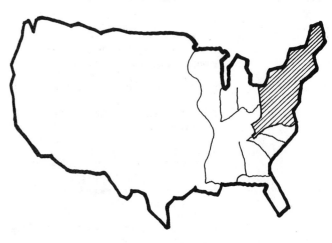

3-4. Northeast Mixture

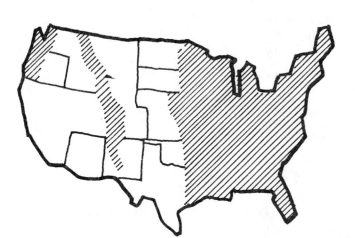

3-2. Moist Mixture (Over 30 Inches Rainfall/Year)

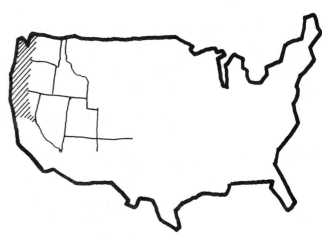

3-5. Northwest Mixture (Below 7,000 Feet)

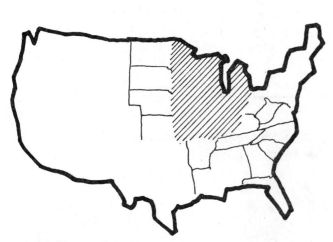

3-3. Midwest Mixture

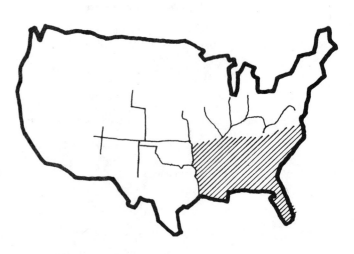

3-6. Southeast Mixture

A. NATIVE WILDFLOWER SPECIES/MIXES

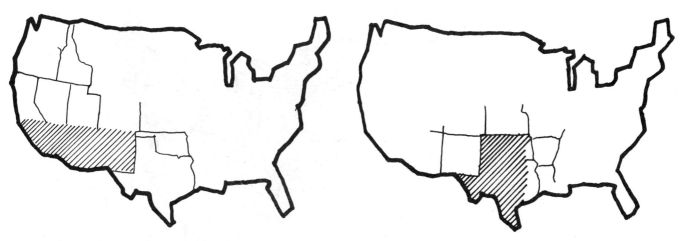

3-7. Southwest Mixture (Below 7,000 Feet)

3-8. Texas/Oklahoma Mixture

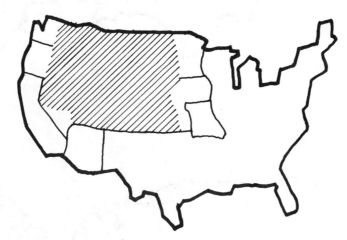

3-9. Western Mixture (Below 7,000 Feet)

B. NORTH AMERICAN FOREST AREAS

3-10. The North American Deciduous Forest

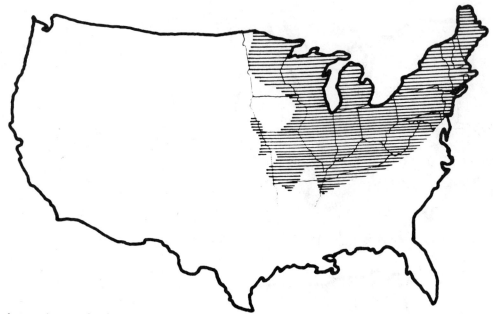

3-11. The North American Upland Region

3-12. The Boreal Coniferous Forest

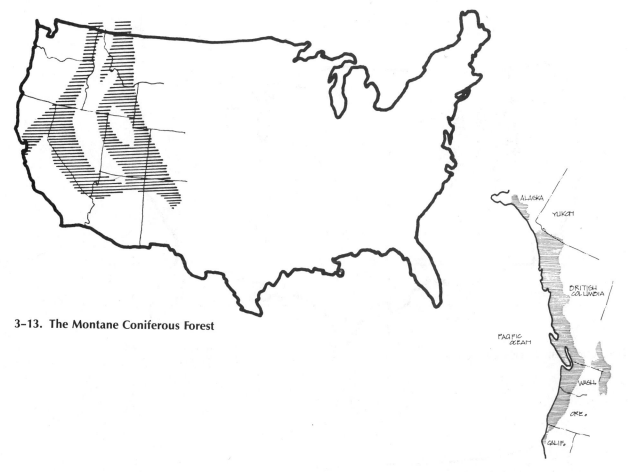

B. NORTH AMERICAN FOREST AREAS

3-13. The Montane Coniferous Forest

3-14. The Northern Pacific Coast/Rainy Western Hemlock Forest

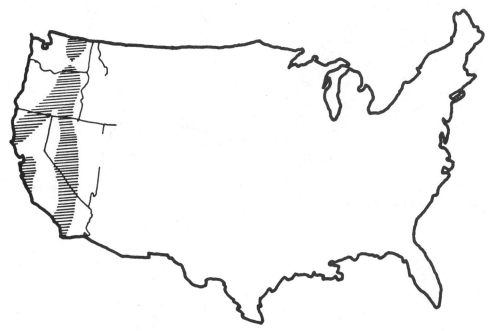

3-15. The Broad Schlerpphyll/Grizzly Bear Community

3–16. Desert and Semidesert Communities

3–17. Woodland and Brushland Communities

B. NORTH AMERICAN FOREST AREAS

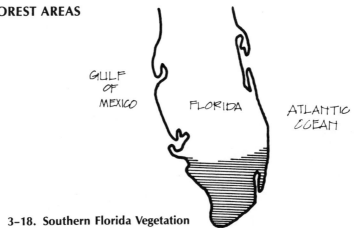

3-18. Southern Florida Vegetation

C. NORTH AMERICAN GRASSLAND AREAS

3-19. The Northern Grasslands

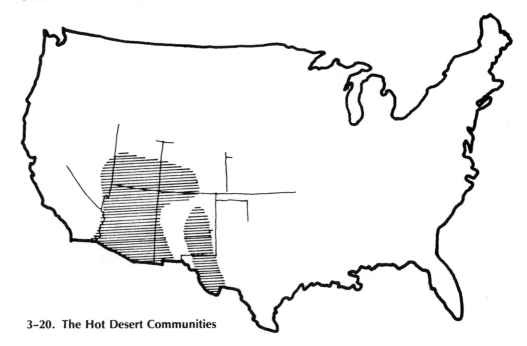

3-20. The Hot Desert Communities

E. LANDSCAPE ILLUMINATION

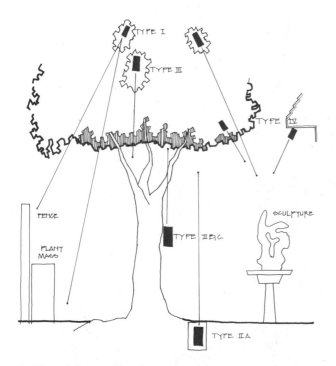

3-21. Landscape Illumination: Lamp Placement (Typical)

G. PLANTING IMPLEMENTATION DETAILS

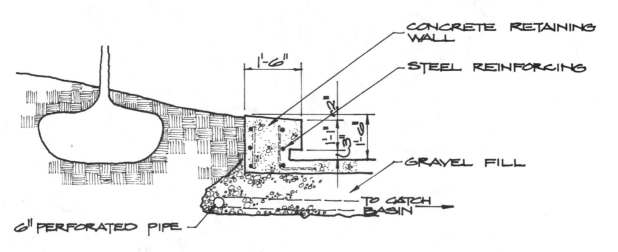

CONCRETE RETAINING WALL

STEEL REINFORCING

GRAVEL FILL

TO CATCH BASIN

6" PERFORATED PIPE

3-22. Concrete Planter

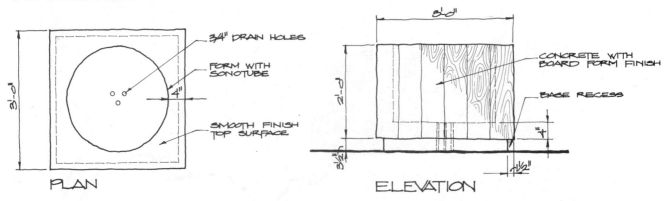

3/4" DRAIN HOLES

FORM WITH SONOTUBE

SMOOTH FINISH TOP SURFACE

CONCRETE WITH BOARD FORM FINISH

BASE RECESS

PLAN

ELEVATION

3-23. Concrete Planter

G. PLANTING IMPLEMENTATION DETAILS

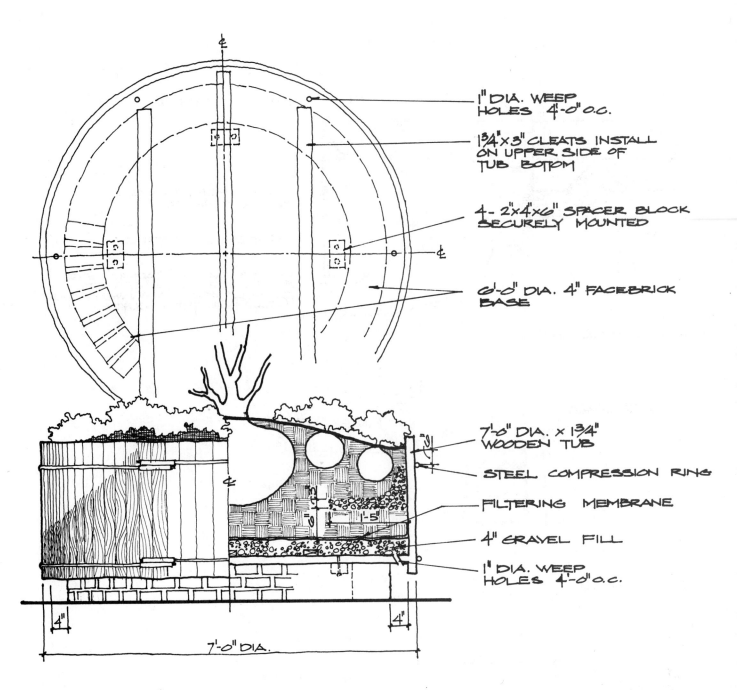

1" DIA. WEEP
HOLES 4'-0" O.C.

1¾"x 3" CLEATS INSTALL
ON UPPER SIDE OF
TUB BOTTOM

4- 2"x4"x6" SPACER BLOCK
SECURELY MOUNTED

6'-0" DIA. 4" FACEBRICK
BASE

7'-0" DIA. x 1¾"
WOODEN TUB

STEEL COMPRESSION RING

FILTERING MEMBRANE

4" GRAVEL FILL

1" DIA. WEEP
HOLES 4'-0" O.C.

4"

4"

7'-0" DIA.

3–24. Wooden Tree Planter

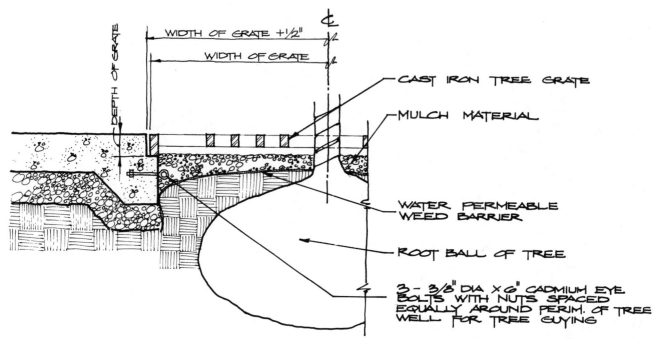

WIDTH OF GRATE +1/2"

WIDTH OF GRATE

DEPTH OF GRATE

CAST IRON TREE GRATE

MULCH MATERIAL

WATER PERMEABLE WEED BARRIER

ROOT BALL OF TREE

3 - 3/8" DIA × 6" CADMIUM EYE BOLTS WITH NUTS SPACED EQUALLY AROUND PERIM. OF TREE WELL FOR TREE GUYING

3-25. Tree Well with Grate

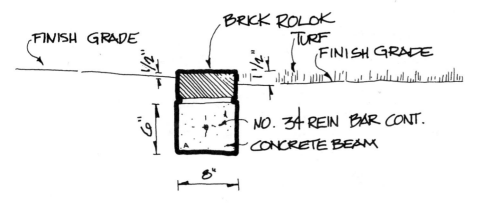

FINISH GRADE

BRICK ROLOK

TURF

FINISH GRADE

1/2"

1/2"

6"

8"

NO. 3Φ REIN BAR CONT.

CONCRETE BEAM

3-26. Brick Mowing Strip

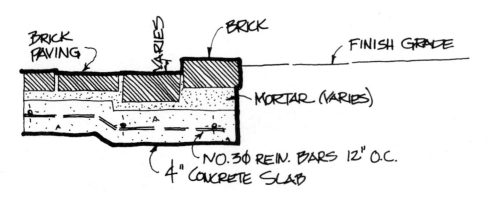

BRICK PAVING

VARIES

BRICK

FINISH GRADE

MORTAR (VARIES)

NO. 3Φ REIN. BARS 12" O.C.

4" CONCRETE SLAB

3-27. Brick Mowing Strip and Brick Walk

G. PLANTING IMPLEMENTATION DETAILS

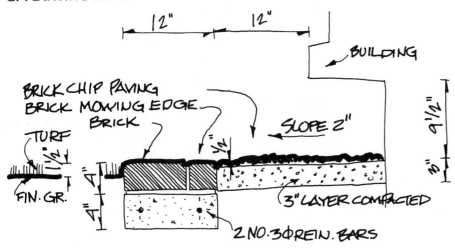

3-28. Brick Planting Edge at Building

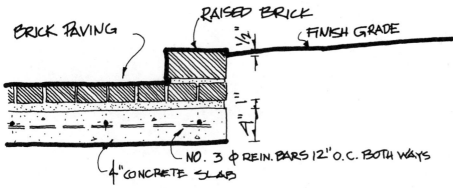

3-29. Raised Brick Planter

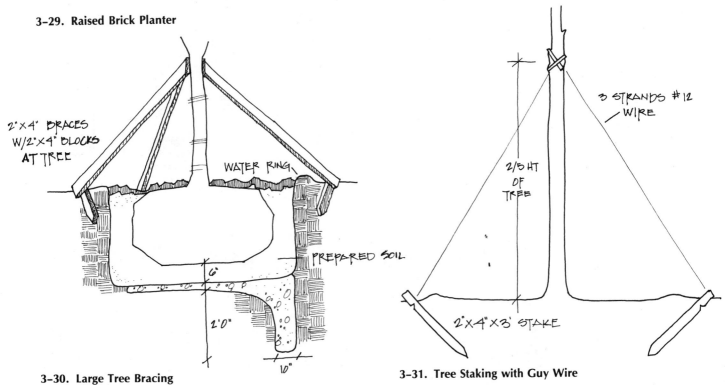

3-30. Large Tree Bracing

3-31. Tree Staking with Guy Wire

G. PLANTING IMPLEMENTATION DETAILS

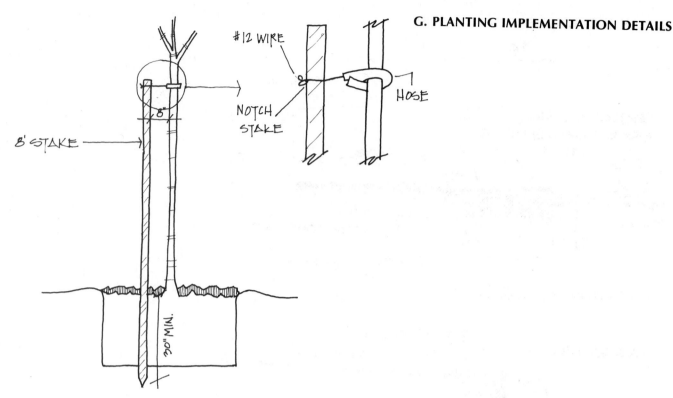

3-32. Tree Staking with Single Stake

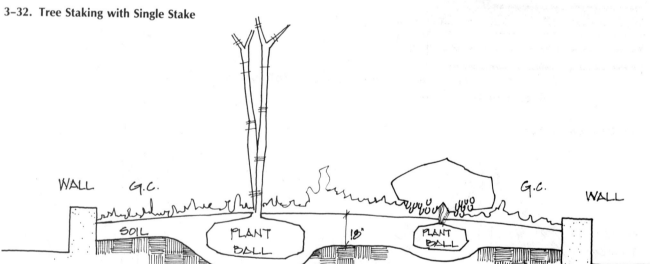

3-33. Raised Planter: Section

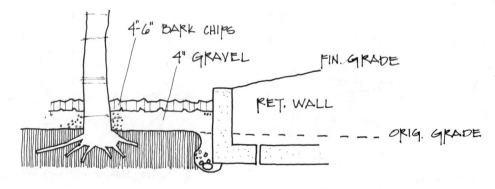

3-34. Soil Fill, Existing Tree

G. PLANTING IMPLEMENTATION DETAILS

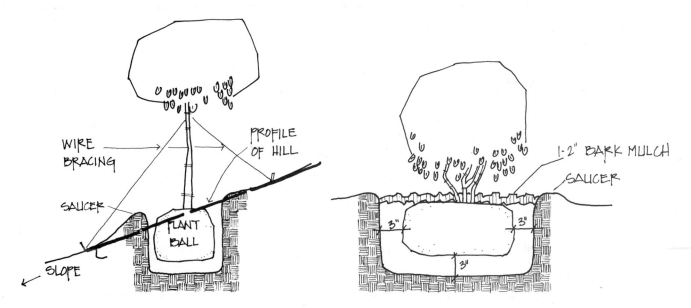

3-35. Tree Planting on Hill/Slope

3-37. Typical Shrub Planting

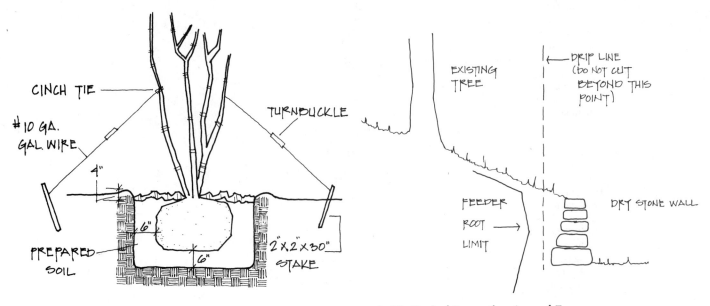

3-36. Multitrunk Tree Bracing

3-38. Typical Excavation Around Tree

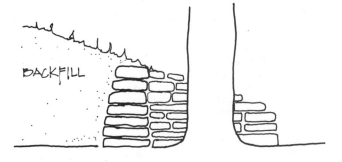

3-39. Drystone Treewell: Section

Earthwork _____

A. SOIL TYPES AND THEIR PROPERTIES
See Table 3–14.

B. RETAINING WALLS
See figures 3–40 to 3–60.

Table 3–14. Soil Types and Their Properties

Division	Soil Description	Value as a Foundation Material	Frost Action	Drainage
Gravel and Gravelly Soils	Well-graded gravel, or gravel-sand mixture, little or no fines	Excellent	None	Excellent
	Poorly graded gravel, or gravel-sand mixtures, little or no fines	Good	None	Excellent
	Silty gravels, gravel-sand-silt mixture	Good	Slight	Poor
	Clayey gravels, gravel-clay-sand mixture	Good	Slight	Poor
Sand and Sandy Soils	Well-graded sands, or gravelly sands, little or no fines	Good	None	Excellent
	Poorly graded sands, or gravelly sands, little or no fines	Fair	None	Excellent
	Silty sands, sand-silt mixtures	Fair	Slight	Fair
	Clayey sands, sand-clay mixtures	Fair	Medium	Poor
Silts and Clays	Inorganic silts, rock flour, silty or clayey silts with slight plasticity	Fair	Very high	Poor
	Inorganic clays of low to medium plasticity, gravelly clays, silty clays, lean clays	Fair	Medium	Impervious
	Organic silt-clays of low plasticity	Poor	High	Impervious
Silts and Clays	Inorganic silts, micaceous or diatomaceous fine sandy or silty soils, elastic silts	Poor	Very high	Poor
	Inorganic clays of high plasticity, fat clays	Very poor	Medium	Impervious
	Organic clays of medium to high plasticity, organic silts	Very poor	Medium	Impervious

B. RETAINING WALLS

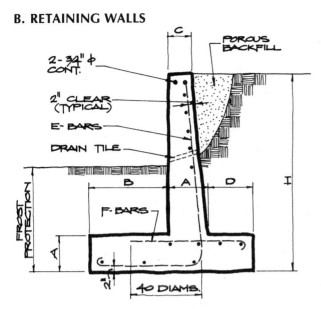

2-¾" ⌀ CONT.

2" CLEAR (TYPICAL)

E- BARS

DRAIN TILE

POROUS BACKFILL

FROST PROTECTION

F- BARS

40 DIAMS.

3-40. Retaining Wall: A

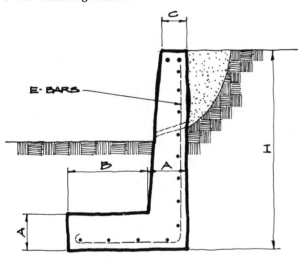

E- BARS

3-41. Retaining Wall: B

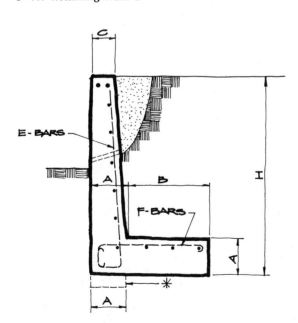

E- BARS

F- BARS

3-42. Retaining Wall: C

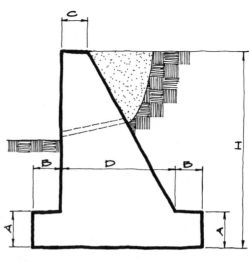

3-43. Retaining Wall: D

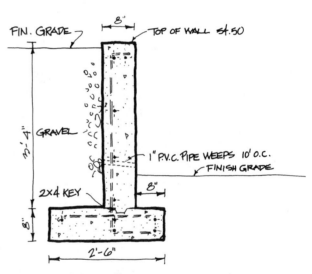

FIN. GRADE

TOP OF WALL 54.50

GRAVEL

1" P.V.C. PIPE WEEPS 10' O.C.

FINISH GRADE

2×4 KEY

2'-6"

3-44. Retaining Wall: E

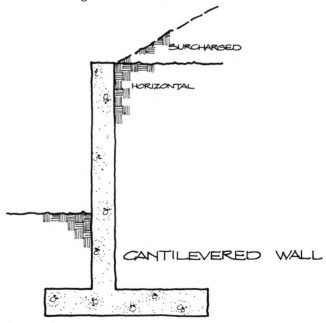

SURCHARGED

HORIZONTAL

CANTILEVERED WALL

3-45. Retaining Wall: F

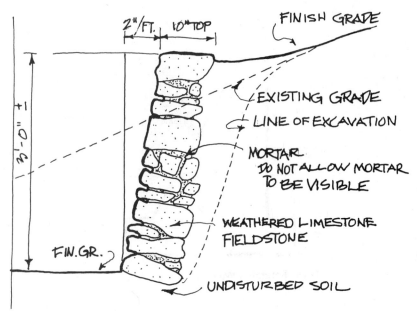

FINISH GRADE

2"/FT. 10"TOP

3'-0" ±

EXISTING GRADE

LINE OF EXCAVATION

MORTAR
DO NOT ALLOW MORTAR
TO BE VISIBLE

WEATHERED LIMESTONE
FIELDSTONE

FIN. GR.

UNDISTURBED SOIL

3-46. Retaining Wall: Stone

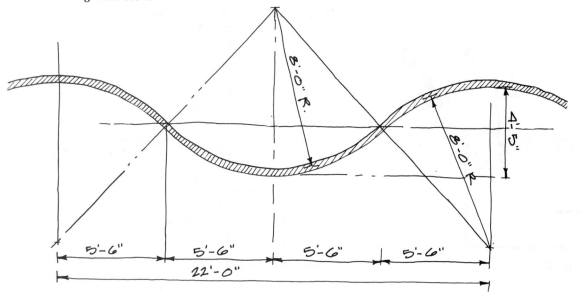

8'-0" R.

8'-0" R.

4'-5"

5'-6"   5'-6"   5'-6"   5'-6"

22'-0"

3-47. Curved Wall: Layout

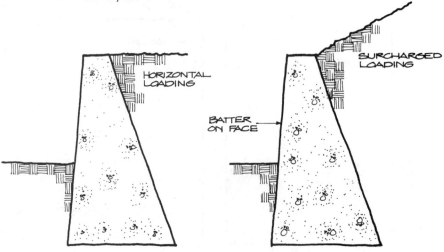

HORIZONTAL
LOADING

SURCHARGED
LOADING

BATTER
ON FACE

3-48. Sections through Gravity Walls

B. RETAINING WALLS

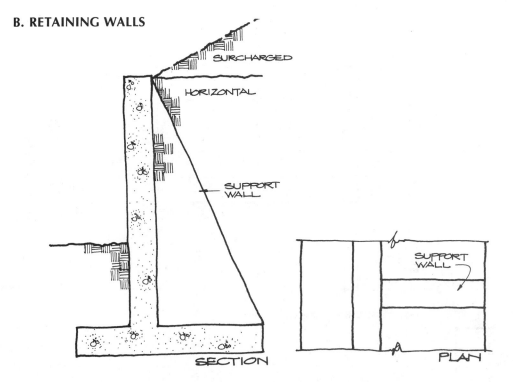

SURCHARGED

HORIZONTAL

SUPPORT WALL

SECTION

SUPPORT WALL

PLAN

3-49. Counterfort Wall

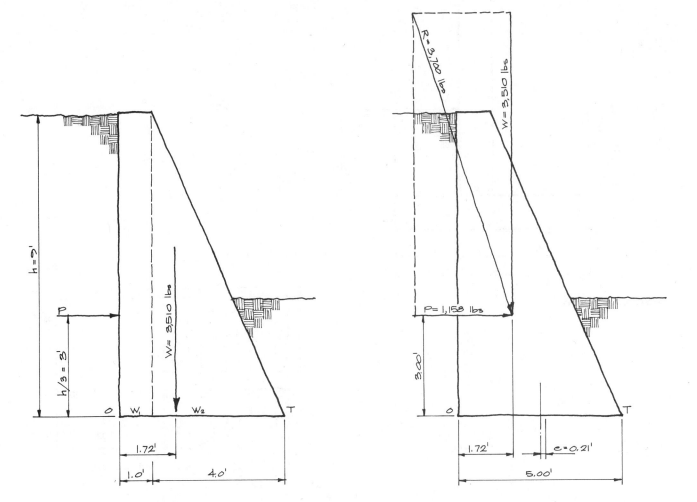

3-50 and 3-51. Gravity Wall

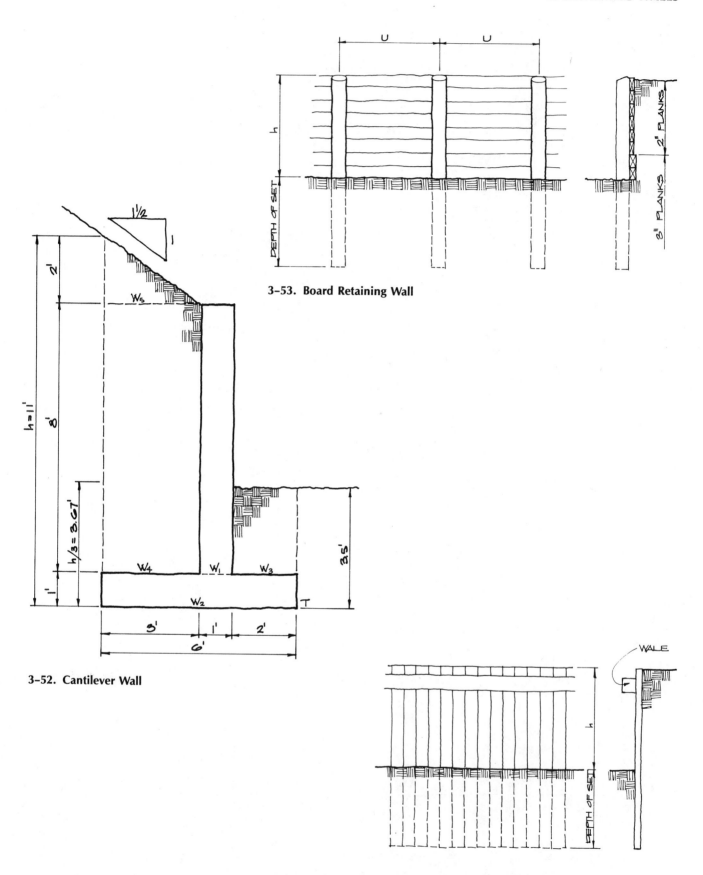

3-53. Board Retaining Wall

3-52. Cantilever Wall

3-54. Timber Retaining Wall

B. RETAINING WALLS

$$P = 0.286 \frac{wh^2}{2}$$

WHERE P = MAGNITUDE OF EARTH PRESSURE, LB

           w = WEIGHT OF RETAINED MATERIAL, PCF

           h = HEIGHT OF RETAINED MATERIAL, FT (MEASURED FROM BOTTOM OF WALL FOOTING)

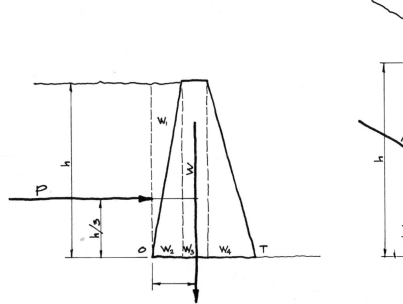
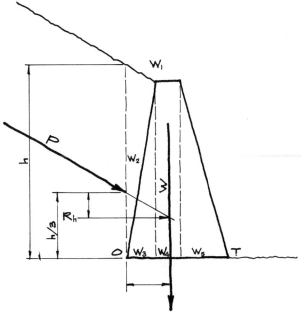

3–55. Retaining Wall, Load Calculation

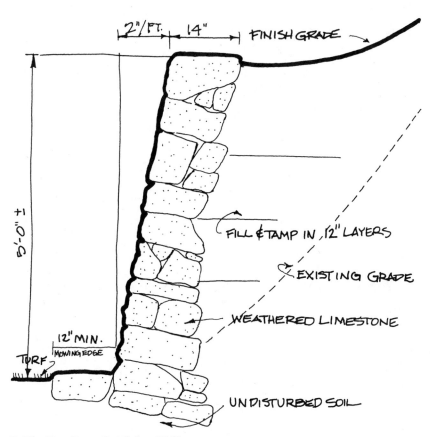

3–56. Dry Stone Retaining Wall

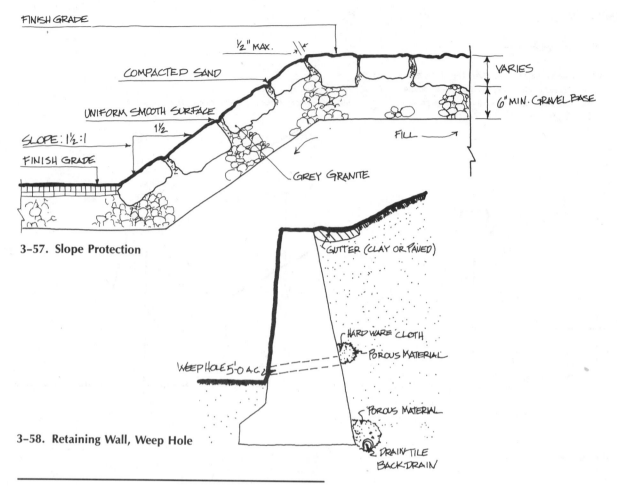

FINISH GRADE

½" MAX.

COMPACTED SAND

UNIFORM SMOOTH SURFACE

1½

SLOPE: 1½:1

FINISH GRADE

VARIES

6" MIN. GRAVEL BASE

FILL

GREY GRANITE

3-57. Slope Protection

GUTTER (CLAY OR PAVED)

HARDWARE CLOTH
POROUS MATERIAL

WEEP HOLE 5'-0 A.C.

POROUS MATERIAL

DRAIN TILE
BACK-DRAIN

3-58. Retaining Wall, Weep Hole

	Stretchers	Units 15⅝" × 7⅝" × ⅜"	Units 11⅝" × 5⅝" × ⅜"
Length	1	1' 4"	1' 0"
	2	2' 8"	2' 0"
	3	4' 0"	3' 0"
	4	5' 4"	4' 0"
	5	6' 8"	5' 0"
	6	8' 0"	6' 0"
	7	9' 4"	7' 0"
	8	10' 8"	8' 0"
	9	12' 0"	9' 0"
	10	13' 4"	10' 0"
	No. Courses	Units 7⅝" (h) × ⅜" (t)	Units 3⅝" (h) × ¾" (t)
Height	1	8"	4"
	2	1' 4"	8"
	3	2' 0"	1' 0"
	4	2' 8"	1' 4"
	5	3' 4"	1' 8"
	6	4' 0"	2' 0"
	7	4' 8"	2' 4"
	8	5' 4"	2' 8"
	9	6' 0"	3' 0"
	10	6' 8"	3' 4"

3-59. Concrete Masonry Wall

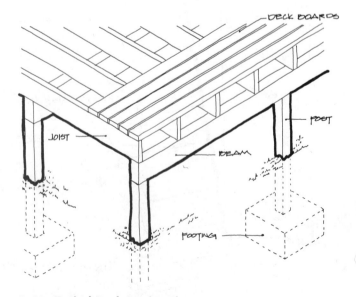

DECK BOARDS

JOIST

POST

BEAM

FOOTING

3-60. Typical Deck Footing Placement

Site Improvements

A. DECKING STRUCTURES

Our experiences with exposed deck construction can be summarized in the following general guidelines for the use of wood and fasteners in outdoor decks. See tables 3–15 and 3–16 as well as figures 3–61 to 3–88.

1. FASTENER USE

a) Guidelines

(1) Use nonstaining fasteners.
(2) Always fasten a thinner member to a thicker member (unless clinched nails are used).
  (a) A nail should be long enough to penetrate the receiving member a distance twice the thickness of the thinner member but not less than 1½ inches (i.e., for a ¾-inch board, the nail should penetrate the receiving member 1½ inches. Use at least a 7-penny nail).
  (b) A screw should be long enough to penetrate the receiving member at least the thickness of the thinner (outside) member but with not less than a 1-inch penetration (i.e., fastening a ¾-inch member to a 2 by 4 would require a 1¾-inch-long screw).
(3) To reduce splitting of boards when nailing:
  (a) Blunt the nail point.
  (b) Predrill (three-quarters of nail diameter).
  (c) Use smaller-diameter nails and a greater number of them.
  (d) Use greater spacing between nails.
  (e) Stagger nails in each row.
  (f) Place nails no closer to the edge than half the board thickness and no closer to the end than the board thickness.
  (g) In wide boards (8 inches or more), do not place nails close to the edge.
(4) Use a minimum of two nails per board (i.e., two nails for 4- and 6-inch widths and three nails for 8- and 10-inch widths).
(5) Avoid end grain nailing. When unavoidable, use screws or side-grain wood cleats adjacent to end grain member (as a post).
(6) When a lag screw is required:
  (a) Use a plain, flat washer under the head.
  (b) Use a lead hole and turn it full distance; do not overturn.
  (c) Do not countersink (this reduces wood section).
(7) When a bolt is required:
  (a) Use flat washers under the nut and head of machine bolts and under the nut of carriage bolts. In softer woods, use a larger washer under carriage bolt heads.
  (b) Holes should be the exact size of the bolt diameter.

2. OUTDOOR WOOD USE

a) Guidelines

(1) When a wide member is required, use edge grain boards because they shrink, swell, and cup less than flat grain boards during moisture changes.
(2) Do not use wood in direct contact with soil unless members are pressure treated.
(3) Provide clearance of wood members (fences, posts, etc.) from plant growth and ground to minimize high moisture content. Bottoms of posts, when supported by piers, for example, should be 6 inches above the grade.
(4) Use forms of flat members that provide natural drainage (a sloped top of a cap rail, for example).
(5) Use rectangular sections with width and thickness as nearly equal as possible (i.e., 3 by 4 instead of 2 by 6).
(6) Dip all ends and points of fabrication in a water-repellent preservative treatment prior to placement.

Table 3–15. Maximum Allowable Spans for Deck Joists*

Species Group**	Joist Size (in.)	JOIST SPACING (IN.) 16	24	32
1	2 × 6	9′–9″	7′–11″	6′–2″
	2 × 8	12′–10″	10′–6″	8′–1″
	2 × 10	16′–5″	13′–4″	10′–4″
2	2 × 6	8′–7″	7′–0″	5′–8″
	2 × 8	11′–4″	9′–3″	7′–6″
	2 × 10	14′–6″	11′–10″	9′–6″
3	2 × 6	7′–9″	6′–2″	5′–0″
	2 × 8	10′–2″	8′–1″	6′–8″
	2 × 10	13′–0″	10′–4″	8′–6″

*Joists are on edge. Spans are center-to-center distances between beams or supports. Based on 40 p.s.f. deck live loads plus 10 p.s.f. dead load. Grade is No. 2 or better; No. 2 medium grain southern pine
**Group 1: Douglas-fir-larch and Southern pine. Group 2: Hem-fir and Douglas-fir and Southern pine. Group 3: Western pines and cedars, redwood, and spruces.

Table 3–16. Maximum Allowable Span (in.)*

Species Group**	LAID FLAT 1 × 4	2 × 2	2 × 3	LAID ON EDGE 2 × 2	2 × 3	2 × 4
1	16	60	60	60	90	144
2	14	48	48	48	78	120
3	12	42	42	42	66	108

*Based on construction grade or better (select structural, appearance, No. 1 or No. 2).
**Group 1: Douglas-fir-larch and southern pine. Group 2: Hem-fir and Douglas-fir south. Group 3: western pines and cedars, redwood, and spruces.

B. SITE FURNITURE

1. BENCHES
See figures 3–89 to 3–93.

2. DRINKING FOUNTAINS
See figures 3–94 and 3–95.

C. CIRCULATION CONTROL

1. BOLLARDS
See figures 3–96 and 3–97.

2. FENCES
See table 3–17. See also figure 3–98.

D. LANDSCAPE IRRIGATION SYSTEMS
See figures 3–99 to 3–103.

E. AREA LIGHTING
See figures 3–104 to 3–106.

F. DRAINAGE SYSTEMS
See figures 3–107 to 3–110.

Table 3–17. Degree of Transparency for Fences and Screens

Use	Solid	Semitrans-parent	Transparent
Entrance	Board Board and Batten Louver Panel Staggered Board Panel	1 × 2 Wood Screen Contempo-rary Picket	
Outdoor Room	Board Board and Batten Louver Panel Staggered Board Panel 1 × 4 Wood Screen	1 × 2 Wood Screen Contempo-rary Picket	
Protection	Staggered Board Board and Batten 1 × 4 Wood Screen	1 × 2 Wood Screen Contempo-rary Picket Picket	Split Rail Contem-porary Rail Wire Mesh Rail and Wire Mesh

A. DECKING STRUCTURES

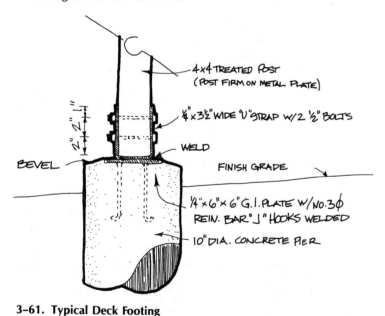

3–61. Typical Deck Footing

4×4 TREATED POST (POST FIRM ON METAL PLATE)

¼"×3½" WIDE "U" STRAP W/2 ½" BOLTS

WELD

BEVEL

FINISH GRADE

¼"×6"×6" G.I. PLATE W/NO.3∅ REIN. BAR "J" HOOKS WELDED

10"DIA. CONCRETE PIER

ALTERNATE BOARD WIDTH PATTERNS

DIAGONAL BOARD DECKING

CHECKERBOARD DECK PATTERN

3–62. Decking Surface Patterns

½" JOINT

POST

¼" SPACING

2×4's
2×4's
(2×6's)
(FLAT OR EDGE)

SPACED BEAM

VERIFY DECK SPANS, BEAMS, AND BEAM SPACING

A. DECKING STRUCTURES

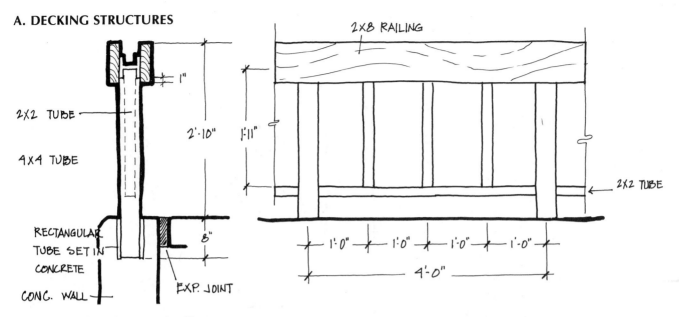

2X8 RAILING

2X2 TUBE

4X4 TUBE

1"

2'-10"

1'-11"

RECTANGULAR TUBE SET IN CONCRETE

CONC. WALL

EXP. JOINT

8"

2X2 TUBE

1'-0"   1'-0"   1'-0"   1'-0"

4'-0"

3-63. Typical Decking Hand Rail

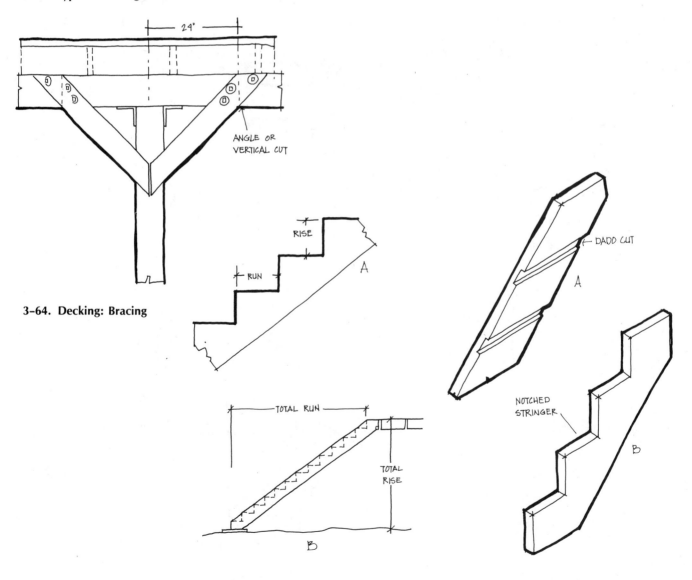

24"

ANGLE OR VERTICAL CUT

3-64. Decking: Bracing

RISE

RUN

A

TOTAL RUN

TOTAL RISE

B

DADO CUT

A

NOTCHED STRINGER

B

3-65. Decking: Step Components—A   **3-66. Decking: Step Components—B**

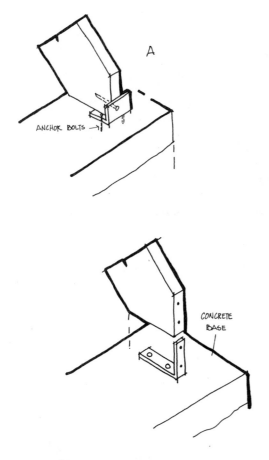

ANCHOR BOLTS →

CONCRETE BASE

3-67. Decking Components: Anchor

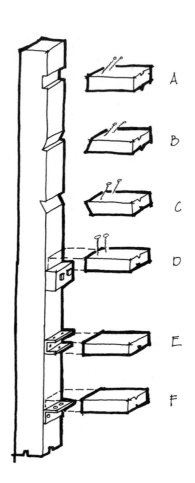

A

B

C

D

E

F

3-68. Decking Components: Ladder

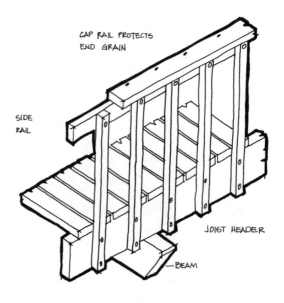

CAP RAIL PROTECTS END GRAIN

SIDE RAIL

JOIST HEADER

BEAM

3-69. Decking Components: Capped Railing

A. DECKING STRUCTURES

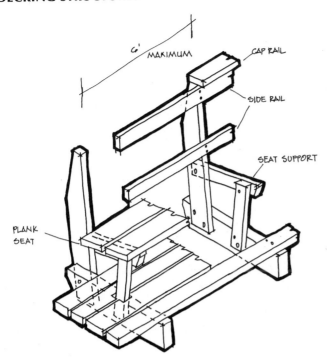

3-70. Decking Components: Bench Detail

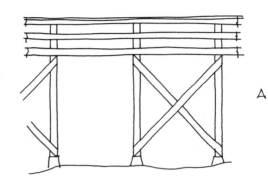

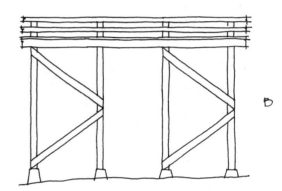

3-72. Decking Components: Cross Supports

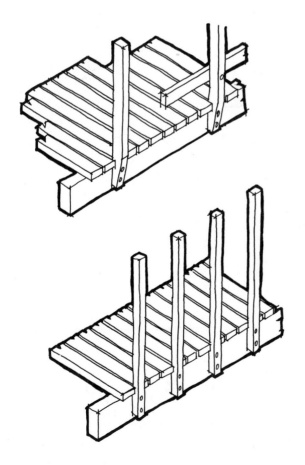

3-71. Decking Components: Rails

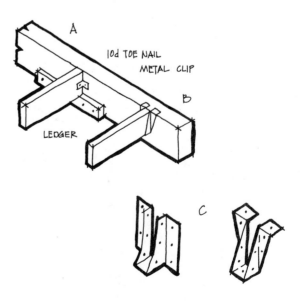

3-73. Decking Components: Joist to Support Beam

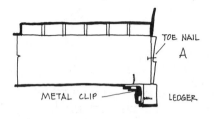
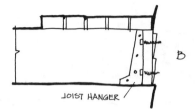
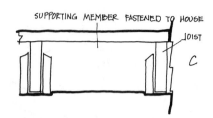

3-74. Decking Components: Joist to Support Beam (Section)

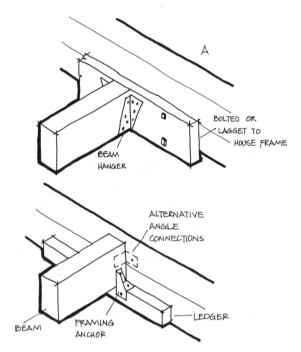

3-75. Decking Components: Joist to Support Beam

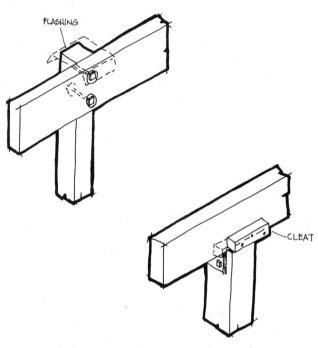

3-77. Decking Components: Railing Attachment

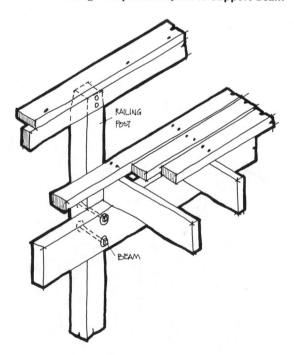

3-76. Decking Components: Bench or Railing

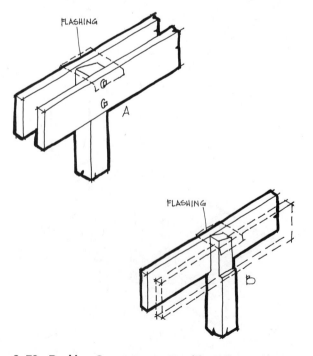

3-78. Decking Components: Double Rail Attachment

A. DECKING STRUCTURES

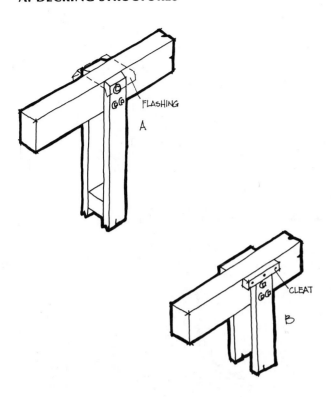

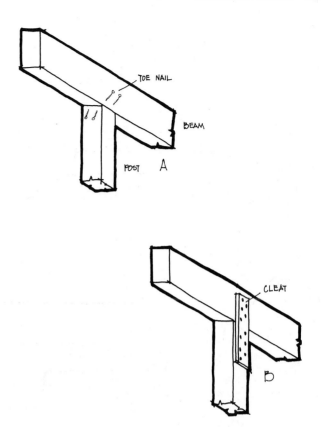

3-79. Decking Components: Double Post

3-81. Decking Components: Beam Joints

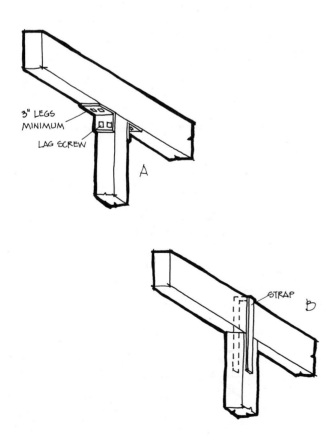

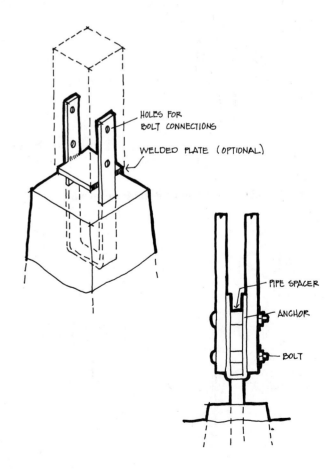

3-80. Decking Components: Support Beams

3-82. Decking Components: Beam Joint at Footing

A. DECKING STRUCTURES

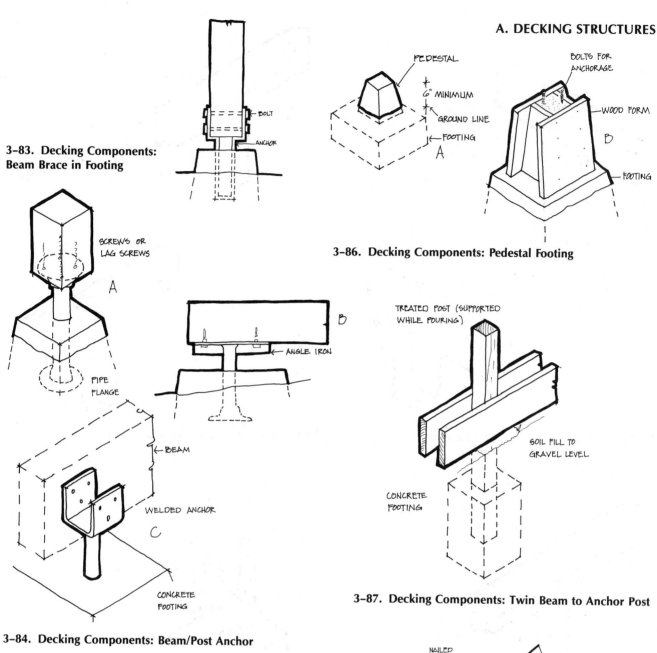

3-83. Decking Components: Beam Brace in Footing

BOLT

ANCHOR

PEDESTAL

6" MINIMUM

GROUND LINE

FOOTING

A

BOLTS FOR ANCHORAGE

WOOD FORM

B

FOOTING

3-86. Decking Components: Pedestal Footing

SCREWS OR LAG SCREWS

A

PIPE FLANGE

B

ANGLE IRON

BEAM

WELDED ANCHOR

C

CONCRETE FOOTING

3-84. Decking Components: Beam/Post Anchor

TREATED POST (SUPPORTED WHILE POURING)

SOIL FILL TO GRAVEL LEVEL

CONCRETE FOOTING

3-87. Decking Components: Twin Beam to Anchor Post

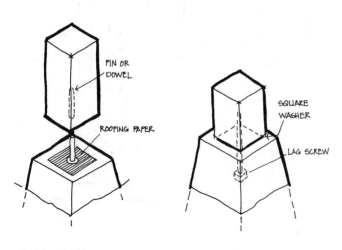

PIN OR DOWEL

ROOFING PAPER

SQUARE WASHER

LAG SCREW

3-85. Decking Components: Post Connection

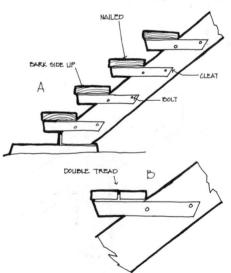

NAILED

BARK SIDE UP

A

CLEAT

BOLT

DOUBLE TREAD

B

3-88. Decking Components: Steps/Risers

B. SITE FURNITURE

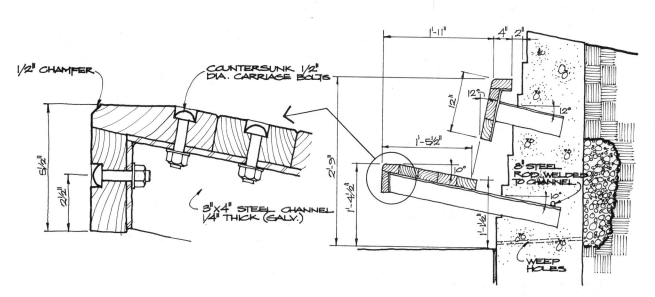

3-89. Seating Component: Bench/Concrete Wall

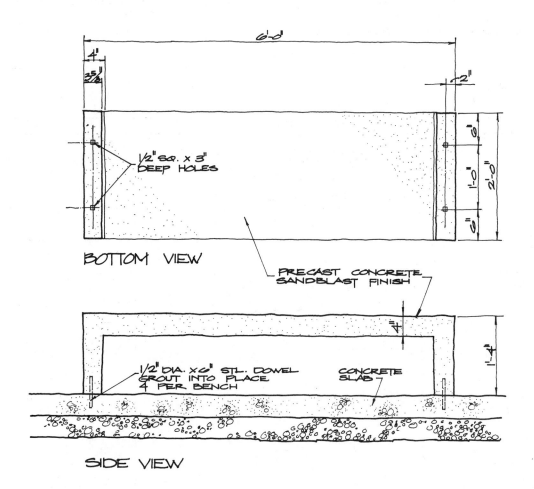

3-90. Seating Component: Precast Concrete Bench

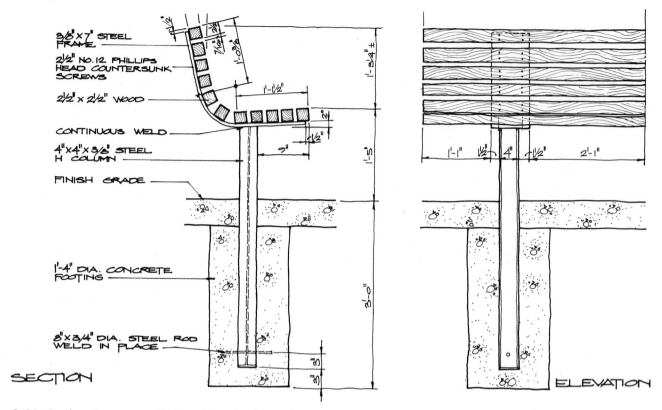

3-91. Seating Component: Redwood Bench with Back

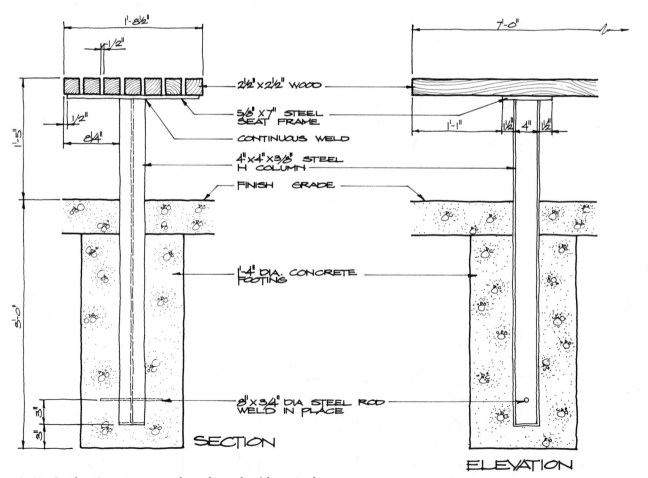

3-92. Seating Component: Redwood Bench without Back

B. SITE FURNITURE

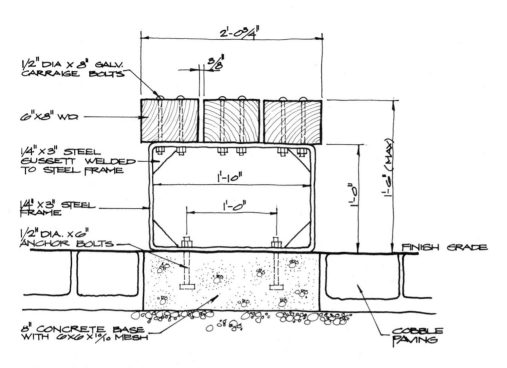

1/2" DIA x 8" GALV. CARRAIGE BOLTS

6"x8" WD.

1/4" x 3" STEEL GUSSETT WELDED TO STEEL FRAME

1/4" x 3" STEEL FRAME

1/2" DIA. x 6" ANCHOR BOLTS

8" CONCRETE BASE WITH 6x6 x 10/10 MESH

2'-0¾"

⅜"

1'-10"

1'-0"

1'-0"

1'-6" (MAX.)

FINISH GRADE

COBBLE PAVING

3-93. Seating Component: Post Bench

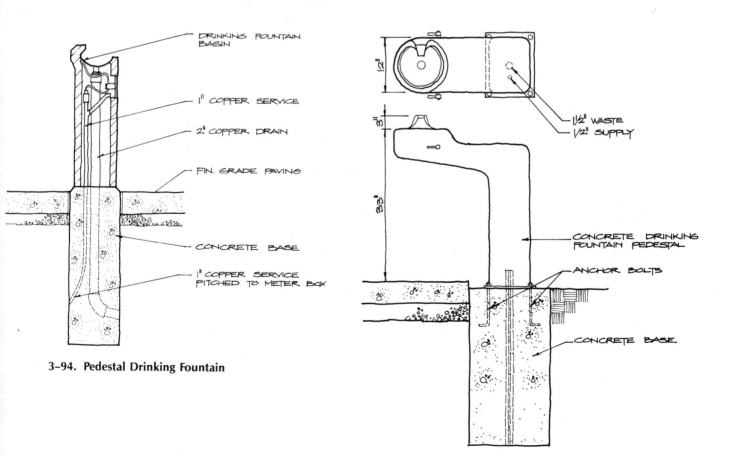

DRINKING FOUNTAIN BASIN

1" COPPER SERVICE

2" COPPER DRAIN

FIN. GRADE PAVING

CONCRETE BASE

1" COPPER SERVICE PITCHED TO METER BOX

3-94. Pedestal Drinking Fountain

12"

3"

33"

1½" WASTE

1½" SUPPLY

CONCRETE DRINKING FOUNTAIN PEDESTAL

ANCHOR BOLTS

CONCRETE BASE

3-95. Angled Drinking Fountain

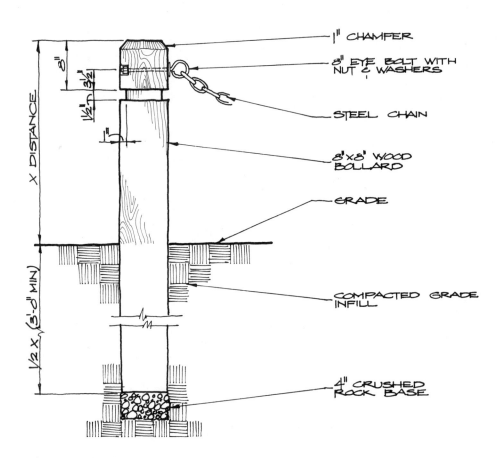

1" CHAMFER

8" EYE BOLT WITH NUT & WASHERS

STEEL CHAIN

8"x8" WOOD BOLLARD

GRADE

COMPACTED GRADE INFILL

4" CRUSHED ROCK BASE

3-96. Wood Bollard: Sculptured with Chain

3-97. Wood Bollards: Sculptured (Typical Designs)

C. CIRCULATION CONTROL

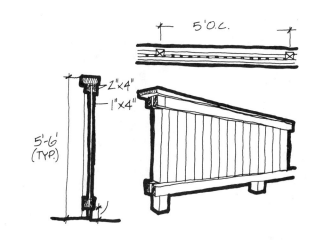

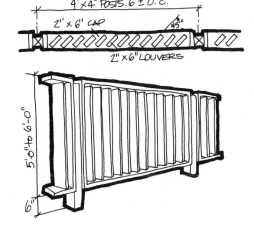

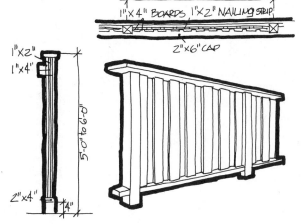

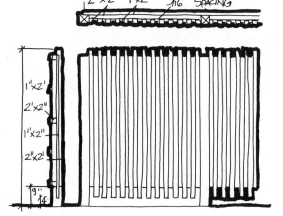

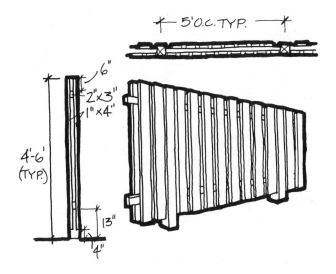

3–98. Fences/Decorative Screens: Concepts

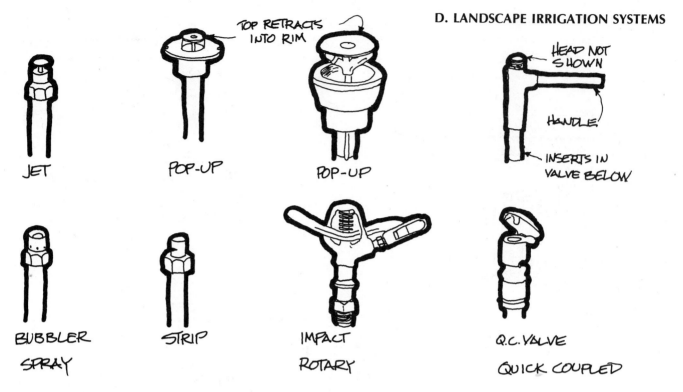

TOP RETRACTS INTO RIM

HEAD NOT SHOWN

HANDLE

INSERTS IN VALVE BELOW

JET

POP-UP

POP-UP

BUBBLER SPRAY

STRIP

IMPACT ROTARY

Q.C. VALVE QUICK COUPLED

3–99. Sprinkler Heads: Types

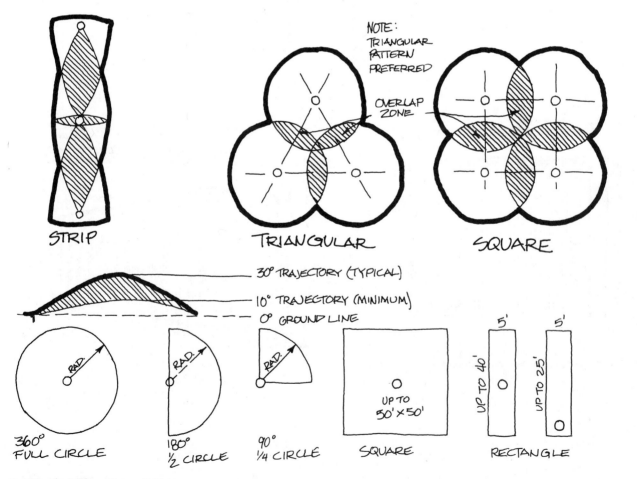

NOTE: TRIANGULAR PATTERN PREFERRED

OVERLAP ZONE

STRIP

TRIANGULAR

SQUARE

30° TRAJECTORY (TYPICAL)

10° TRAJECTORY (MINIMUM)

0° GROUND LINE

RAD.

RAD.

RAD.

360° FULL CIRCLE

180° ½ CIRCLE

90° ¼ CIRCLE

SQUARE
UP TO 50'×50'

5'
UP TO 40'

5'
UP TO 25'

RECTANGLE

3–100. Sprinklers: Spray Patterns

E. AREA LIGHTING

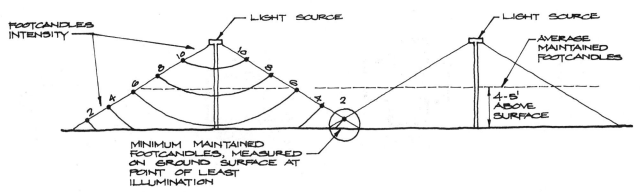

FOOTCANDLES INTENSITY

LIGHT SOURCE

LIGHT SOURCE

AVERAGE MAINTAINED FOOTCANDLES

4-5' ABOVE SURFACE

MINIMUM MAINTAINED FOOTCANDLES, MEASURED ON GROUND SURFACE AT POINT OF LEAST ILLUMINATION

3-105. Lighting Systems: Footcandle Measurement

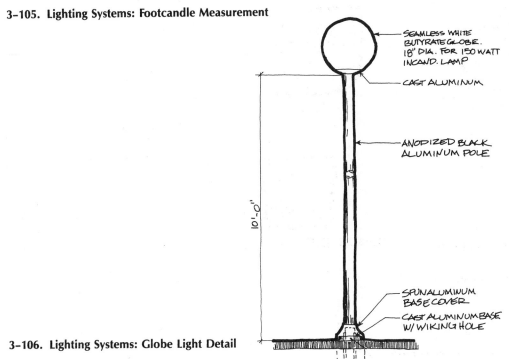

SEAMLESS WHITE BUTYRATE GLOBE. 18" DIA. FOR 150 WATT INCAND. LAMP

CAST ALUMINUM

ANODIZED BLACK ALUMINUM POLE

10'-0"

SPUN ALUMINUM BASE COVER

CAST ALUMINUM BASE W/ WIRING HOLE

3-106. Lighting Systems: Globe Light Detail

F. DRAINAGE SYSTEMS

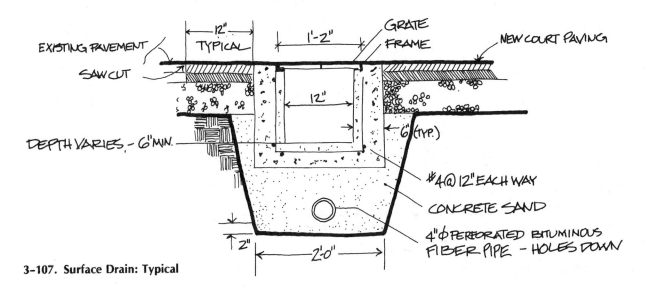

EXISTING PAVEMENT

SAW CUT

12" TYPICAL

1'-2"

GRATE FRAME

NEW COURT PAVING

12"

DEPTH VARIES, - 6" MIN.

6" (TYP.)

#4 @ 12" EACH WAY

CONCRETE SAND

4" Ø PERFORATED BITUMINOUS FIBER PIPE - HOLES DOWN

2"

2'-0"

3-107. Surface Drain: Typical

D. LANDSCAPE IRRIGATION SYSTEMS

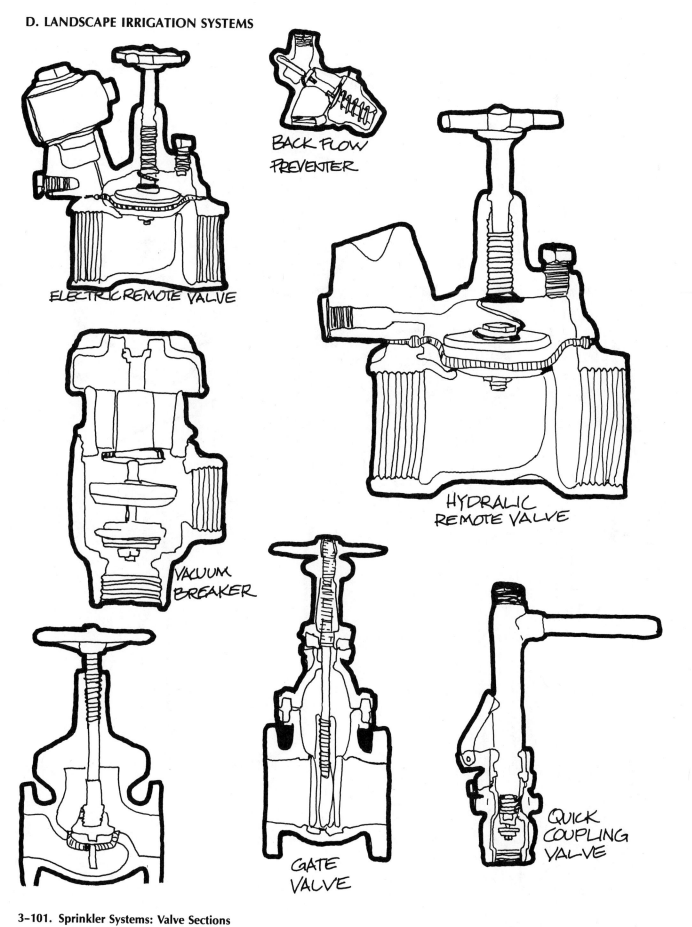

ELECTRIC REMOTE VALVE

BACK FLOW PREVENTER

HYDRALIC REMOTE VALVE

VACUUM BREAKER

GATE VALVE

QUICK COUPLING VALVE

3-101. Sprinkler Systems: Valve Sections

D. LANDSCAPE IRRIGATION SYSTEMS

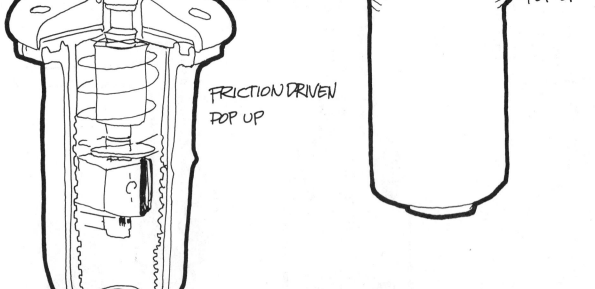

IMPACT DRIVE HEAD

IMPACT DRIVE POP UP

SHRUB HEAD

FIXED SPRAY HEAD

FIXED SPRAY POP UP

BUBBLER

GEAR DRIVEN POP UP

FRICTION DRIVEN POP UP

3-102. Sprinkler Systems: Head Sections

D. LANDSCAPE IRRIGATION SYSTEMS

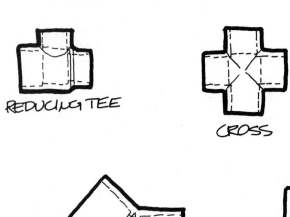

REDUCING TEE

CROSS

STANDARD TEE

SLIP TO THREAD ADAPTOR

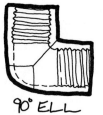

45° ELL

90° ELL

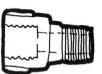

MALE REDUCER BUSHING

FEMALE REDUCER BUSHING

3-103. Sprinkler Systems: Pipe Connectors

E. AREA LIGHTING

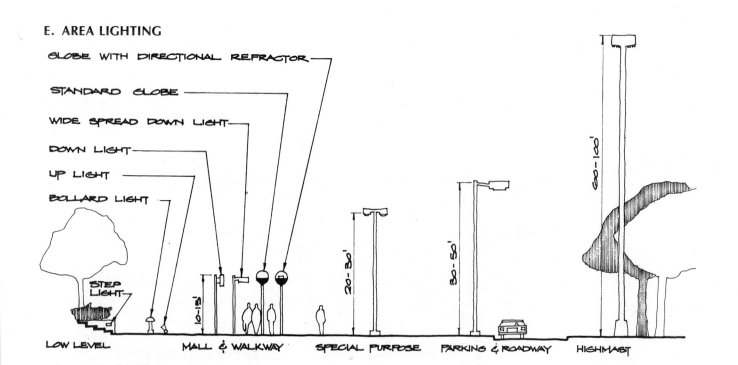

GLOBE WITH DIRECTIONAL REFRACTOR

STANDARD GLOBE

WIDE SPREAD DOWN LIGHT

DOWN LIGHT

UP LIGHT

BOLLARD LIGHT

STEP LIGHT

60-100'

20-30'

30-50'

10-15'

LOW LEVEL

MALL & WALKWAY

SPECIAL PURPOSE

PARKING & ROADWAY

HIGHMAST

3-104. Lighting Systems: Unit Types

F. DRAINAGE SYSTEMS

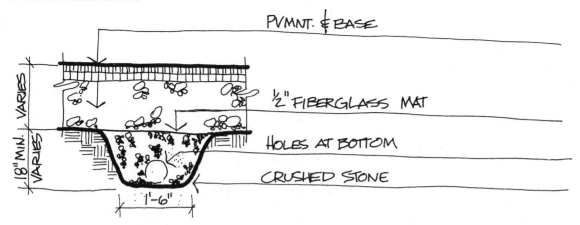

3-108. Surface Drain: Recreation Court

PVMNT. & BASE

½" FIBERGLASS MAT

HOLES AT BOTTOM

CRUSHED STONE

VARIES

18" MIN. VARIES

1'-6"

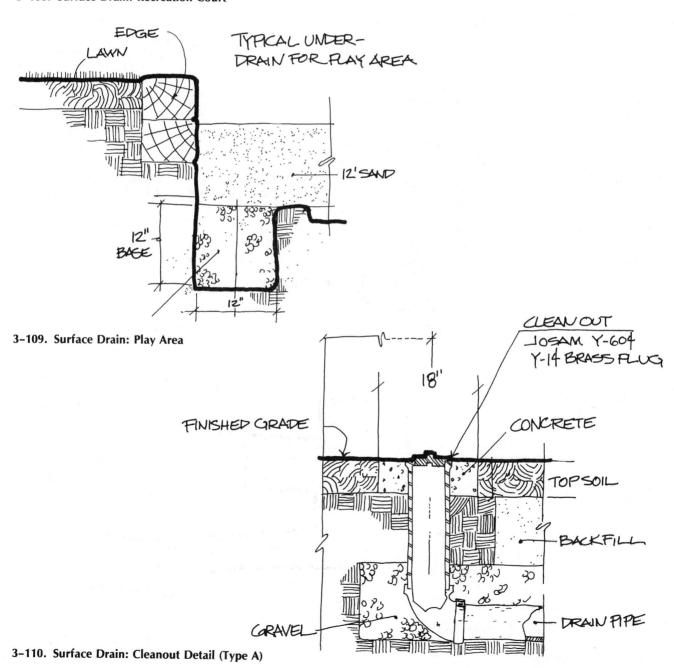

EDGE

LAWN

TYPICAL UNDER-
DRAIN FOR PLAY AREA

12' SAND

12"
BASE

12"

3-109. Surface Drain: Play Area

CLEAN OUT
JOSAM Y-604
Y-14 BRASS PLUG

18"

FINISHED GRADE

CONCRETE

TOPSOIL

BACKFILL

GRAVEL

DRAIN PIPE

3-110. Surface Drain: Cleanout Detail (Type A)

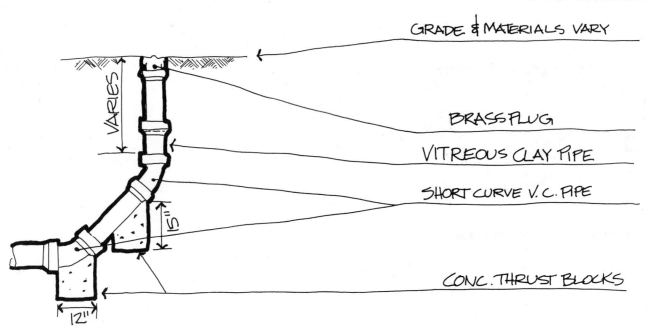

GRADE & MATERIALS VARY

BRASS PLUG

VITREOUS CLAY PIPE

SHORT CURVE V. C. PIPE

CONC. THRUST BLOCKS

VARIES

15"

12"

3–111. Surface Drain: Cleanout Detail (Type B)

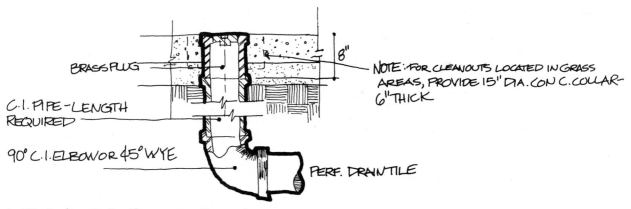

BRASS PLUG

C.I. PIPE-LENGTH REQUIRED

90° C.I. ELBOW OR 45° WYE

8"

NOTE: FOR CLEANOUTS LOCATED IN GRASS AREAS, PROVIDE 15" DIA. CONC. COLLAR-6" THICK

PERF. DRAINTILE

3–112. Surface Drain: Cleanout Detail (Type C)

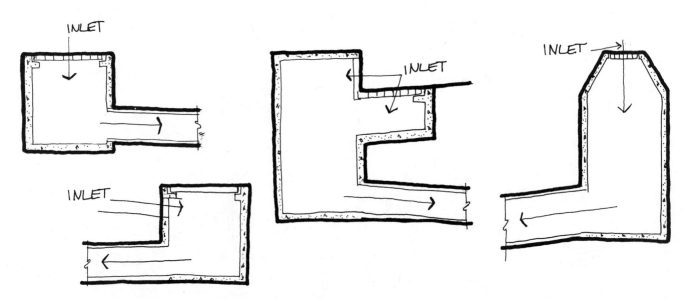

INLET

INLET

INLET

INLET

3–113. Catch Basin Types

F. DRAINAGE SYSTEMS

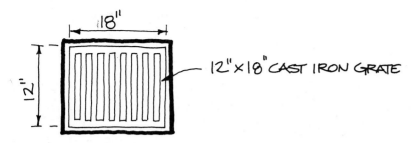

3-114. Cast Iron Grate

18"

12"

12" X 18" CAST IRON GRATE

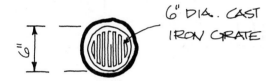

3-115. Cast Iron Site Drain (Typical)

6" DIA. CAST IRON GRATE

FINISH GRADE

6" DIA. CONCRETE PIPE

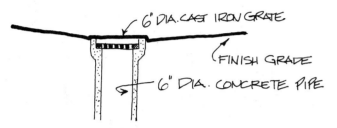

3-116. Cast Iron Site Drain Grate

6"

6" DIA. CAST IRON GRATE

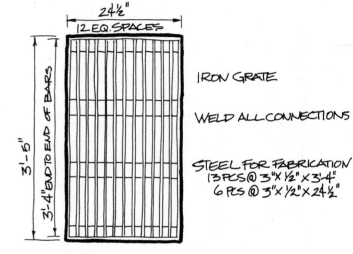

3-118. Catch Basin: Iron Grate (Typical)

24½"

12 EQ. SPACES

3'-5"

3'-4" END TO END OF BARS

IRON GRATE

WELD ALL CONNECTIONS

STEEL FOR FABRICATION
13 PCS @ 3"X ½" X 3'-4"
6 PCS @ 3"X ½"X 24½"

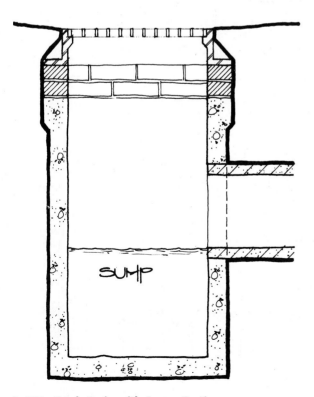

SUMP

3-117. Catch Basin with Sump: Section

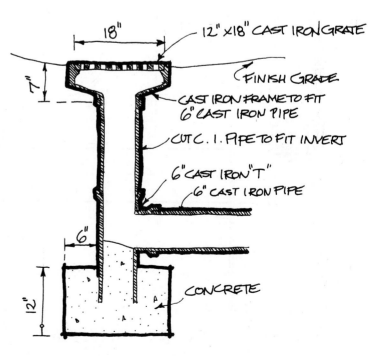

18"

7"

6"

12"

12" X 18" CAST IRON GRATE

FINISH GRADE

CAST IRON FRAME TO FIT
6" CAST IRON PIPE

CUT C. I. PIPE TO FIT INVERT

6" CAST IRON "T"
6" CAST IRON PIPE

CONCRETE

3-119. Catch Basin: Drain Inlet

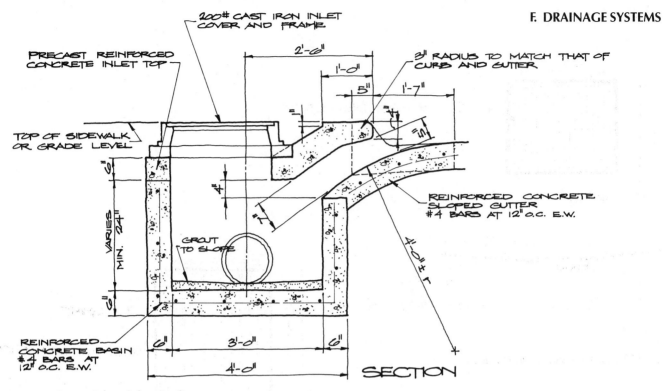

3–120. Storm Sewer Inlet: Section

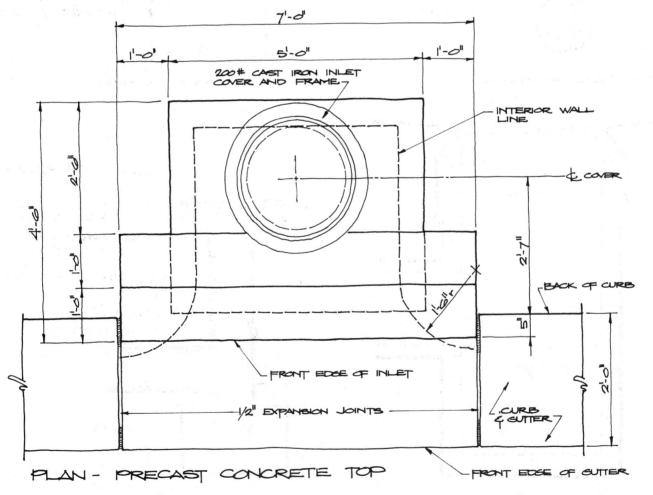

3–121. Storm Sewer Inlet: Plan

F. DRAINAGE SYSTEMS

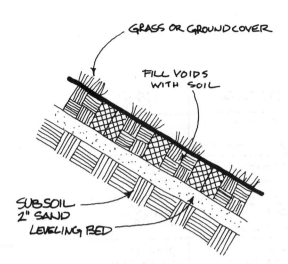

GRASS OR GROUNDCOVER

FILL VOIDS WITH SOIL

SUBSOIL
2" SAND
LEVELING BED

3-122. Erosion Control: Brick Pavers

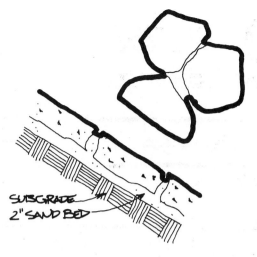

SUBGRADE
2" SAND BED

3-124. Erosion Control: Stone Pavers

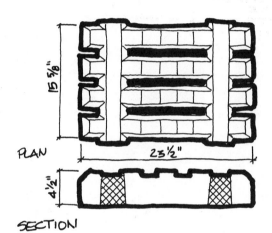

15 5/8"

PLAN

23 1/2"

4 1/2"

SECTION

3-123. Erosion Paver: Typical

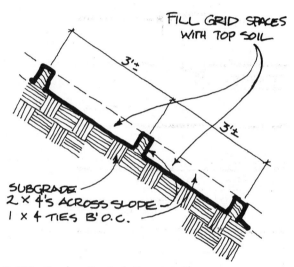

FILL GRID SPACES WITH TOP SOIL

3'±

3'±

SUBGRADE
2 x 4's ACROSS SLOPE
1 x 4 TIES 8' O.C.

3-125. Erosion Control: Concrete Pavers

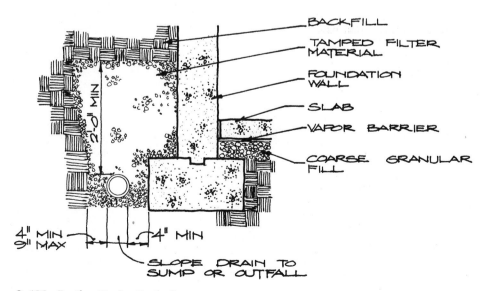

BACKFILL

TAMPED FILTER MATERIAL

FOUNDATION WALL

SLAB

VAPOR BARRIER

COARSE GRANULAR FILL

2'-0" MIN

4" MIN
9" MAX

4" MIN

SLOPE DRAIN TO SUMP OR OUTFALL

3-126. Footing Drain: Typical

PERFORATED 4 TO 6 ROWS OF 1/4" HOLES

DRAIN SECTION

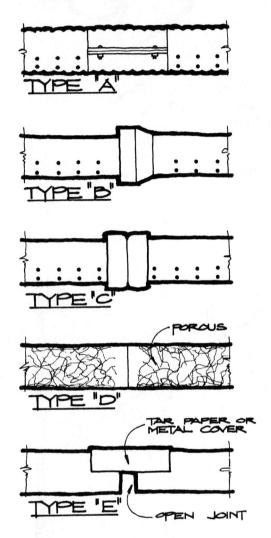

TYPE "A"

TYPE "B"

TYPE "C"

POROUS

TYPE "D"

TAR PAPER OR METAL COVER

TYPE "E"

OPEN JOINT

DRAIN TYPE	MATERIAL	JOINT
A	CORRUGATED METAL FLEXIBLE PLASTIC	COLLARS
B	CONCRETE CLAY TILE	BELL AND SPIGOT
C	ASBESTOS CEMENT RIGID PLASTIC	SLEEVE SOCKET
D	POROUS CONCRETE	TONGUE & GROOVE
E	UNPERFORATED CLAY TILE CONCRETE PLASTIC	BUTT

3–127. Subsurface Drain Pipes: Typical

appendixes

A: STEEL WIRE SIZES AND GAUGES

A. S. & W Gauge	DIAMETER		WEIGHT PER FOOT
	in	cm	lb.
00	0.3310	0.8407	0.2922
0	0.3065	0.7785	0.2506
1	0.2830	0.7188	0.2136
2	0.2625	0.6668	0.1829
- (¼")	0.2500	0.6350	0.1667
3	0.2437	0.6190	0.1584
4	0.2253	0.5723	0.1354
5	0.2070	0.5258	0.1143
6	0.1920	0.4877	0.0983
7	0.1770	0.4496	0.0836
8	0.1620	0.4115	0.0700
9	0.1483	0.3767	0.0587
10	0.1350	0.3429	0.0486
11(⅛")	0.1250	0.3175	0.0387
12	0.1055	0.2680	0.0297
13	0.0915	0.2324	0.0223
14	0.0800	0.2032	0.0171
15	0.0720	0.1838	0.0138
16(1/16)"	0.0625	0.1583	0.0104

Drainage systems are provided to intercept and dispose of the water flow to the degree necessary to prevent damage to an area facility from seepage and runoff. Each of these two sources requires its own method of control and competent engineering design to ensure a degree of protection commensurate with the hazard potential.

B: MATERIALS WEIGHTS

Materials		
MASONRY		PSF
4" Brickwork		40
4" Concrete Block, Heavy		34
4" Concrete Block, Lightweight		22
4" Concrete Brick, Heavy		46
4" Concrete Brick, Lightweight		33
6" Concrete Block, Heavy		50
6" Concrete Block, Lightweight		31
8" Concrete Block, Heavy		55
8" Concrete Block, Lightweight		35
12" Concrete Block, Heavy		85
12" Concrete Block, Lightweight		55
CONCRETE		PCF
Plain Concrete	Cinder	108
	Expanded Clay	90
	Stone and Cast Stone	144
Reinforced	Cinder	111
Concrete	Slag	138
	Stone	150
CONCRETE, LIGHTWEIGHT		PSF
Cinder Concrete		60
Expanded Clay Concrete		85–100
Perlite Concrete		35–50
Vermiculite Concrete		25–60
LIQUIDS AND FUELS		PCF
Ice		57.2
Gasoline		75
Snow		8
Water, Fresh		62.4
METALS		PCF
Aluminum		165
Brass		534
Bronze, Statuary		509
Gold, Solid		1,205
Iron, Wrought		480
SOIL, SAND, AND GRAVEL		PCF
Ashes		40–50
Clay, Wet		110
Clay, Dry		63
Earth, Friable		76
Earth, Dry		95
Earth, Packed		96
Sand/Gravel, Loose		90–105
Silt, Moist		96

C: DESIRABLE SLOPES

	PERCENT SLOPE	
	Maximum	Minimum
Streets, Service Drives, and Parking Areas	8.00	0.50[a]
Collector and Approach Walks	10.00[b]	0.50
Entrance Walks	4.00[c]	1.00
Ramps	15.00	—
Paved Play and Sitting Areas	2.00	0.50
Paved Laundry Yard	5.00	0.50
Paved Gutters	—	0.50
Project Lawn Areas	25.00[d]	1.00
Tenant Yards	10.00	1.00
Grassed Playgrounds	4.00	0.50
Swales	10.00[e]	1.00[f]
Grassed Banks	4 to 1 Slope	
Planted Banks	2 to 1 Slope (3 to 1 Preferable)	

[a]0.75% for dished section.
[b]Less where icy conditions may occur frequently.
[c]Slopes up to 10% or more are satisfactory provided walks are long enough to employ a curved profile, so that a slope not exceeding 4% can be used adjoining the building platform. See also preceding note.
[d]Steepest grade recommended for power mower.
[e]Less for drainage areas of more than approximately ½ acre.
[f]2% preferable in all cases, particularly so where swales cross walks.

D: STANDARD REINFORCING BAR SIZES

Bar Size Designation (#)	WEIGHT PER FOOT		DIAMETER	
	lb.	kg	in.	cm
3	0.376	0.171	0.375	0.953
4	0.6668	0.303	0.500	1.270
5	1.043	0.473	0.625	1.588
6	1.502	0.681	0.750	1.905
7	2.044	0.927	0.875	2.223
8	2.670	1.211	1.000	2.540
9	3.400	1.542	1.128	2.865
10	4.303	1.952	1.270	3.226
11	5.313	2.410	1.410	3.581
14	7.650	3.470	1.693	4.300
18	13.600	6.169	2.257	5.733

Concrete Reinforcing Bars: Standard Sizes

Bar No.	Diameter
2	¼″ (0.635 cm)
3	⅜″ (0.952 cm)
4	½″ (1.27 cm)
5	⅝″ (1.59 cm)
6	¾″ (1.90 cm)
7	⅞″ (2.22 cm)
8	1″ (2.54 cm)

E: DEPTH AND SPACING OF SUBDRAINS FOR VARIOUS SOIL CLASSES

Soil Classes	PERCENTAGE OF SOIL SEPARATES			Depth of Bottom of Drain (ft.)	Distance Between Subdrains (ft.)
	Sand	Silt	Clay		
Sand	80–100	0–20	0–20	3–4	150–300
				2–3	100–150
Sandy Loam	50–80	0–50	0–20	3–4	100–150
				2–3	85–100
Loam	30–50	30–50	0–20	3–4	85–100
				2–3	75–85
Silt Loam	0–50	50–100	0–20	3–4	75–85
				2–3	65–75
Sandy Clay Loam	50–80	0–30	20–30	3–4	65–75
				2–3	55–65
Clay Loam	20–50	20–50	20–30	3–4	55–65
				2–3	45–65
Silty Clay Loam	0–30	50–80	20–30	3–4	45–55
				2–3	40–45
Sandy Clay	50–70	0–20	30–50	3–4	40–45
				2–3	35–40
Silty Clay	0–20	50–70	30–50	3–4	35–40
				2–3	30–35
Clay	0–50	0–50	30–100	3–4	30–35
				2–3	25–30

F: COMMON NAILS*

Length	Penny	Gauge	Diameter of Head	No. of Nails per Pound
1	2	15	¹¹⁄₆₄	847
1¼	3	14	¹³⁄₆₄	543
1½	4	12½	¼	296
1¾	5	12½	¼	254
2	6	11½	¹⁷⁄₆₄	167
2¼	7	11½	¹⁷⁄₆₄	150
2½	8	10¼	⁹⁄₃₂	101
2¾	9	10¼	⁹⁄₃₂	92.1
3	10	9	⁵⁄₁₆	66
3¼	12	9	⁵⁄₁₆	66.1
3½	16	8	¹¹⁄₃₂	47.4
4	20	6	¹³⁄₃₂	29.7
4½	30	5	⁷⁄₁₆	22.7
5	40	4	¹⁵⁄₃₂	17.3
5½	50	3	½	13.5
6	60	2	¹⁷⁄₃₂	10.7

*See figures F–1 to F–3.

F–1. Common Nail Measurements

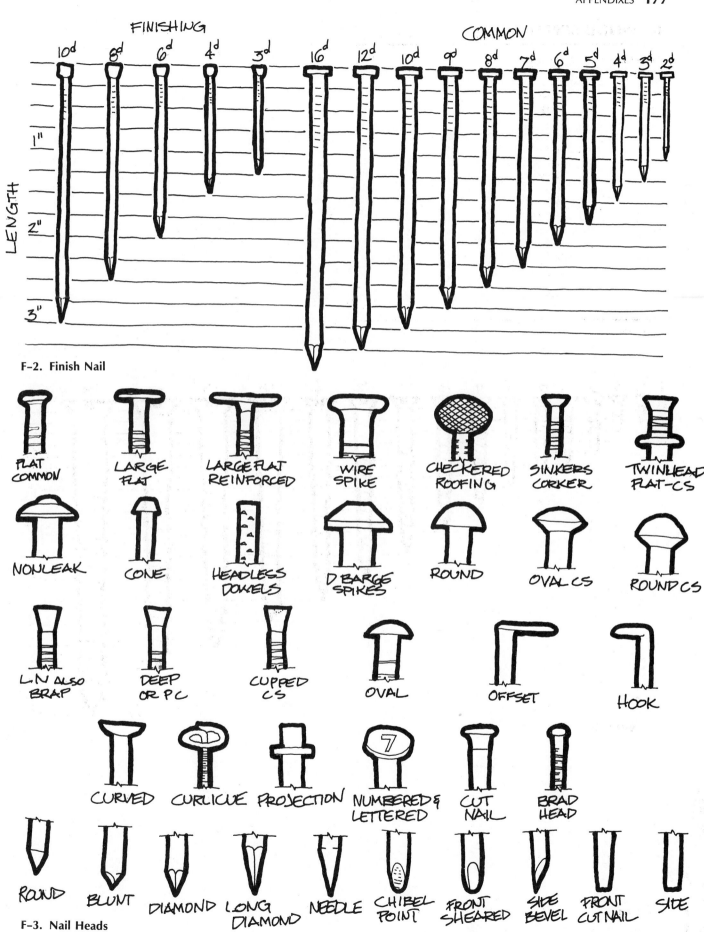

FINISHING

COMMON

LENGTH

1"

2"

3"

10ᵈ 8ᵈ 6ᵈ 4ᵈ 3ᵈ 16ᵈ 12ᵈ 10ᵈ 9ᵈ 8ᵈ 7ᵈ 6ᵈ 5ᵈ 4ᵈ 3ᵈ 2ᵈ

F–2. Finish Nail

PLAT COMMON
LARGE FLAT
LARGE FLAT REINFORCED
WIRE SPIKE
CHECKERED ROOFING
SINKERS CORKER
TWINHEAD FLAT-CS

NONLEAK
CONE
HEADLESS DOWELS
D BARGE SPIKES
ROUND
OVAL CS
ROUND CS

L.N ALSO BRAP
DEEP OR P.C
CUPPED CS
OVAL
OFFSET
HOOK

CURVED
CURLICUE
PROJECTION
NUMBERED & LETTERED
CUT NAIL
BRAD HEAD

ROUND
BLUNT
DIAMOND
LONG DIAMOND
NEEDLE
CHIBEL POINT
FRONT SHEARED
SIDE BEVEL
FRONT CUT NAIL
SIDE

F–3. Nail Heads

G: WOOD SCREWS*

Diameter (in.)	Length (in.)
0	¼–⅜
1	¼–½
2	¼–¾
3	¼–1
4	¼–1½
5	⅜–1½
6	⅜–2½
7	⅜–2½
8	⅜–3
9	½–3
10	½–3½
11	⅝–3½
12	⅝–4
14	¾–5
16	1–5
18	1¼–5
20	1½–5
24	3–5

*See figure G–1.

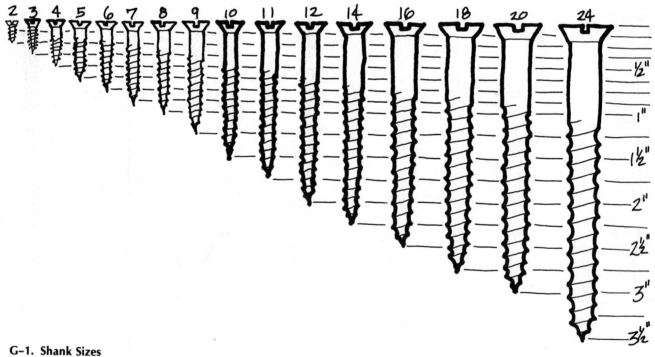

G–1. Shank Sizes

H: TURNBUCKLES AND BOLTS*

Diameter	¼″	⁵⁄₁₆″	⅜″	½″	⅝″	¾″	⅞″	1″
A	4	4¼	6	6	6	6	6	6
				9	9	9		
				12	12	12	12	12
B	⁷⁄₁₆	½	⁹⁄₁₆	¾	²⁹⁄₃₂	1¹⁄₁₆	1⁷⁄₃₂	1⅜
C	¾	⅞	³¹⁄₃₂	1⁷⁄₃₂	1½	1²³⁄₃₂	1⅞	2¹⁄₃₂

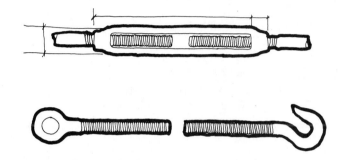

H–1. Turnbuckles

LAG BOLT	
Diameter (in.)	Length (in.)
¼	1–6
⁵⁄₁₆	1–10
⅜	1–12
⁷⁄₁₆	1–12
½	1–12
⅝	1½–16
¾	1½–16
⅞	2–16
1	2–16

CARRIAGE	
Diameter (in.)	Length (in.)
¼	¾–8
⁵⁄₁₆	¾–8
⅜	3¾–12
⁷⁄₁₆	1–12
½	1–20
⁹⁄₁₆	1–20
⅝	1–20
¾	1–20

MACHINE	
Diameter (in.)	Length (in.)
¼	½–8
⁵⁄₁₆	½–8
⅜	¾–12
⁷⁄₁₆	¾–12
½	¾–24
⁹⁄₁₆	1–30
⅝	1–30
¾	1–30
⅞	1½–30
1	1½–30

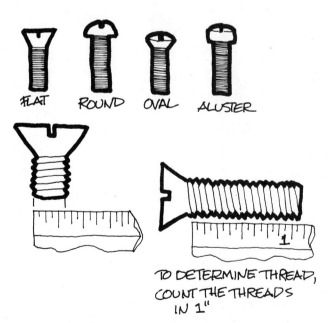

FLAT ROUND OVAL ALUSTER

TO DETERMINE THREAD, COUNT THE THREADS IN 1″

H–2. Head Styles

*See figures H–1 and H–2.

I: CONVERSION FACTORS/TABLES

SURFACE MEASURE

1 inch	=	2.54 centimeters
1 foot	=	.3048 meter
1 yard	=	.9144 meter
1 kilometer	=	.6214 mile
1 square inch	=	6.452 square centimeters
1 square foot	=	.093 square meter

1 centimeter	=	.3937 inch
1 decimeter	=	.3281 foot
1 meter	=	1.094 yards
1 mile	=	1.609 kilometers
1 square yard	=	0.836 square meter
1 square mile	=	2.590 square kilometers

CUBIC MEASURE

1 cubic meter	=	1,000 cubic decimeters
1 cubic decimeter	=	100 cubic centimeters
1 cubic centimeter	=	1,000 cubic millimeters
1 cubic foot	=	1,728 cubic inches
	=	0.037 cubic yards
	=	7.48 gallons
	=	28.32 liters
1 cubic yard	=	27 cubic feet
	=	46,656 cubic inches
	=	202 gallons

To convert cubic feet to gallons:
  # cubic feet × 7.48
To convert gallons to cubic feet:
  # gallons × 0.1337

SQUARE MEASURE

1 square foot	=	144 square inches
1 square yard	=	1,296 square inches
	=	9 square feet
1 square mile	=	640 acres
1 acre	=	43,560 square feet
	=	4,840 square yards

ANGULAR MEASURE

60 seconds	=	1 minute
60 minutes	=	1 degree
360 degrees	=	1 circle
60 degrees	=	1 sextant
90 degrees	=	1 quadrant

LAND AND SEA MEASURE
U. S. Land Measure*

1 township	=	36 square miles
1 square mile	=	1 section or 640 acres
1 acre	=	43,560 square feet or 10 square chains
1 square chain	=	16 square poles
1 square pole	=	625 square links

Metric Land Measure

1 square kilometer	=	100 hectares
1 hectare	=	100 acres
1 acre	=	100 centiares
1 centiare	=	1 square meter

Chain Measure (Gunter's, Surveyors')*

1 mile	=	80 chains
1 furlong	=	10 chains
1 chain	=	100 links or 4 rods
1 rod	=	16½ feet
1 link	=	0.66 feet or 7.92 inches

Nautical Measure

1 degree longitude at equator	=	60 nautical miles
1 nautical mile	=	1.15078 statute miles
1 fathom	=	6 feet

*Chains, poles, rods, and links are no longer used in land surveys. Acres and feet, and decimals thereof, have been the units of choice since the 1930s. Today, all land measure is being converted to the metric system as rapidly as possible.

MISCELLANEOUS AREA AND VOLUME FORMULAS
Areas of Plane Geometric Figures

1. Area of a triangle = ½ base × altitude (altitude measured perpendicular to the side selected as the base).

2. Area of an irregular quadrilateral = sum of areas of two triangles formed by either diagonal.

3. Area of a parallelogram = length of any side × altitude (as measured perpendicular to the selected side).

4. Area of a regular polygon = ½ sum of all sides × radius of inscribed circle.

5. Area of a circle = $\pi \times r^2$.

6. Area of a sector of a circle = $\alpha°/360° \times \pi r^2$ or arc length × $r/2$.

7. Area of a segment of a circle = area of sector less area of triangle, or $r^2/2$ ($\alpha°/180° - \sin \alpha$).

8. Area of an ellipse = 0.7854 × long axis × short axis.

9. Area of a parabola = base × ⅔ altitude.

10. Area of pavement at each curb return = $0.2146r^2$.

VOLUMES OF GEOMETRICAL SOLIDS

1. Volume of a cylinder, cube, or prism = area of base × altitude (as measured perpendicularly from base to center of top area if bases are not parallel).

2. Volume of a cone or pyramid = area of base × ⅓ altitude.

3. Volume of a sphere = ⅘ πr^3 or $0.5236D^3$.

4. Volume of a sector of a sphere = $2/3\pi r^2 b$.

5. Volume of a sector of a sphere = volume of sector of sphere less volume of cone, of ⅓πb^2 × $(3r - b)$.

6. Volume of an ellipsoid = $\pi abc/6$.

7. Surface area of a cylinder = $2\pi r^2 + \pi D$ × altitude (includes top and bottom).

8. Surface area of a pyramid = sum of areas of all sides, or perimeter of base × ½ altitude.

9. Surface area of a cone = perimeter of base × ½ altitude.

10. Surface area of a sphere = $4\pi r^2$.

11. Surface area of a sector of a sphere = ½$\pi r(4b + c)$ (includes surface area of cone plus surface area of sphere).

12. Surface area of a segment of a sphere = $2\pi rb$ (does not include area of circular base).

Given	Sought	Formula
A,B,a	b,c	$b = \dfrac{a}{\sin A} = \sin B$ $c = \dfrac{a}{\sin A}\sin(A+B)$
A,B,b	a,c	$a = b\dfrac{\sin A}{\sin B}$ $c = b\dfrac{\sin(A+B)}{\sin B}$
A,B,c	a,b	$a = c\dfrac{\sin A}{\sin(A+B)}$ $b = c\dfrac{\sin B}{\sin(A+B)}$
a,b,c	A	$\sin\frac{A}{2} = \sqrt{\dfrac{(s-b)\,(s-c)}{bc}}$
		$\cos\frac{A}{2} = \sqrt{\dfrac{s\,(s-a)}{bc}}$
		$\tan\frac{A}{2} = \sqrt{\dfrac{(s-b)\,(s-c)}{s(s-a)}}$
		$\sin A = \dfrac{2\sqrt{s(s-a)\,(s-b)\,(s-c)}}{bc}$
a,b,c	d,c	$d = \dfrac{b^2+c^2+a^2}{2b}$ $c = \dfrac{a^2+b^2-c^2}{2b}$
	Area	Area $= \sqrt{s(s-a)\,(s-b)\,(s-c)}$
A,B,C,a	Area	Area $= \dfrac{a^2 = \sin B\bullet\sin C}{2\sin A}$
C,a,b	Area	Area $= \dfrac{ab\bullet\sin C}{2}$

MISCELLANEOUS TRIGONOMETRIC FORMULAS
Right Triangles

1. $\sin \alpha = \dfrac{y}{r}$

2. $\cos \alpha = \dfrac{x}{r}$

3. $\tan \alpha = \dfrac{y}{x}$

4. $\csc \alpha = \dfrac{r}{y}$

5. $\sec \alpha = \dfrac{r}{x}$

6. $\cot \alpha = \dfrac{x}{y}$

7. $\csc \alpha = \dfrac{1}{\sin \alpha}$

8. $\sec \alpha = \dfrac{1}{\sin \alpha}$

9. $\cot \alpha = \dfrac{1}{\tan \alpha}\dfrac{\cos \alpha}{\sin \alpha}$

10. $\tan \alpha = \dfrac{\sin \alpha}{\cos \alpha}$

11. $\text{vers } \alpha = \dfrac{CD}{r} = 1 - \cos \alpha$

12. $\text{exsec } \alpha = \dfrac{EB}{x} = \sec \alpha - 1$

13. $r = \dfrac{y}{\sin \alpha} = \dfrac{x}{\cos \alpha}$

14. $x = r \bullet \cos \alpha = y \bullet \cot \alpha$

15. $y = r \bullet \sin \alpha = x \bullet \tan \alpha$

16. $EB = x \bullet \text{exsec } \alpha$

17. $CD = r \bullet \text{vers } \alpha$

Oblique Triangles

$s = \dfrac{a + b + c}{2}$

FLUID MEASURE

(Milliliters and cubic centimeters are equivalent, but it is customary to use milliliters for liquids.)

1 cubic inch = 16.39 milliliters
1 fluid ounce = 29.6 milliliters
1 cup = 237 milliliters
1 pint = 473 milliliters
1 quart = 946 milliliters
 = .946 liters
1 gallon = 3,785 milliliters
 = 3.785 liters

Formula = Fluid ounces × 29.5735295625
     = milliliters

LINEAR MEASURE

FEET	CENTIMETERS	METERS
1	30.48	.3048
2	61	.61
3	91	.91
4	122	1.22
5	152	1.52
6	183	1.83
7	213	2.13
8	244	2.44
9	274	2.74
10	305	3.05
50	1,524	15.24
100	3,048	30.48

Formula: meters × 3.2808 = feet
1 kilometer = 3280.8398 feet = .621371 miles

INCHES	CENTIMETERS
1	2.54
2	5.1
3	7.6
4	10.2
5	12.7
6	15.2
7	17.8
8	20.3
9	22.9
10	25.4
11	27.9
12	30.5

INCHES	MILLIMETERS
1/16	1.5875
1/8	3.2
3/16	4.8
1/4	6.35
5/16	7.9
3/8	9.5
7/16	11.1
1/2	12.7
9/16	14.3
5/8	15.9
11/16	17.5
3/4	19.05
13/16	20.6
7/8	22.2
15/16	23.8
1	25.4

Feet to Meters (1 ft. = 0.3048 m)

Feet	0	1
1	—	0.305
10	3.048	3.353
20	6.096	6.401
30	9.144	9.449
40	12.192	12.497
50	15.240	15.545
60	18.288	18.593
70	21.336	21.641
80	24.384	24.689
90	27.432	27.737
100	30.480	30.785

Feet and Inches to Millimeters (1 ft. = 304.8 mm; 1 in. = 25.4 mm)

Feet	0	1
1	—	305
10	3,048	3,353
20	6,096	6,401
30	9,144	9,449
40	12,192	12,497
50	15,240	15,545
60	18,288	18,593
70	21,336	21,641
80	24,384	24,689
90	27,432	27,737
100	30,480	30,785

Decimals of an Inch

Fraction	Decimal	Fraction	Decimal
1/64	0.015625	33/64	0.515625
1/32	0.03125	17/32	0.53125
3/64	0.046875	35/64	0.546875
1/16	0.0625	9/16	0.5625
5/64	0.078125	37/64	0.578125
3/32	0.09375	19/32	0.59375
7/64	0.109375	39/64	0.609375
1/8	0.125	5/8	0.625
9/64	0.140625	41/64	0.640625
5/32	0.15625	21/32	0.65625
11/64	0.171875	43/64	0.671875
3/16	0.1875	11/16	0.6875
13/64	0.203125	45/64	0.703125
7/32	0.21875	23/32	0.17875
15/64	0.234375	47/64	0.734375
1/4	0.250	3/4	0.750
17/64	0.265625	49/64	0.765625
9/32	0.28125	25/32	0.78125
19/64	0.296875	51/64	0.796875
5/16	0.3125	13/16	0.8125
21/64	0.328125	53/64	0.828125
11/32	0.34375	27/32	0.84375
23/64	0.359375	55/64	0.859375
3/8	0.375	7/8	0.875
25/64	0.390625	57/64	0.890625
13/32	0.40625	29/32	0.90625
27/64	0.421875	59/64	0.921875
7/16	0.4375	15/16	0.9375
29/64	0.453125	61/64	0.953125
15/32	0.46875	31/32	0.96875
31/64	0.484375	63/64	0.984375
1/2	0.500	1	1.0000

Acres to Hectares (1 Acre = 0.4046856 hectare)

Acres	Hectares
1	0.404
100	40.47
200	80.94
300	121.41
400	161.87
500	202.34

Drawing Scales

Metric	Ratio	Scale
1:5	1:4	3″ = 1′0″
1:10	1:18	1½″ = 1′0″
	1:12	1″ = 1′0″
1:20	1:16	¾″ = 1′0″
	1:24	½″ = 1′0″
1:50	1:48	¼″ = 1′0″
1:100	1:96	⅛″ = 1′0″
1:500	1:384	1/32″ = 1′0″
	1:480	1″ = 40′0″
	1:600	1″ = 50′0″
1:1000	1:960	1″ = 80′0″
	1:1200	1″ = 100′0″
1:2000	1:2400	1″ = 200′0″
1:5000	1:4800	1″ = 400′0″
	1:6000	1″ = 500′0″
1:10,000	1:10,560	6″ = 1 mile
	1:12,000	1″ = 1000′0″
1:25,000	1:21,120	3″ = 1 mile
	1:24,000	1″ = 2000′0″
1:50,000	1:63,360	1″ = 1 mile
1:100,000	1:126,720	½″ = 1 mile

Slope Ratios

Ratio Y/X	Angle	Percentage
1:100	0°34′	1
1:50	1°09′	2
1:25	2°17′	4
1:20	2°52′	5
1:15	3°48′	6.7
1:10	5°54′	10
1:5	11°19′	20
1:3	18°26′	33.3
1:2	26°34′	50
1:1	45°	100
2:1	63°26′	200
3:1	71°34′	300
4:1	75°58′	400
5:1	78°42′	500

Decimals of a Foot

Fraction	Decimal	Fraction	Decimal	Fraction	Decimal
1/16	0.0052	4 1/16	0.3385	8 1/16	0.6719
1/8	0.0104	4 1/8	0.3438	8 1/8	0.6771
3/16	0.0156	4 3/16	0.3490	8 3/16	0.6823
1/4	0.0208	4 1/4	0.3542	8 1/4	0.6875
5/16	0.0260	4 5/16	0.3594	8 5/16	0.6927
3/8	0.0313	4 3/8	0.3646	8 3/8	0.6979
7/16	0.0365	4 7/16	0.3750	8 7/16	0.7031
1/2	0.0417	4 1/2	0.3750	8 1/2	0.7083
9/16	0.0469	4 9/16	0.3802	8 9/16	0.7135
5/8	0.0521	4 5/8	0.3854	8 5/8	0.7188
11/16	0.0573	4 11/16	0.3906	8 11/16	0.7240
3/4	0.0625	4 3/4	0.3958	8 3/4	0.7292
13/16	0.0677	4 13/16	0.4010	8 13/16	0.7344
7/8	0.0729	4 7/8	0.4063	8 7/8	0.7396
15/16	0.0781	4 15/16	0.4115	8 15/16	0.7448
1	0.0833	5	0.4167	9	0.7500
1 1/16	0.0885	5 1/16	0.4219	9 1/16	0.7552
1 1/8	0.0938	5 1/8	0.4271	9 1/8	0.7604
1 3/16	0.0990	5 3/16	0.4323	9 3/16	0.7656
1 1/4	0.1042	5 1/4	0.4375	9 1/4	0.7708
1 5/16	0.1094	5 5/16	0.4427	9 5/16	0.7760
1 3/8	0.1146	5 3/8	0.4479	9 3/8	0.7813
1 7/16	0.1198	5 7/16	0.4531	9 7/16	0.7865
1 1/2	0.1250	5 1/2	0.4583	9 1/2	0.7917
1 9/16	0.1302	5 9/16	0.4635	9 9/16	0.7969
1 5/8	0.1354	5 5/8	0.4688	9 5/8	0.8021
1 11/16	0.1406	5 11/16	0.4740	9 11/16	0.8073
1 3/4	0.1458	5 3/4	0.4792	9 3/4	0.8125
1 13/16	0.1510	5 13/16	0.4844	9 13/16	0.8177
1 7/8	0.1563	5 7/8	0.4896	9 7/8	0.8229
1 15/16	0.1615	5 15/16	0.4948	9 15/16	0.8281
2	0.1667	6	0.5000	10	0.8333
2 1/16	0.1719	6 1/16	0.5052	10 1/16	0.8385
2 1/8	0.1771	6 1/8	0.5104	10 1/8	0.8438
2 3/16	0.1823	6 3/16	0.5156	10 3/16	0.8490
2 1/4	0.1875	6 1/4	0.5208	10 1/4	0.8542
2 5/16	0.1927	6 5/16	0.5260	10 5/16	0.8594
2 3/8	0.1979	6 3/8	0.5313	10 3/8	0.8646
2 7/16	0.2031	6 7/16	0.5365	10 7/16	0.8698
2 1/2	0.2083	6 1/2	0.5417	10 1/2	0.8750
2 9/16	0.2135	6 9/16	0.5469	10 9/16	0.8802
2 5/8	0.2188	6 5/8	0.5521	10 5/8	0.8854
2 11/16	0.2240	6 11/16	0.5573	10 11/16	0.8906
2 3/4	0.2292	6 3/4	0.5625	10 3/4	0.8958
2 13/16	0.2344	6 13/16	0.5677	10 13/16	0.9010
2 7/8	0.2396	6 7/8	0.5729	10 7/8	0.9063
2 15/16	0.2448	6 15/16	0.5781	10 15/16	0.9115
3	0.2500	7	0.5833	11	0.9167
3 1/16	0.2552	7 1/16	0.5885	11 1/16	0.9219
3 1/8	0.2604	7 1/8	0.5938	11 1/8	0.9271

Decimals of a Foot (continued)

Fraction	Decimal	Fraction	Decimal	Fraction	Decimal
3 3/16	0.2656	7 3/16	0.5990	11 3/16	0.9323
3 1/4	0.2708	7 1/4	0.6042	11 1/4	0.9375
3 5/16	0.2760	7 5/16	0.6094	11 5/16	0.9427
3 3/8	0.2813	7 3/8	0.6146	11 3/8	0.9479
3 7/16	0.2865	7 7/16	0.6198	11 7/8	0.9531
3 1/2	0.2917	7 1/2	0.6250	11 1/2	0.9583
3 9/16	0.2969	7 9/16	0.6302	11 9/16	0.9635
3 5/8	0.3021	7 5/8	0.6354	11 5/8	0.9688
3 11/16	0.3073	7 11/16	0.6406	11 11/16	0.9740
3 3/4	0.3125	7 3/4	0.6458	11 3/4	0.9792
3 13/16	0.3177	7 13/16	0.6510	11 13/16	0.9844
3 7/8	0.3229	7 7/8	0.6563	11 7/8	0.9896
3 15/16	0.3281	7 15/16	0.6615	11 15/16	0.9948
4	0.333	8	0.6667	12	1.0000

Gallons to Liters (1 Gal. [U.S.] = 3.78541 L)

Gallons	Liters
1	3.785
10	37.85
20	75.71
30	113.56
40	151.42
50	189.27

Cubic Feet to Cubic Meters (1 cu. ft. = 0.0283 cu. m.)

Cubic Feet	Cubic Meters
1	0.0283
10	0.283
20	0.566
30	0.850
40	1.133
50	1.416
60	1.699
70	1.982
80	2.265
90	2.549
100	2.832

Miles to Kilometers (1 mile = 1.609344 km.)

Miles	Kilometers
1	1.609
10	16.093
20	32.187
30	48.280
40	64.374
50	80.467
60	96.561
70	112.654
80	128.748
90	144.841
100	160.934

Square Feet to Square Meters
(1 sq. ft. = 0.0929 sq. m.)

Feet	Meters
1	0.93
100	9.29
200	18.58
300	27.87
400	37.16
500	46.45
600	55.74
700	65.03
800	74.32
900	83.61
1000	92.90
1100	102.19
1200	111.48
1300	120.77
1400	130.06
1500	139.35

Conversion Factors: Metric to U.S.

If You Know:	Multiply by:	To obtain:
Centimeters	0.03281	Feet
	0.3937	Inches
Centimeters per second	0.02237	Miles per hour
	1.969	Feet per minute
Cubic meters	35.31	Cubic feet
	1.308	Cubic yards
	264.2	Gallons (U.S. liquid)
Grams per square centimeter	2.0481	Pounds per square foot
Hectares	2.4713	Acres
Kilograms	2.205	Pounds
Kilograms per square centimeter	14.223	Pounds per square inch
Kilograms per square meter	0.0014223	Pounds per square inch
Kilometer	3,280.87	Feet
	0.62137	Miles
	1,093.62	Yards
Kilometers per hour	54.68	Feet per minute
	0.9113	Feet per second
Liters	0.02838	Bushels (U.S. dry)
	61.02	Cubic inches
	0.03531	Cubic feet
	0.2642	Gallons (U.S. liquid)
	1.0567	Quarts (U.S. liquid)
Meters	3.281	Feet
	39.37	Inches
	1.094	Yards
Meters per second	2.237	Miles per hour
	0.03728	Miles per minute
Square centimeters	0.1550	Square inches
Square kilometers	0.3861	Square miles
Tons (metric)	2,205	Pounds

Conversion Factors: U.S. to Metric

If you know:	Multiply by:	To obtain:
Acres	4,046.461	Square meters
	0.404646	Hectares
Acre-feet	1,233.49	Cubic meters
Atmospheres	76	Centimeters of mercury
	10,333	Kilograms per square meter
Cubic feet	28.316	Liters
	0.02832	Cubic meters
Cubic inches	16.39	Cubic centimeters
	0.01639	Liters
Feet	30.48	Centimeters
	0.0003048	Kilometers
	0.3048	Meters
Feet per minute	0.5080	Centimeters per second
	0.3048	Meters per minute
Feet per second	18.29	Meters per minute
Gallons	3.785	Liters
Gallons per minute	0.06308	Liters per second
Inches	2.54	Centimeters
	0.0254	Meters
	25.40	Millimeters
Knots	1.852	Kilometers per hour
Miles	1.6093	Kilometers
Ounces (avoirdupois)	28.349527	Grams
Pounds per cubic inch	27.68	Grams per cubic centimeter
Quarts	0.945	Liters
Square miles	2.590	Square kilometers
Yards	0.9144	Meters

Conversion Factors

If You Know:	Multiply by:	To obtain:
Acres	43,560	Square feet
	0.0015625	Square miles
	4,840	Square yards
Acre-feet	43,560	Cubic feet
	325,851	Gallons
Atmospheres	29.92	Inches of mercury
	33.90	Feet of water
	14.70	Pounds per square inch
Cubic feet	1,728	Cubic inches
	7.48052	Gallons
Cubic feet per second	448.831	Gallons per minute
Cubic yards	27	Cubic feet
Degrees (angle)	0.01745	Radians
Fathoms	6	Feet
Feet	0.0001394	Miles
Feet of water (head)	62.43	Pounds per square foot
	0.4335	Pounds per square inch
Feet per minute	0.0113636	Miles per hour
Furlongs	660	Feet
	0.125	Miles
Gallons	0.1337	Cubic feet
	231	Cubic inches
Gallons, imperial	1.20095	Gallons, U.S.

Conversion Factors (continued)

If You Know:	Multiply By:	To obtain:
Gallons of water	8.3453	Pounds of water
Gallons per minute	0.002228	Cubic feet per second
	8.0208	Cubic feet per hour
Grains (troy)	0.0648	Grams
	0.0020833	Ounces (avoirdupois)
Grams	15.43	Grains
Horsepower	550	Foot-pounds per second
Inches	1,000	Mils
Inches of mercury	0.4912	Pounds per square inch
Inches of water	0.03613	Pounds per square inch
Knots	1	Nautical miles per hour
	1.15078	Statute miles per hour
Links (Gunter's)	7.92	Inches
	0.66	Feet
Microns	0.000001	Meters
Miles, nautical	6,076.1033	Feet
Miles, statute	5,280	Feet
Miles per hour	83	Feet per minute
Miles per minute	83	Feet per second
Ounces (avoirdupois)	16	Drams
	437.5	Grains
	28.349527	Grams
	0.9115	Ounces (troy)
Ounces (fluid)	1.805	Cubic inches

Conversion Factors (continued)

If You Know:	Multiply By:	To obtain:
Pounds per square inch	2.307	Feet of water
	2.036	Inches of mercury
Pounds of water	0.01602	Cubic feet
Pounds (troy)	12	Ounces (troy)
	13.1657	Ounces (avoirdupois)
	5,760	Grains
Quart (dry)	67.20	Cubic inches
Quart (liquid)	57.75	Cubic inches
Quire	25	Sheets
Radians	57.29578	Degrees (angle)
Ream	500	Sheets
Rods	0.25	Chains (Gunter's)
	16.5	Feet
Square chains (Gunter's)	16	Square rods
Square feet	0.00002296	Acres
Square miles	640	Acres
Temperature, centigrade + 273	1	Absolute temperature, centigrade
Temperature, centigrade + 17.78	1.8	Temperature, fahrenheit
Temperature, fahrenheit + 460	1	Absolute temperature, fahrenheit
Temperature, fahrenheit − 32	5/9	Temperature, centigrade
Watts	0.05692	Btu per minute
	44.26	Foot-pounds per minute
	0.001341	Horsepower
Watt-hours	3.415	Btu
	2,655	Foot-pounds

J: COMMON BRICKS AND STONES
See figures J–1 to J–5.

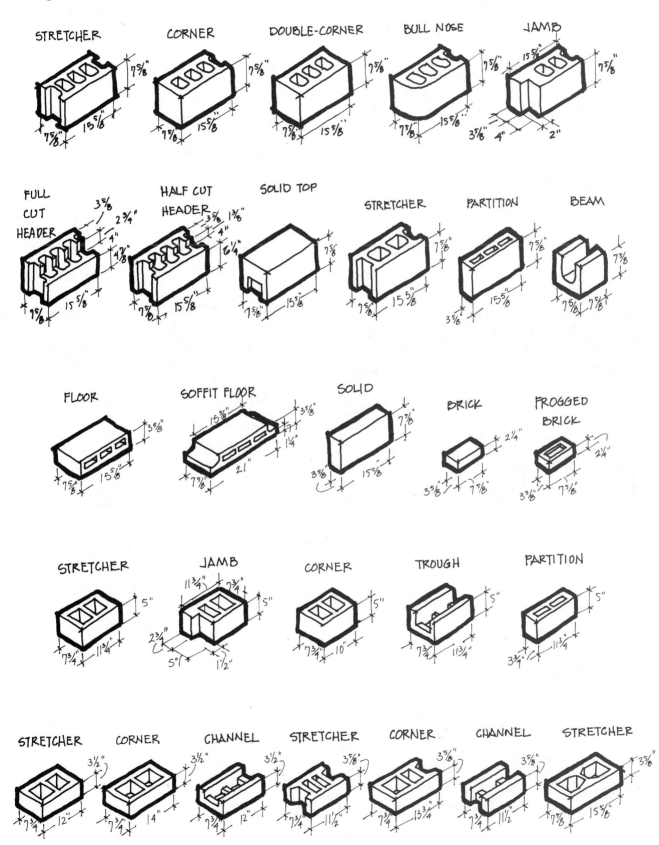

J–1. Concrete Bricks and Blocks

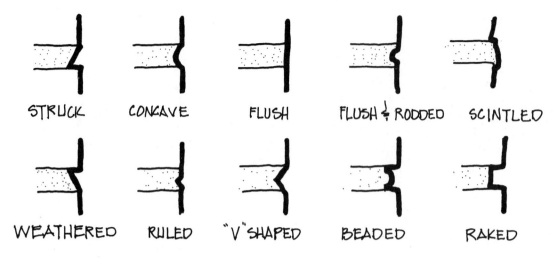

STRUCK   CONCAVE   FLUSH   FLUSH & RODDED   SCINTLED

WEATHERED   RULED   "V"SHAPED   BEADED   RAKED

J–2. Brick Bonds

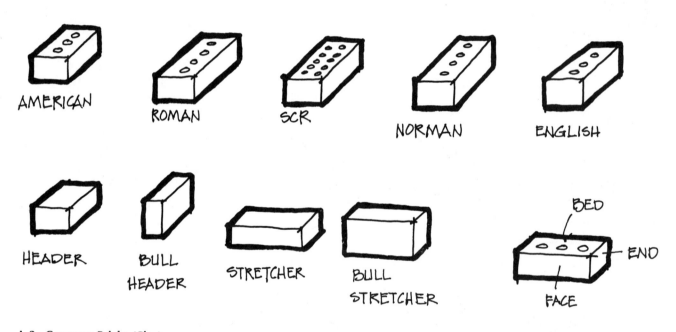

AMERICAN   ROMAN   SCR   NORMAN   ENGLISH

HEADER   BULL HEADER   STRETCHER   BULL STRETCHER

BED   END   FACE

J–3. Common Bricks (Clay)

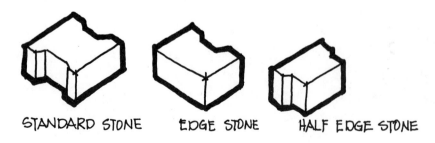

STANDARD STONE   EDGE STONE   HALF EDGE STONE

J–4. Brick/Stone Pavers

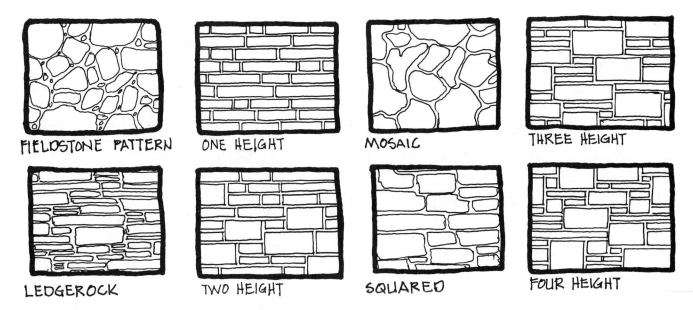

FIELDSTONE PATTERN · ONE HEIGHT · MOSAIC · THREE HEIGHT

LEDGEROCK · TWO HEIGHT · SQUARED · FOUR HEIGHT

J–5. Stone Patterns

K: STANDARD LUMBER SIZES AND JOINTS

See figures K–1 to K–7.

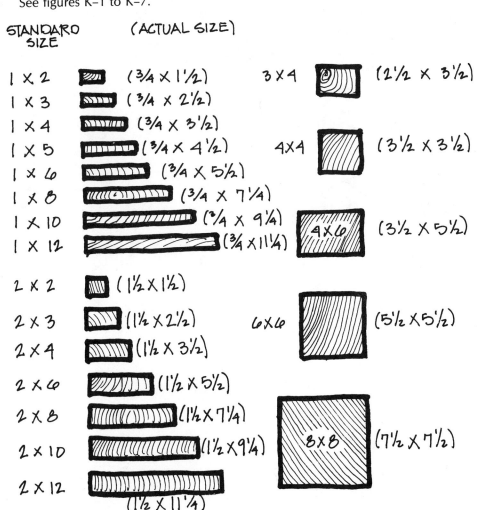

STANDARD SIZE — (ACTUAL SIZE)

1 × 2 (3/4 × 1 1/2)
1 × 3 (3/4 × 2 1/2)
1 × 4 (3/4 × 3 1/2)
1 × 5 (3/4 × 4 1/2)
1 × 6 (3/4 × 5 1/2)
1 × 8 (3/4 × 7 1/4)
1 × 10 (3/4 × 9 1/4)
1 × 12 (3/4 × 11 1/4)

2 × 2 (1 1/2 × 1 1/2)
2 × 3 (1 1/2 × 2 1/2)
2 × 4 (1 1/2 × 3 1/2)
2 × 6 (1 1/2 × 5 1/2)
2 × 8 (1 1/2 × 7 1/4)
2 × 10 (1 1/2 × 9 1/4)
2 × 12 (1 1/2 × 11 1/4)

3 × 4 (2 1/2 × 3 1/2)
4 × 4 (3 1/2 × 3 1/2)
4 × 6 (3 1/2 × 5 1/2)
6 × 6 (5 1/2 × 5 1/2)
8 × 8 (7 1/2 × 7 1/2)

K–1. Standard Lumber Sizes

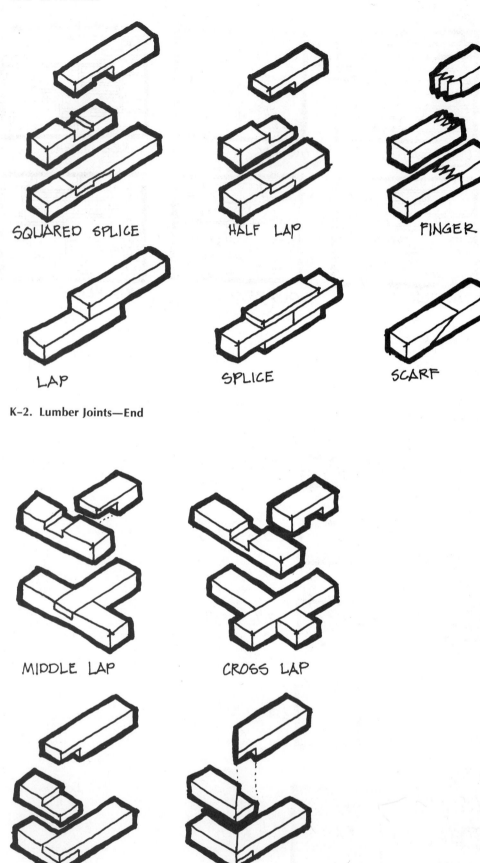

SQUARED SPLICE   HALF LAP   FINGER

LAP   SPLICE   SCARF

K-2. Lumber Joints—End

MIDDLE LAP   CROSS LAP

END LAP   MITER HALF LAP

K-3. Lumber Joints—Right Angle

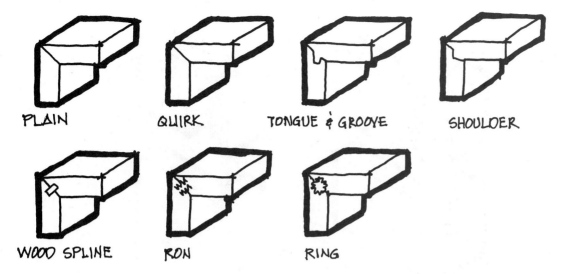

PLAIN QUIRK TONGUE & GROOVE SHOULOER

WOOD SPLINE RON RING

K-4. Lumber Joints—Miters

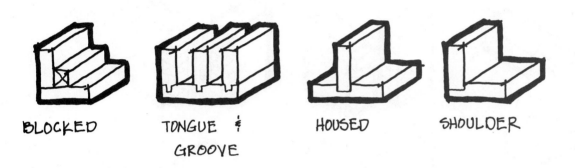

BLOCKED TONGUE & GROOVE HOUSED SHOULOER

K-5. Tongue & Groove

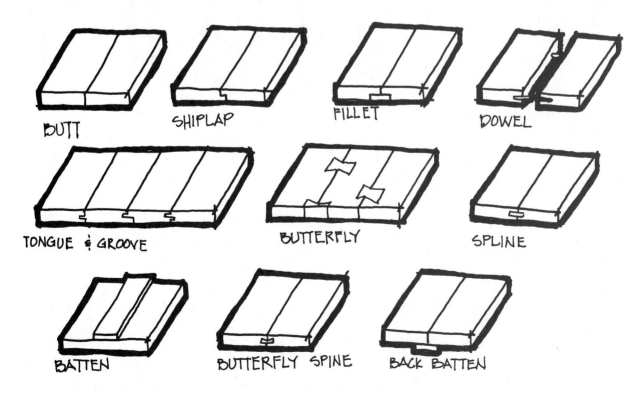

BUTT SHIPLAP FILLET DOWEL

TONGUE & GROOVE BUTTERFLY SPLINE

BATTEN BUTTERFLY SPINE BACK BATTEN

K-6. Lumber Joints—Edge

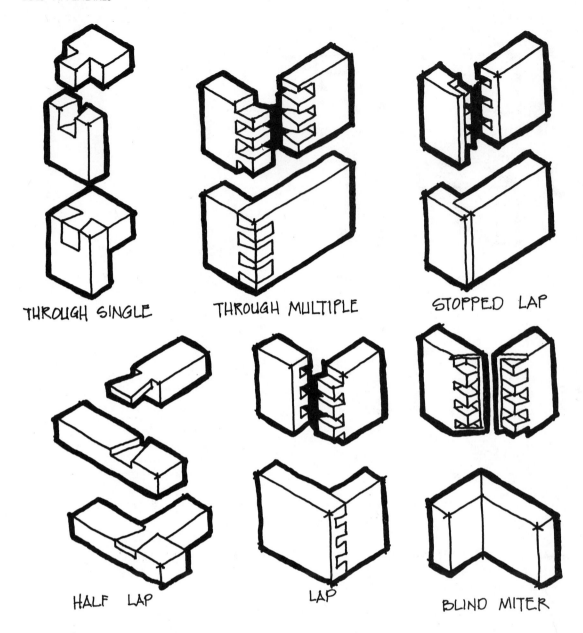

THROUGH SINGLE

THROUGH MULTIPLE

STOPPED LAP

HALF LAP

LAP

BLIND MITER

K-7. Lumber Joints—Dovetail

Index